GW01561181

# THE ORIGIN OF BUDDHIST MEDITATION

The historic authenticity of the early Buddhist sources is a much disputed topic. Although many modern scholars of Indian Buddhism are highly sceptical about the possibility of identifying and recovering authentic early teachings, this book maintains that such an objective is possible. Having identified early material that goes back to the Buddha himself, the author argues that the two teachers of the Buddha were historical figures. Based on the early Brahminic literature, namely the early Upaniṣads and *Mokṣadharma*, the author asserts the origin of the method of meditation learned by the Buddha from these teachers, and attempts to use them to identify some authentic teachings of the Buddha on meditation.

The following claims are put forward in this book, which will stimulate a debate within the field of Buddhist Studies:

- The claim Buddha was taught by Āḷāra Kālāma and Uddaka Rāmaputta, as stated in the literature of numerous early Buddhist sects, is historically authentic.
- Āḷāra Kālāma and Uddaka Rāmaputta taught a form of early Brahminic meditation.
- The Buddha must consequently have been trained in a meditative school whose ideology was provided by the philosophical portions of early Upaniṣads.
- This hypothesis is confirmed in *Pārāyanavagga*, where the Buddha teaches an adapted practice of Āḷāra Kālāma's goal to some Brahmins, and appears to be fully conversant with the philosophical presuppositions of early Brahminic meditation.

The book will be of significant interest to academics in the field of Buddhist Studies, Asian Religion and South Asian Studies.

**Alexander Wynne** is a translator for the Clay Sanskrit Library. He was awarded a DPhil in Oriental Studies from the University of Oxford in 2003 and was a Junior Research Fellow at St John's College, Oxford, from 2002–2006.

# ROUTLEDGE CRITICAL STUDIES IN BUDDHISM
## General Editors: Charles S. Prebish and Damien Keown

*Routledge Critical Studies in Buddhism* is a comprehensive study of the Buddhist tradition. The series explores this complex and extensive tradition from a variety of perspectives, using a range of different methodologies.

The series is diverse in its focus, including historical studies, textual translations and commentaries, sociological investigations, bibliographic studies and considerations of religious practice as an expression of Buddhism's integral religiosity. It also presents materials on modern intellectual historical studies, including the role of Buddhist thought and scholarship in a contemporary, critical context and in the light of current social issues. The series is expansive and imaginative in scope, spanning more than two and a half millennia of Buddhist history. It is receptive to all research works that inform and advance our knowledge and understanding of the Buddhist tradition.

A SURVEY OF VINAYA LITERATURE
*Charles S. Prebish*

THE REFLEXIVE NATURE OF AWARENESS
*Paul Williams*

ALTRUISM AND REALITY
*Paul Williams*

BUDDHISM AND HUMAN RIGHTS
*Edited by Damien Keown, Charles Prebish, Wayne Husted*

WOMEN IN THE FOOTSTEPS OF THE BUDDHA
*Kathryn R. Blackstone*

THE RESONANCE OF EMPTINESS
*Gay Watson*

AMERICAN BUDDHISM
*Edited by Duncan Ryuken Williams and Christopher Queen*

IMAGING WISDOM
*Jacob N. Kinnard*

PAIN AND ITS ENDING
*Carol S. Anderson*

EMPTINESS APPRAISED
*David F. Burton*

THE SOUND OF LIBERATING TRUTH
*Edited by Sallie B. King and Paul O. Ingram*

BUDDHIST THEOLOGY
*Edited by Roger R. Jackson and John J. Makransky*

THE GLORIOUS DEEDS OF PURNA
*Joel Tatelman*

EARLY BUDDHISM - A NEW APPROACH
*Sue Hamilton*

CONTEMPORARY BUDDHIST ETHICS
*Edited by Damien Keown*

INNOVATIVE BUDDHIST WOMEN
*Edited by Karma Lekshe Tsomo*

TEACHING BUDDHISM IN THE WEST
*Edited by V. S. Hori, R. P. Hayes and J. M. Shields*

EMPTY VISION
*David L. McMahan*

SELF, REALITY AND REASON IN TIBETAN PHILOSOPHY
*Thupten Jinpa*

IN DEFENSE OF DHARMA
*Tessa J. Bartholomeusz*

BUDDHIST PHENOMENOLOGY
*Dan Lusthaus*

RELIGIOUS MOTIVATION AND THE ORIGINS OF BUDDHISM
*Torkel Brekke*

DEVELOPMENTS IN AUSTRALIAN BUDDHISM
*Michelle Spuler*

ZEN WAR STORIES
*Brian Victoria*

THE BUDDHIST UNCONSCIOUS
*William S. Waldron*

INDIAN BUDDHIST THEORIES OF PERSONS
*James Duerlinger*

ACTION DHARMA
*Edited by Christopher Queen, Charles Prebish and Damien Keown*

TIBETAN AND ZEN BUDDHISM IN BRITAIN
*David N. Kay*

THE CONCEPT OF THE BUDDHA
*Guang Xing*

THE PHILOSOPHY OF DESIRE IN THE BUDDHIST PALI CANON
*David Webster*

THE NOTION OF DITTHI IN THERAVADA BUDDHISM
*Paul Fuller*

THE BUDDHIST THEORY OF SELF-COGNITION
*Zhihua Yao*

MORAL THEORY IN ŚĀNTIDEVA'S ŚIKṢĀMUCCAYA
*Barbra R. Clayton*

BUDDHIST STUDIES FROM INDIA TO AMERICA
*Edited by Damien Keown*

DISCOURSE AND IDEOLOGY IN MEDIEVAL JAPANESE BUDDHISM
*Edited by Richard K. Payne and Taigen Dan Leighton*

BUDDHIST THOUGHT AND APPLIED PSYCHOLOGICAL RESEARCH
*Edited by D. K. Nauriyal, Michael S. Drummond and Y. B. Lal*

BUDDHISM IN CANADA
*Edited by Bruce Matthews*

BUDDHISM, CONFLICT AND VIOLENCE IN MODERN SRI LANKA
*Edited by Mahinda Deegalle*

THERAVĀDA BUDDHISM AND THE BRITISH ENCOUNTER
Religious, missionary and colonial experience in nineteenth century Sri Lanka
*Elizabeth Harris*

BEYOND ENLIGHTENMENT
Buddhism, religion, modernity
*Richard Cohen*

BUDDHISM IN THE PUBLIC SPHERE
Reorienting global interdependence
*Peter D. Hershock*

BRITISH BUDDHISM
Teachings, practice and development
*Robert Bluck*

BUDDHIST NUNS IN TAIWAN AND SRI LANKA
A critique of the feminist perspective
*Wei-Yi Cheng*

NEW BUDDHIST MOVEMENTS IN THAILAND
Toward an understanding of Wat Phra Dhammakāya and Santi Asoke
*Rory Mackenzie*

The following titles are published in association with the *Oxford Centre for Buddhist Studies*

Oxford Centre for Buddhist Studies
*a project of* The Society for the Wider Understanding of the Buddhist Tradition

EARLY BUDDHIST METAPHYSICS
*Noa Ronkin*

MIPHAM'S DIALECTICS AND THE DEBATES ON EMPTINESS
*Karma Phuntsho*

HOW BUDDHISM BEGAN
The conditioned genesis of the early teachings
*Richard F. Gombrich*

BUDDHIST MEDITATION
An anthology of texts from the Pāli canon
*Sarah Shaw*

REMAKING BUDDHISM FOR MEDIEVAL NEPAL
The fifteenth-century reformation of Newar Buddhism
*Will Tuladhar-Douglas*

METAPHOR AND LITERALISM IN BUDDHISM
The doctrinal history of nirvana
*Soonil Hwang*

THE BIOGRAPHIES OF RECHUNGPA
The evolution of a Tibetan hagiography
*Peter Alan Roberts*

THE ORIGIN OF BUDDHIST MEDITATION
*Alexander Wynne*

# THE ORIGIN OF BUDDHIST MEDITATION

*Alexander Wynne*

Routledge
Taylor & Francis Group
LONDON AND NEW YORK

First published 2007
by Routledge
2 Park Square, Milton Park, Abingdon, Oxon OX14 4RN

Simultaneously published in the USA and Canada
by Routledge
270 Madison Ave, New York, NY 10016

*Routledge is an imprint of the Taylor & Francis Group, an informa business*

Transferred to Digital Printing 2009



Typeset in Times New Roman by
Florence Production Ltd, Stoodleigh, Devon



*British Library Cataloguing in Publication Data*
A catalogue record for this book is available
from the British Library

*Library of Congress Cataloging in Publication Data*
Wynne, Alexander, 1974–
The origin of Buddhist mediation/Alexander Wynne
p. cm. (Routledge critical studies in Buddhism)
Includes bibliography references and index
1. Meditation – Buddhism – History. 2. Buddhist literature – History and criticism. 3. Gautama Buddha. 4. Brahmanism – Relations – Buddhism. 5. Buddhism – Relations – Brahmanism.
I. Title
BQ5612.W86 2007
294.3′.443509 – dc22 2006031390

ISBN10: 0–415–42387–2 (hbk)
ISBN10: 0–415–54467–X (pbk)
ISBN10: 0–203–96300–8 (ebk)

ISBN13: 978–0–415–42387–8 (hbk)
ISBN13: 978–0–415–54467–2 (pbk)
ISBN13: 978–0–203–96300–5 (ebk)

# CONTENTS

*Acknowledgements* ix
*Abbreviations* x

**1 Introduction** **1**

The problem of the earliest form of Buddhism 1
The study of Buddhist origins 4
Texts and conventions 7
A note on terminology 8

**2 Āḷāra Kālāma and Uddaka Rāmaputta** **9**

Textual sources and the historical problem 9
Arguments for the historical authenticity of the biographical account in the *Mahīśāsaka Vinaya* 10
Further texts on the two teachers 12
Uddaka Rāmaputta and Rāma 14
Other peculiarities in the *Ariyapariyesana Sutta* 16
The APS as a description of the Buddha's awakening 24
The terms 'nothingness' and 'neither perception nor non-perception' as epithets of liberation 25
Conclusion to Chapter 2 26

**3 Formless meditation and early Brahminism** **27**

Verses on meditation in the Mahābhārata and early Buddhist literature 27
The elements and formless spheres 29
The *kasiṇāyatana-s* 31
Element meditation and early Brahminism 34
Element meditation in the *Mokṣadharma* 37

Cosmology and meditation in early Brahminism 39
The goals of the two teachers: early Upaniṣadic parallels 42
The aphorism *passan na passati* 45
Conclusion to Chapter 3 49

**4 The philosophy of early Brahminic *yoga*** **51**

Cosmogony in the *Vasiṣṭha-Karālajanakasaṃvādaḥ* (Mbh XII.291) 52
Cosmogony in the *Nāsadīyasūkta* 57
Cosmogony in the *Śukānupraśnaḥ* (Mbh XII.224) 64
Conclusion to Chapter 4 66
Appendix to Chapter 4: the early yogic doctrine of *karman* 67

**5 Meditation in the *Pārāyanavagga*** **72**

The antiquity of the *Pārāyanavagga* 73
The *Upasīvamāṇavapucchā* (Sn 1069–76) 75
Sn 1071–72: *vimutto/'dhimutto* 78
Sn 1071–72: *anānuyāyī* 80
Sn 1073–74: *sītisiyā* 84
Sn 1073–76: the metaphors 'becoming cool' (*sīti* +√*bhū*) and 'going out' (*atthaṃ* + √*gam*) 90
The indefinability of the sage 95
The historical significance of the *Upasīvamāṇavapucchā* 98
The *Udayamāṇavapucchā* (Sn 1105–11) 100
The *Posālamāṇavapucchā* (Sn 1112–15) 103
Conclusion to Chapter 5 106

**6 Conclusion: the origin of Buddhist meditation and early Buddhism** **108**

The relationship between early Buddhism and Brahminism 113
An early Buddhist controversy: meditation or intellectualism? 117
The intellectual tendency in early Buddhism 120
The four *jhāna-s* and their development 122
The identification of authentic teachings of the Buddha 125

*Notes* 129
*Bibliography* 159
*Index* 165

# ACKNOWLEDGEMENTS

This book is a revised version of a thesis of the same name for which I was awarded a DPhil degree at the University of Oxford in 2003. I am greatly indebted to my DPhil examiners, Prof. Lambert Schmithausen and Prof. Joanna Jurewicz for their helpful and valuable suggestions, many of which I have tried to incorporate into this book. Although I began work for my DPhil thesis in 2000, its origins go back to my undergraduate studies at Bristol University, where I was first taught courses in Buddhism by Prof. Paul Williams and Dr Rupert Gethin. I remain indebted to these scholars for introducing me to the academic study of Buddhism. My studies in Oxford have been aided by many individuals; in particular, I would like to thank Dr Jim Benson and my DPhil supervisor, Prof. Richard Gombrich. Without Prof. Gombrich's support and advice, this book would never have been written.

# ABBREVIATIONS

| | |
|---|---|
| A | *Aṅguttara Nikāya* |
| Akbh | Abhidharmako'Sabhāùya |
| Ap | Apadāna |
| APS | *Ariyapariyesana Sutta* |
| Apte | V.S. Apte, Practical Sanskrit–English Dictionary |
| Āyār | Āyāraṅga Sutta |
| Be | Burmese edition |
| BhG | *Bhagavadgītā* |
| BHS | Buddhist Hybrid Sanskrit |
| BHSD | Buddhist Hybrid Sanskrit Dictionary |
| BR | Böhtlingk and Roth, Sanskrit-Wörterbuch |
| BU | *Bṛhadāraṇyaka Upaniṣad* |
| Bud | *Buddhacarita* |
| CPD | Critical Pāli Dictionary |
| CU | *Chāndogya Upaniṣad* |
| D | *Dīgha Nikāya* |
| Dhp | *Dhammapada* |
| DOP | Dictionary of Pāli |
| DPPN | Dictionary of Pāli Proper Names |
| GDhp | *Gāndhārī Dhammapada* |
| It | *Itivuttaka* |
| Ja | Jātaka |
| KaU | *Kaṭha Upaniṣad* |
| KeU | *Kena Upaniṣad* |
| KN | *Khuddaka Nikāya* |
| M | *Majjhima Nikāya* |
| Mai U | *Maitrāyaṇīya Upaniṣad* |
| MāU | Māṇḍūkya Upaniṣad |
| Mbh | Mahābhārata |
| MMW | Monier Monier-Williams, a Sanskrit–English dictionary |
| Mp | Manorathapūraṇī (Aṅguttaranikāya-aṭṭhakathā) |
| MSS | *Mahā-Saccaka Sutta* |

| | |
|---|---|
| MuU | *Muṇḍaka Upaniṣad* |
| Mvu | *Mahāvastu* |
| Ne | Nālandā edition |
| Nett | Nettipakaraõa |
| Nidd II | *Cūḷāniddesa* |
| Pañis | Pañisambhidhāmagga |
| PED | Pāli English dictionary |
| Pj II | *Paramatthajotikā* (*Suttanipāta*-aṭṭhakathā) |
| Ps | Papañcasūdanī (Majjhimanikāya-aṭṭhakathā) |
| PTS | Pali Text Society |
| ṚV | *Ṛg Veda* |
| S | Saṃyutta Nikāya |
| ŚB | Śatapatha Brāhmaṇa |
| SBhV | *Saṅghabhedavastu* |
| Skt | Sanskrit |
| Sn | *Suttanipāta* |
| ŚU | *Śvetāśvatara Upaniṣad* |
| Sv | Sumaṅgalavilāsinī (Dīghanikāya-aṭṭhakathā) |
| Th | *Theragāthā* |
| Thī | Therīgāthā |
| TU | Taittirīya Upaniṣad |
| Ud | *Udāna* |
| Vin | Vinaya |
| VRI | Vipassana Research Institute |

# 1

# INTRODUCTION

## The problem of the earliest form of Buddhism

The biggest problem in Buddhist Studies is that nobody knows what the Buddha taught. This is not because of an absence of early literary sources (in Pāli, Sanskrit, Chinese, Tibetan, etc.) that claim to contain his teachings. The problem rather, is that recent studies have shown that the early texts appear to contain a number of doctrinal differences,[1] and it is not clear which formulations might be authentic and go back to the Buddha. The historical claims of the early Buddhist sects only add to the general scepticism. All claim that their canonical literature was compiled at the first council of Rājagṛha, shortly after the Buddha's death. Unfortunately, however, there are numerous differences between the various canons, even in the details about the extent and classification of the canon supposedly compiled at the first council. Because of this Lamotte has commented: 'It would be absurd to claim that all those canons were fixed at the very beginnings of Buddhism.'[2] It seems that the composition of early Buddhist literature was ongoing, and this casts doubt on the antiquity of any canonical text.

To have any chance of recovering the teachings of the Buddha, the early Buddhist literature must be chronologically stratified. But it is not clear how even the oldest stratum in the early texts could be attributed to the Buddha, should it be identified to some degree of satisfaction. For there appear to be no criteria, internal (e.g. a text whose authenticity is obvious) or external (e.g. an inscription from the very early period), that could connect any text or idea to the historical Buddha.[3] The problem this creates has been summed up by J. W. de Jong:

> One either selects some texts which are considered to reflect the earliest Buddhist doctrines, or one assumes that some doctrines are the original ones and tries to trace their development in the canonical texts. In both cases the point of departure is determined by a subjective decision.[4]

Somewhat inevitably, de Jong concludes: 'We will never be able to know the contents of the teachings of the Buddha himself.'[5] A slightly earlier, and simpler, version of this claim is found in A. B. Keith's statement that any attempt to ascribe texts to the Buddha is futile: 'All that we can do is to indulge in the legitimate, if somewhat useless, exercise of conjecturing what part of the doctrines which pass later as Buddhist is most likely to have been his own.'[6]

If these sceptical opinions are to be believed, the early Buddhist literature defies any satisfactory chronological stratification, and none of it can be ascribed to the Buddha. The sceptics presuppose, therefore, that the early literature lacks sufficient historical information to assign texts and ideas to different periods. But it seems to me that this overstates the matter somewhat: even by the most sceptical reckoning, it is unlikely that the early literature is devoid of all historical content. The *Mahāparinibbāna Sutta*, for example, is probably in many respects a quite reliable record of the last few months of the Buddha's life. It is likely that some of the events recorded in it are historically authentic, e.g. the Buddha's death in Kusinārā[7] and his last words on that occasion,[8] for there is no reason to believe that such polemically neutral passages would have been invented. There are other ways of identifying passages in the early literature that almost certainly go back to the Buddha. Richard Gombrich has pointed out that humorous statements attributed to the Buddha are probably authentic. As he puts it: 'Are jokes ever composed by committees?'[9] But it is one thing to establish historical facts and another to identify teachings of the Buddha. Jokes or facts about the Buddha's death do not establish whether the Buddha taught the Noble Eightfold Path, or even the Four Noble Truths. In short, then, it is difficult to see how the passages of outstanding historical significance – and there are not many obvious examples – could be used as the criterion by which to attribute any of the early doctrinal formulations to the Buddha.

It is undoubtedly the case, therefore, that the most important problem facing a historian of early Buddhism is that of establishing a relationship between early Buddhist doctrine and historical fact. In this book I will reconsider this problem and propose a new solution to it. I will attempt to prove that facts about the Buddha's early life are historically authentic and can be used to identify some of his teachings in the early literature. The historical facts in question concern the mysterious figures who are said to have taught meditation to the Buddha-to-be (the Bodhisatta), Āḷāra Kālāma and Uddaka Rāmaputta. I will claim that the primary text in which this account is contained, the *Ariyapariyesana Sutta*, is probably the earliest and most historically valuable biographical tract in the early Buddhist literature. This being the case, it is quite likely that the Bodhisatta really was taught meditation by these two men. This text does not say anything about the content of the earliest Buddhist teachings, but I will use it to provide a historical background to early Buddhist thought in another way. I will attempt to show correspondences between the early literature on the two teachers and some of the speculations contained in the philosophical literature of early Brahminism. By this means I will try to reconstruct the philosophical presuppositions of the two teachers' meditative practices. This will lead to a much improved understanding of the teachings that the Bodhisatta rejected and thus, I will claim, some idea of his intellectual development. Such a reconstruction will not provide us with the criteria that will allow us to determine the teachings of the Buddha with absolute certainty. But facts about the Buddha's intellectual development can help us investigate the early Buddhist literature on meditation afresh. They provide the criteria that make it possible to reconsider the historical authenticity of the early literature.

In the early Buddhist literature the meditative states related to the teachers of the Bodhisatta are termed 'formless spheres'. These four states are listed as follows in the Pāli canon:

| | |
|---|---|
| *ākāsānañcāyatana* | the sphere of the infinity of space |
| *viññāṇañcāyatana*[10] | the sphere of the infinity of consciousness |
| *ākiñcaññāyatana* | the sphere of nothingness |
| *nevasaññānāsaññāyatana* | the sphere of neither perception nor non-perception. |

Teachings containing these meditative states are numerous in the early Buddhist literature. This is of some historical significance. If the Bodhisatta rejected the goals of his teachers ('the sphere of nothingness' taught by Āḷāra Kālāma, and 'the sphere of neither perception nor non-perception' taught by Uddaka Rāmaputta), as the early biographies claim, then we must ask why so many practices including them are outlined in the early literature. There seem to be two possible answers. Either the Buddha allowed his followers to practise the pre-Buddhist sort of meditation taught by his teachers, in which case he must have taught a modified version of the practices, or he rejected the practice of the formless spheres and not just their goals, which would mean that their presence in the early Buddhist literature is not a true reflection of his teachings. If so, an investigation of the literature on the formless spheres would not reveal authentic teachings of the Buddha. But the former hypothesis is more intriguing, and it is this that I will investigate in this book. Based on the theory that the Bodhisatta was taught these meditative states by two teachers and later allowed them to be practised by his disciples, I will analyse a few old Buddhist texts from the *Suttanipāta*. In these texts the Buddha teaches an adapted form of the pre-Buddhist practices; I will attempt to show that these teachings are historically authentic.

## The study of Buddhist origins

A basic presupposition of this book is that the early Buddhist literature is heterogeneous. Despite this, I see no reason to deny the historicity of the literature as a matter of course,[11] although nowadays scholars are generally sceptical of the antiquity and authenticity of early Buddhist literature. The modern sceptical view has been articulated most notably by Gregory Schopen as follows:

> We know, and have known for some time, that the Pāli canon as we have it – and it is generally conceded to be our oldest source – cannot be taken back further than the last quarter of the first century BCE, the date of the Alu-vihāra redaction, the earliest redaction we can have some knowledge of, and that – for a critical history – it can serve, at the very most, only as a source for the Buddhism of this period. But we also know that even this is problematic since, as Malalasekera has pointed out: '. . . how far the *Tipiṭaka* and its commentary reduced to writing at Alu-vihāra resembled them as they have come down to us, no one can say.' In fact, it is not until the time of the commentaries of Buddhaghosa, Dhammapāla, and others – that is to say, the fifth to sixth centuries CE – that we can know anything definite about the actual contents of [the Pāli] canon.[12]

This view is now so common that many scholars do not see the need to justify it. This can be seen in the *Encyclopedia of Religion* where the authors of the entry 'Buddhism in India' note the following:

> Unfortunately, we do not possess reliable sources for most of the history of Buddhism in its homeland; in particular, we have precious little to rely on for its early history. Textual sources are late, dating at the very least five hundred years after the death of the Buddha.[13]

Such are the sceptical assumptions made by modern scholars of Indian Buddhism. It is easy to understand certain aspects of this scepticism, since no manuscripts of our most complete source – the Pāli canon – date back to the fifth century AD. Thus it makes it theoretically possible that this canon was periodically revised up to and beyond its commentators (*c.* fifth century AD). Nevertheless, I do not see this as a sufficient reason to reject its antiquity. Scholars such as Schopen would have us believe that the Pāli canon is evidence for Buddhism up to the time of the commentators, a view that implies that texts commented upon by fifth-century authors are not necessarily older than the commentaries themselves. But this is absurd. The very existence of the commentaries presupposes a textual tradition of some antiquity. If so, it is only to be assumed that the early Buddhist literature contains passages of considerable antiquity, even if it is possible that such passages have been corrupted in the course of time. To be sure, the sceptics, whose arguments are based on the lack of textual sources from the early period, can only go so far as to doubt the possibility of identifying very old parts of the canonical literature. But that passages of genuine antiquity exist cannot be categorically denied. Indeed, it seems to me that the opposite can be proved. The internal evidence of the texts themselves, as well as archaeological and epigraphical evidence, suggests that ancient texts have been preserved in the early literature, in spite of the corrosive effects of time.

The evidence concerning the transmission of the Pāli canon can be summed up as follows. The first remarkable fact, as has been noted by T. W. Rhys Davids, is that the texts seem to belong to a period of Indian history before the third century BC: they do not mention Aśoka, which is hardly likely if they were still open in his time.[14] This evidence is supplemented by epigraphical and textual evidence suggesting that Buddhism arrived in Sri Lanka in the middle of the third century BC.[15] Moreover, Pāli is a North Indian language that appears to show no traces of a Sinhalese dialect.[16] If the language of the canon was not changed in spite of its Sinhalese surroundings, it is reasonable to assume that its contents were not changed either. This suggestion is supported by the fact that texts received by the Buddhists of Sri Lanka from other Buddhist sects in India were not placed in the Pāli canon, even when there were good reasons for doing so.[17] This suggests that the early Sri Lakan Buddhists regarded some of the Pāli literature as canonical and transmitted it conservatively. Furthermore, if literature borrowed from other sects was kept outside the Pāli canon, it means that correspondences between the Pāli canon and the canonical literature of other sects probably predate the formation of the sects.[18] The evidence suggests, then, that the literature introduced to Sri Lanka in the third century BC was changed very little after its introduction.

According to another sceptical argument, the early Buddhist literature cannot be used to construct historical events, no matter how old it is. Proponents of this argument claim that antiquity is no guarantee of historicity, since religious literature is normative rather than descriptive. Indeed, according to Schopen:

> Scholars of Indian Buddhism have taken canonical monastic rules and formal literary descriptions of the monastic ideal preserved in very late manuscripts and treated them as if they were accurate reflections of the religious life and career of actual practising Buddhist monks in early India.[19]

As he puts it, 'Even the most artless formal narrative text has a purpose, and . . . in "scriptural" texts, especially in India, that purpose is almost never "historical" in our sense of the term.'[20] This view is widely accepted and implies that any attempt to read Buddhist texts as historical documents is flawed. In more recent times, some scholars have even argued that the tendency is based on the suspect political motives of the early Orientalists. According to King:

> Western scholars located 'Buddhism' in classical texts, which they then tended to accept uncritically as accurate *descriptions* of 'primitive Buddhism' rather than as *prescriptive* and ideological representations of Buddhist belief and practice. This provided a justification for those accounts that emphasized the apparent degradation and corruption of contemporary Buddhist religion and society.[21]

If this opinion is to be believed, the historical study of early Buddhist texts was part of an Orientalist plot to belittle the society and culture of the modern East.[22] This sort of suspicion about the methods of the early Orientalists is of course a development of Edward Said's argument that 'all academic knowledge about India and Egypt is somehow tinged and impressed by the gross political fact'.[23] Such a critique of Orientalism has been taken very seriously in recent times. Following Said, some Buddhist scholars have declared that they have moved beyond the old textual methods, which they see as 'inadequate',[24] and others have lamented the methods of the early Orientalists and subsequent dominance of textualist approaches, the adherents of which have been dubbed 'Pāli text puritans'.[25]

No matter what the modern critics say, it seems to me that there is very little evidence that 'Orientalist' methods of studying Buddhist texts are invalid. The early Orientalists assumed that the early Buddhist texts contain historical facts that could be revealed by text-critical means.[26] Some modern scholars have taken the opposite view, i.e. that Buddhist texts have little or no historical value. They take it as axiomatic that Buddhist texts are prescriptive and idealistic, and because of this imply that any attempt to construct history from them is deeply flawed. But this opinion is based on an a priori assumption that religious literature is normative and prescriptive. Such an assumption does not seem to be proved by the evidence of the early Buddhist texts, however. As I mentioned earlier, facts about the Buddha's death as well as jokes attributed to him are probably historically authentic.[27] Such facts do not establish that the early Buddhist literature is entirely descriptive rather than normative, but they show that the literature contains descriptive elements that can be used to construct historical events. Besides this, there are other ways of extracting historical information from the texts. I have argued elsewhere that historical facts can be inferred from the circumstantial evidence contained in them.[28] Facts that can be inferred about the transmission of the early Pāli literature are particularly suggestive: they seem to show that the early Buddhists attempted to compose and transmit texts in a form that could preserve information accurately, indeed word by word.[29] For example, one of the rules in the *Bhikkhu-pātimokkha* forbids the teaching of the *dhamma* 'word to word' to a layman.[30] From this evidence we cannot conclude that such things never happened: we do not know, and never will know, if *bhikkhus* taught lay people in such a fashion. However, in stipulating that the teaching ought not to be 'word for word' (*padaso*), the rule indirectly indicates the manner of teaching the *dhamma* to ordained monastics. This indirect evidence is supported by more textual evidence of a similar kind,[31] and implies that Suttas were transmitted 'word for word' even in the earliest period, thus raising the possibility that some of the Buddha's teachings, and perhaps even his words, have been preserved verbatim. Such methods of literary transmission, as well as descriptive portions of the texts, suggest that the application of the modern critique of Orientalism to Buddhist Studies is naive.

For the reasons given above, I see no reason to deny the possibility that the early Buddhist literature contains passages of genuine historical authenticity. If even a small number of passages of clear historical significance can be identified, it follows that an attempt to determine the historical reality of primitive Buddhism through the textual evidence is not based on faulty presuppositions about the nature of this evidence. In fact, the opposite is true: the critique of historical (or 'Orientalist') studies of Buddhist texts is based on the faulty presupposition that religious literature is wholly normative. Therefore, in this study of early Buddhism I see no reason to doubt the validity of the 'Orientalist' methods used to study Buddhist literature. It is to be hoped that the time has passed when it could be said of an empirical study of Buddhist texts that 'the ghost of Mrs Rhys Davids' stalks its pages.[32] Subsequent criticism of this work should be directed at its arguments, rather than the fact that it is based on an approach that modern sceptics believe to be 'tinged and impressed by the gross political fact'.

## Texts and conventions

All citations of Pāli texts refer to the volume, page and line numbers of PTS editions. I have also consulted the Nālandā and VRI editions of the Suttapiṭaka; both are editions of the Burmese Chaṭṭhasaṅgāyana. Quotations from the early Upaniṣads are taken from the edition of Limaye and Vadekar, and those from the *Mokṣadharma* are taken from the Poona critical edition of the Mahābhārata. All translations are my own unless otherwise indicated.

## A note on terminology

The word 'meditation' has multiple meanings and can be applied to various sorts of religious practice described in the early Indian texts. The particular sort of meditative practices under consideration here can be described as 'enstatic':[33] the aim is for the practitioner to desist from awareness of the outside world by focusing his awareness on an inner object. Various indigenous words indicate this practice, and most of them are common to both Buddhist and Brahminic texts (e.g. Skt *samādhi* (concentration) and *dhyāna* (meditation)), although the definitive Brahminic word – *yoga* – is hardly found in that sense in the Suttapiṭaka.[34] While the various Sanskrit and Pāli words have a clear meaning, their translations into English are often confusing. The terms 'absorption' and 'inner-concentration' bring to mind the sense of these practices; I use them as the general terms under which all the practices are considered. The Buddhist practices considered are collectively termed 'formless meditation', for they are concentrations on incorporeal objects. Hence, I refer to their objects as 'formless spheres', for, according to the Buddhist texts, these objects are non-physical 'planes' of reality (*āyatana-s*) that exist outside the thoughts of the meditating *bhikkhu*. As for the Brahminic practices, I generally use the word *yoga* in order to designate them. This word is first used in the sense of 'inner-concentration' in the *Kaṭha Upaniṣad* (KaU II.12), but thereafter is ubiquitous in Brahminic writings on the subject. Nowadays, it is usually found in an English dictionary and may have different connotations from the sense in which I use it. But in the early Indian religious and philosophical texts, it refers to the 'work' or 'discipline' of inner concentration.

# 2

# ĀḶĀRA KĀLĀMA AND UDDAKA RĀMAPUTTA

In some of the earliest biographies of the Buddha, it is claimed that the Bodhisatta was taught the 'sphere of nothingness' by Āḷāra Kālāma and the 'sphere of neither perception nor non-perception' by Uddaka Rāmaputta. Since these two persons do not appear outside the early Buddhist literature, their historicity is somewhat dubious. However, the two teachers have an incidental appearance in a number of early Buddhist texts besides the early biographies, and this supports the hypothesis that they really existed. In this chapter I will investigate the historical significance of all these passages; I hope to show that the two teachers really were historical persons, and that they almost certainly taught the Bodhisatta.

## Textual sources and the historical problem

The main source for the account of the Bodhisatta's training under the two teachers is the *Ariyapariyesana Sutta* (M no. 26: APS),[1] although the same account is repeated in the *Mahā-Saccaka Sutta* (M no. 36), the *Bodhi-Rājakumāra Sutta* (M no. 85) and the *Saṅgārava Sutta* (M no. 100). There are also Sarvāstivādin and Dharmaguptaka versions of the story in Chinese translation,[2] and Sanskrit versions in the Mahāsāṅghika *Mahāvastu*[3] and the Mūlasarvāstivādin *Saṅghabhedavastu*.[4] Both men are also mentioned in the Vinayas and Sūtras of some of these different schools when the recently awakened Buddha wonders to whom he can teach his doctrine: at first he thinks of the two men, but then he realizes that they have died.[5] It seems that the account of the Bodhisatta's training under the two teachers was embedded in the pre-sectarian Buddhist tradition. A correct understanding of the historicity of these accounts is vital for a correct understanding of early Buddhist meditation.

Scholarly opinion on the historical authenticity of this account is split. Louis de La Vallée Poussin seems to have accepted that there is some truth in its authenticity,[6] and more recently Zafiropulo has outlined a number of arguments in support of its veracity.[7] But according to scholars such as André Bareau, Johannes Bronkhorst and Tilmann Vetter,[8] the story of the

Bodhisatta's training under the two men is a fabrication.[9] Bronkhorst, following Bareau, explains that the *Mahīśāsaka Vinaya* relates the story about the Buddha's intention to teach the two men first, although it says nothing about his training under them, and this is despite the fact that it says a number of other things about the Bodhisattva prior to his awakening.[10] For this reason he concludes: 'One suspects that the names of these two men originally occurred only where the Buddha thinks of possible persons with whom to start his missionary activity. In order to give some content to these mysterious names, the account of the Bodhisatta's training under teachers with these names was added.'[11]

This argument, based on the evidence of the *Mahīśāsaka Vinaya*, is a version of the argument from silence. According to such arguments the absence of information in a source is held to be of exceptional significance; in this case, the absence of the account of the training under the two teachers in the *Mahīśāsaka Vinaya* is thought to show that the account found in the other texts was a later fabrication. Arguments from silence are, however, notoriously difficult to prove and are best used in support of a theory based on other, more reliable, evidence. It seems to me that this particular version of the argument from silence is fundamentally flawed, since it presupposes the antiquity of the *Mahīśāsaka Vinaya*, although this is far from clear.

## Arguments for the historical authenticity of the biographical account in the *Mahīśāsaka Vinaya*

The argument of Bareau *et al.* is based on two related facts. First of all, the account of the awakening in the *Mahīśāsaka Vinaya* does not mention the training under the two teachers. In addition to this, all the versions of the account of the Buddha's decision to teach these two men first do not mention that they had previously been his teachers. Bareau believed that the absence of the training under the two teachers in the *Mahīśāsaka Vinaya*'s account of the awakening was a sign of its antiquity. Thus, he assumed that the composers of the early biographical tracts invented the fact that the two men had been teachers of the Bodhisatta because of their appearance in the account of the decision to teach.

The fact that the *Mahīśāsaka Vinaya* does not mention the training under the two teachers is clearly the most important part of Bareau's argument. But there is a more plausible explanation for this omission than the one given by Bareau. It is more likely that the training under the two teachers was not mentioned in this text because its ancient guardians removed all accounts of the Bodhisatta's strivings from its beginning. This can be seen in the structure of the *Mahīśāsaka Vinaya*'s biographical account.[12] According to Bareau, it begins with the Bodhisatta's arrival at Uruvilvā, an event that all the other sources unanimously agree occurs after the training under the two teachers. It is therefore not a source for events before that. Worse still, according to most of the other sources (apart from the APS and its Sarvāstivādin version preserved in Chinese), the Bodhisatta's arrival at Uruvilvā initiates a period in which he practises harsh austerities. This is not mentioned in the *Mahīśāsaka Vinaya*, which therefore lacks almost all the details of the Bodhisatta's strivings. Why is this?

According to Frauwallner, the *Mahīśāsaka Vinaya* is simply corrupt: 'Of all the Vinaya works we have studied, the Vinaya of the Mahīśāsaka has the worst tradition.'[13] If we accept Frauwallner's judgement, it means that the apparent simplicity of the *Mahīśāsaka Vinaya* is due to the fact that much of its original material has been lost in transmission. Its redactors, either by accident or deliberately, omitted biographical material on the Bodhisattva's strivings. It seems, then, that the differences between it and the other biographical accounts of the awakening may not be due to its antiquity, and are instead likely to be the result of the redactional activity of its textual guardians. In fact, the *Mahīśāsaka Vinaya* appears most like the biographical account in the Theravādin Vinaya, which also lacks the details of the Bodhisatta's strivings and begins with the awakening.[14] Like the Theravādin Vinaya, the *Mahīśāsaka Vinaya* is not a reliable source for the biographical incidents occurring before the awakening. It is easy to see why this biographical material was not preserved in the Theravādin Vinaya: the relevant material has been preserved in the Suttapiṭaka. Similarly, the apparent lack of any information on the strivings of the Bodhisattva in the *Mahīśāsaka Vinaya* is probably due to the fact that the relevant material was preserved in the Mahīśāsaka Sūtrapiṭaka.

It appears that the *Mahīśāsaka Vinaya* is not a reliable source on the strivings of the Bodhisattva. The first part of Bareau's argument, therefore, is refuted. What about Bareau's second argument? Why is it not mentioned, in the account of the Bodhisatta's decision to teach, that the two men had been teachers of the Bodhisatta? Before answering this, it must be noted that Bareau was unaware that the *Saṅghabhedavastu* account of the Buddha's decision to teach the two men first does include a reference to the fact that the two had previously taught the Bodhisatta.[15] This suggests that we ought not to attach much importance to the failure of any of the other Vinaya or Sūtra accounts to refer to this episode. There is, however, a very simple reason for the fact that the other accounts fail to mention it.

In the account of the Buddha's decision to teach the two men in the APS (M I.169.33ff), there is no need to mention the training under them for it is found just a few pages earlier (M I.163.27ff). This suggests that the men may not have been named as teachers of the Bodhisatta in the various accounts of the decision to teach because the two episodes – the striving and the decision to teach – were originally part of the same biographical account, and there was no need for repetition. It seems to me that this explanation is more plausible than Bareau's use of the argument from silence: we can suppose that an early, pre-sectarian account of the Buddha's decision to teach did not name the two men as teachers of the Bodhisattva because the teachers had already been mentioned earlier in the same account. In this case, repetition was not required for the information had already been supplied.

These arguments, which explain the texts without recourse to the argument from silence, imply that the tradition of the two teachers ought to be taken seriously. If we discount Bareau's sceptical arguments based on the *Mahīśāsaka Vinaya*, there appear to be few reasons for doubting either the fact that the two teachers were historical figures or that they taught the Bodhisatta. It is certainly surprising the early Buddhists did not claim that the meditative states of 'nothingness' and 'neither perception nor non-perception' were the original discoveries of the Bodhisatta. Such a claim, which would have exalted the Buddha's position, is only to be expected of a new religious movement. The claim that the Bodhisatta was taught by two teachers impresses one as a statement of historical fact rather than zealous hagiography. This impression is supported by a number of peculiarities found in the APS. Before considering these peculiarities, I will examine other texts on the two teachers preserved in the early Buddhist literature. This material has been overlooked by previous scholars but is historically significant because it is not an attempt to fabricate the teachers' historicity. It is incidental evidence that, we can safely assume, was composed without any hidden agenda. Although the material is limited, it reveals some telling historical facts about the two men.

## Further texts on the two teachers

The commentary on the APS tells us that the personal name of Āḷāra Kālāma was Āḷāra, and that Kālāma was his *gotta* name.[16] The name 'Kālāma' appears a few times in the Suttapiṭaka. According to Malalasekera, Kālāma was a clan or family name.[17] The Buddha is said to have given a discourse to the Kālāmas in their town of Kesaputta in Kosala:[18] the commentary on this Sutta tells us that the Kālāmas were *khattiya-s*, but does not relate them to Āḷāra Kālāma.[19] We do not know the location of Kesaputta in Kosala, or even if Āḷāra Kālāma came from there, but we do know that in the Buddha's time Kapilavatthu had been annexed by the kingdom of Kosala. There are at least three pieces of evidence suggesting this. At Sn 422, the Buddha tells King Bimbisāra that his countrymen (*janapado*) live on the slopes of the Himālayas, '[vassals] of the one possessing an abode (*niketino*) among the Kosalans'.[20] In the *Dhammacetiya Sutta* (M no. 89), King Pasenadi of Kosala is reported to have said: 'The Blessed One is a Kosalan, I too am a Kosalan.'[21] And the *Bharaṇḍu-Kālāma Sutta* begins by stating: 'At one time the Blessed One, wandering among the Kosalans, arrived in Kapilavatthu.'[22] Thus we can assume that the city of Kapilavatthu was included within the kingdom of Kosala in the Buddha's lifetime. If Āḷāra

Kālāma belonged to the Kālāma clan situated in the town of Kesaputta in the kingdom of Kosala, and if Kapilavatthu formed part of Kosala in the Buddha's lifetime, then it is possible that the two towns were near each other, and that Āḷāra Kālāma lived near to Kapilavatthu. Such a possibility is supported by other evidence.

In the *Bharaṇḍu-Kālāma Sutta* it is stated that the Buddha stayed at the hermitage (*assama*) of a certain Bharaṇḍu Kālāma in Kapilavatthu.[23] The text tells us that Bharaṇḍu Kālāma used to be one of the Buddha's fellow renouncers (*purāṇasabrahmacārī*). The commentary expands upon this and tells us that Bharaṇḍu had been an associate of the Buddha in the time of Āḷāra Kālāma; in those days, he had lived in the very same hermitage in which he was still living.[24] If the story is true, it seems that by staying in the hermitage of Bharaṇḍu Kālāma, the Buddha was visiting the hermitage of his former teacher Āḷāra Kālāma and conversing with his old companion Bharaṇḍu. This evidence lends plausibility to the tradition that the Bodhisatta first of all sought out Āḷāra Kālāma after his renunciation: if the latter lived nearby, he was probably well known in the immediate area.[25] It is even possible that Bharaṇḍu, and not the Buddha (who had forsaken the community), was the son or spiritual heir of Āḷāra.

Āḷāra Kālāma is also mentioned in the *Mahāparinibbāna Sutta* (D no. 16), in a story recounted by his disciple Pukkusa Mallaputta to the Buddha.[26] Pukkusa is said to have told the Buddha that when a caravan of 500 carts once passed by Āḷāra Kālāma, he claimed that he did not see or hear the caravan. When asked if he was asleep (*sutto*), he said that he was not, but when asked if he was conscious (*saññī*), he agreed (*evam āvuso*). The Buddha's reply to this elevates himself at the expense of his supposed former teacher: he is said to have retorted that once he did not hear the thunder and lightning that killed two farmers nearby. It is hardly possible that this story was composed when the fabricated person 'Āḷāra Kālāma' had been accepted in Buddhist circles as a real, pre-Buddhist figure, long after the knowledge of his invention had been forgotten. The story works only if the audience, Buddhist or non-Buddhist, had in mind a real figure whom they could place in a contemporary milieu. This evidence, as well as that contained in the *Bharaṇḍu-Kālāma Sutta*, supports the suggestion that Āḷāra Kālāma was a historical figure.[27]

There is also further information on Uddaka Rāmaputta. He is mentioned in the *Uddaka Sutta* (S IV.83–84) and the *Vassakāra Sutta* (A II.180–81). In the former a verse is ascribed to him in which he claims that he is 'wise' (*vedagū*) and an 'all-conqueror' (*sabbajī*), terms indicating liberation. The Buddha says that Uddaka is not liberated, and reinterprets the terms in the verse to show this. In the *Vassakāra Sutta* the Brahmin Vassakāra, chief minister of Magadha, visits the Buddha in Rājagaha and tells him that the *rājā* Eḷeyya has faith in the *samaṇa* Rāmaputta; the commentary names the latter as Uddaka Rāmaputta.[28] Vassakāra also appears in the *Mahāparinibbāna Sutta* as the chief minister of King Ajātasattu of Magadha.[29] Vassakāra's connection with Rājagaha and Magadha suggests that the *rājā* Eḷeyya was a local chieftain in Magadha, probably situated somewhere close to Rājagaha. If so, it is likely that Uddaka Rāmaputta was based in or around Rājagaha. This suggestion is confirmed by the *Mahāvastu*, which states that Udraka Rāmaputra lived in Rājagṛha (Mvu II.119.8). The coincidence of this different evidence from the Theravādin and Mahāsāṅghika sources is not to be overlooked. It suggests a common early tradition that Uddaka Rāmaputta was based in Rājagaha, no doubt as a famous sage of Magadha.[30] This diverse information on the two teachers supports the notion that they were historical figures. This claim is supported by other features in the APS, the most notable of these being the appearance in the narrative of a certain Rāma, the father or spiritual teacher of Uddaka Rāmaputta.

## Uddaka Rāmaputta and Rāma

A peculiar detail, preserved in almost all the biographical accounts, can be seen when the accounts of the Buddha's visits to the two teachers in the APS are compared. It suggests beyond any reasonable doubt that the two men were historical figures.[31]

The account of the visit to Āḷāra Kālāma begins immediately after the Bodhisatta has renounced the world and joined this teacher's hermitage. At first the Bodhisatta is said to attain an intellectual mastery of the teaching (*taṃ dhammaṃ pariyāpuniṃ*), but he then reflects that it consists of 'just that much striking of the lips, that much talk about talk'.[32] The Bodhisatta is then said to realize that Āḷāra Kālāma did not proclaim his doctrine because of mere faith but because of direct realization.[33] Thus the Bodhisatta asks his teacher how far he had realized his teaching, and the latter replies that he has attained the sphere of 'nothingness'.[34] This attainment is termed *dhamma* throughout the account: the Bodhisatta endeavours to attain the meditative realization of this *dhamma*, and soon does so.[35] The account of the training under Uddaka Rāmaputta is almost exactly the same: the Bodhisatta first of all gains an intellectual understanding of the teaching, before attaining the direct realization of the sphere of 'neither perception nor non-perception'. But there is a subtle difference between the two accounts, a difference that lends plausibility to the notion that the teachers were historical figures. It is quite obvious that it was not Uddaka Rāmaputta who had attained the sphere of 'neither perception nor non-perception' but Rāma, his father or spiritual teacher.

This becomes clear in the following exchange. The Bodhisatta is said to have contemplated that Rāma (not Rāmaputta) did not proclaim (*pavedesi*) his attainment because of mere faith, but because he dwelt (*vihāsi*) knowing and seeing it himself.[36] The corresponding passage in the account of the training under Āḷāra Kālāma uses the same verbs in the present tense (*pavedeti*, *viharati*), indicating that Āḷāra was living and Rāma was dead, and that Rāmaputta had not realized the *dhamma* that he taught. The same phenomenon is found in the rest of the passage. Thus the Bodhisatta is said to have asked Rāmaputta: 'To what extent (*kittāvatā*) did the venerable Rāma proclaim (*pavedesī*): "I pass my time having understood, realized and attained this *dhamma*"?'[37] The reply, of course, is as far as the sphere of 'neither perception nor non-perception'. The Bodhisatta is then said to have contemplated that not only did Rāma have faith, energy, mindfulness, concentration and insight, but that he too possesses these virtues. And at the end of the episode, after the Bodhisatta has attained the sphere of 'neither perception nor non-perception', Uddaka Rāmaputta is reported to have said: 'Thus the *dhamma* that Rāma knew (*aññāsi*), that *dhamma* you [the Bodhisatta] know (*jānāsi*); the *dhamma* you know, that *dhamma* Rāma knew.'[38] This is different from the corresponding speech that Āḷāra Kālāma is reported to have made to the Bodhisatta: 'Thus the *dhamma* that I know (*jānāmi*), that *dhamma* you know (*jānāsi*); the *dhamma* you know, that *dhamma* I know.'[39] And whereas Āḷāra Kālāma is willing to establish the Bodhisatta as an equal to him (*samasamaṃ*), so that they can lead the ascetic group together (*imaṃ gaṇaṃ pariharāmā ti*),[40] Uddaka Rāmaputta acknowledges that the Bodhisatta is equal to Rāma (*iti yādiso rāmo ahosi tādiso tuvaṃ*), not himself, and asks the Buddha to lead the community alone (*imaṃ gaṇaṃ pariharā ti*).[41]

The distinction between Uddaka Rāmaputta and Rāma is also found in the Sarvāstivādin, Dharmaguptaka and Mahāsāṅghika accounts of the Bodhisattva's training.[42] The *Saṅghabhedavastu* (plus parallel Tibetan translations) and the *Lalitavistara* fail to distinguish Rāmaputta from Rāma,[43] but this is probably because of a later obfuscation of the tradition. Oral or scribal transmitters of the text would have tended to identify the two accounts, after some significant period of time. Thus, it is likely that the distinction between Uddaka Rāmaputta and Rāma would have dropped out of the account at a later point. This is much more likely than the opposite scenario, i.e. that the distinction between Uddaka Rāmaputta and Rāma was invented in the majority of texts at a later date. Indeed, exactly the same mistake has been made by I. B. Horner, the PTS translator of the *Majjhima Nikāya*, who has been duped by the repetitive oral style into believing that the accounts of the training under the two teachers must be exactly the same, apart from the difference between the names of the two men and their meditative attainments.[44] It is an easy mistake to make.

Although previous scholars have noticed the distinction between Uddaka Rāmaputta and Rāma, the significance of this fact has not yet been clearly stated. It must be pointed out that there is no need to trouble over these details in an oral tradition where adjacent passages are often composed in exactly the same way, with one passage usually being a verbatim repetition of the previous one. Reciters of this autobiographical episode would have tended to make the two accounts identical, apart from substituting the name Uddaka Rāmaputta for Āḷāra Kālāma. An effort has been made to make sure that the repetitive oral style does not interfere with the distinction between Uddaka Rāmaputta and Rāma. The distinction can only be explained if Rāma and Rāmaputta were two different people, and the effort to maintain it must surely go back to the beginning of the tradition of composing biographical Suttas. Otherwise, it is part of an elaborate hoax – a most unlikely state of affairs. Bareau maintained that the correspondence between the descriptions of the training under the two teachers proved their artificial (i.e. unhistorical) nature.[45] But repetition is normal in Pāli oral literature. The preservation of the distinction between Rāmaputta and Rāma, in spite of the normal Pāli repetition, does not give the impression that the tract is contrived. On the coutrary, it seems that the account has preserved valuable historical information. The conclusion must be that the three men were real.[46] It seems that the early Buddhist literature contains the earliest reliable information on teachers of meditation in ancient India.

## Other peculiarities in the *Ariyapariyesana Sutta*

The existence in fifth century BC northern India of two teachers of meditation called Āḷāra Kālāma and Uddaka Rāmaputta can hardly be doubted. But did they really teach the Bodhisatta? According to Zafiropulo, the biographical episodes most likely to be historically authentic are those containing the names of the Bodhisatta's teachers and aspects of their teaching.[47] In support of this claim, it can be shown that the APS contains further peculiarities, suggesting that it is the oldest account of the awakening. These do not definitely prove that the two teachers instructed the Bodhisatta in meditation, but they add to the historical worth of the account.

### *Philological peculiarities*

One of the most peculiar episodes in the early Buddhist literature is found in the APS. Besides its peculiarity the account contains an anomalous linguistic form; both features suggest that the episode is archaic. The account in question is that of the Buddha's first meeting after the awakening, with Upaka the Ājīvika. Upon being asked 'Who is your teacher?' (M I.170.37: *ko vā te satthā*), the Buddha is reported to have made the famous declaration that he has no teacher or equal (M I.171.7: *na me ācariyo atthi, sadiso me na vijjati*). In response to this, Upaka is said to have shaken his head and replied 'It may be, sir' (M I.171.16: *huveyya p' āvuso ti*). The form *huveyya* is an anomaly in the Pāli canon. In his notes on the APS, Trenckner records the textual variant *hupeyya*, which is also the form given in the VRI as well as the version of the account contained in the PTS edition of the Vinaya (Vin I.8.30). According to Norman, the form *hupeyya* is probably 'the correct form of Upaka's reply', whereas the form *huveyya* is probably 'the result of normalising *hupeyya* to make it conform to the Pāli pattern.'[48] Thus the word *hupeyya* seems to be a dialect form of the more normal Pāli *bhaveyya* (third singular optative, √*bhū*); Oberlies describes it as 'the rustic slang of an ājīvika ascetic'.[49] It is probably an obscure word from some old, 'backwater' Magadhan dialect.[50] Apart from this linguistic anomaly, the episode itself is most peculiar. It is not the sort of story that would have been invented – surely the early Buddhists would not have portrayed the recently awakened Buddha as someone who was not able to convert or even make an impression on his first interlocutor. The account probably records an historical fact. If so, it suggests that the biographical tract contained in the APS is of considerable historical worth.

It is worth pointing out that a further philological peculiarity in the APS occurs in the account of the training under the two teachers. This account is the only prose passage in which the second personal pronoun has been preserved in the form *tuvaṃ*; elsewhere, this form is only found in verse.[51] If the insertion of an epenthetic vowel (*svarabhakti*) is a phenomenon connected with eastern dialects,[52] the word *tuvaṃ* could indicate that the account was composed in the homeland of Buddhism (Magadha). Its position in a prose passage is certainly unusual. No doubt other 'Māgadhisms' in the early Buddhist texts were ironed out in the translation/transformation of the early oral compositions into different dialects. But why was the anomalous form in the APS not changed? Because of an historical accident? This is possible. But it is also possible that it was left in on purpose, because this account was known to be archaic and not to be tampered with.[53]

### *Narrative peculiarities*

Alone among the Pāli texts on awakening of the Bodhisatta, the APS is peculiar in that it contains only the account of the Bodhisatta's visit to the two teachers in its section on the strivings. Moreover, it has an exact parallel in a Chinese Sarvāstivādin Sūtra.[54] This most probably means that one text on the strivings – the ancestor to both the APS and its Chinese Sarvāstivādin parallel – was already closed to other accounts of the strivings in pre-sectarian times.[55] This is most peculiar. Why did the ancient compilers/redactors of the texts exclude other tracts on the strivings from the pre-sectarian version of the APS? There is no obvious reason why the APS should not follow the order of events stated in the other three autobiographical texts of the *Majjhima Nikāya* (the MSS *et al*: the *Mahā-Saccaka Sutta*, the *Bodhirājakumāra Sutta* and the *Saṅgārava Sutta*). In these Suttas, after departing from the two teachers and then arriving at Uruvelā, three similes are said to have occurred to the Bodhisatta; they provide the reason for his practice of breathless meditation and emaciation.[56] Why is this account of the Bodhisatta's asceticism not also found in the APS at the same point (M I.167.8)? It is hardly likely that this information dropped out of the pre-sectarian version of the APS because of some accident in its transmission, for the biographical accounts in the MSS *et al.* would have acted as a check against this.[57] The omission must be due to a redactional decision: for some reason or other, the compilers/redactors of the pre-sectarian version of the APS decided that the account of the austerities – as well as the account of the awakening following it – was not to be added to it. Why did they do this?

One possible explanation is that the narrative form of the APS prevented any easy addition of further accounts of the strivings. Indeed, narrative considerations probably played some part in the exclusion of accounts of the strivings from two of the other biographical Suttas of the *Majjhima Nikāya*, the *Bhayabharava Sutta* (M no. 4) and the *Dvedhāvitakka Sutta* (M no. 19). These Suttas are both autobiographical accounts of events in the Bodhisatta's life before the awakening. Like the MSS *et al.*, they culminate in the attainment of the four *jhāna-s* and three knowledges that constitute liberating insight.[58] They do not, however, include any of the accounts of the Bodhisatta's strivings found in the APS or the MSS *et al.* But this is probably because the narrative form of these texts prevented the addition of other strivings attempted by the Bodhisatta. The *Bhayabharava Sutta* is an account of how the Bodhisatta overcame the fear of living in the wilderness, while the *Dvedhāvitakka Sutta* is an account of the Bodhisatta's introspection of his own good and bad thoughts. Unlike the other biographical accounts of the Bodhisatta's strivings in the *Majjhima Nikāya*, neither of these texts are sequential accounts of the Bodhisatta's strivings that begin with the renunciation and end with the awakening. The narratives in both these Suttas are such that other accounts of the strivings could not have been added without making substantial changes to the texts. It appears that rather than make these changes, the ancient redactors of the early Buddhist literature left the two texts as they were.

It could be argued that narrative considerations similar to these prevented the addition of further accounts of the Bodhisatta's strivings to the pre-sectarian version of the APS. This is perhaps possible since the strivings in the APS are based around a peculiar formula that occurs immediately after the Bodhisatta's arrival at Uruvelā (M I.167.9) and describes the awakening:

> Then, bhikkhus, I thought: 'Lovely indeed is this stretch of earth, delightful is this forest thicket, and the river flows clear, with accessible banks, lovely, near to a village for alms. This indeed is suitable for the striving of a son of a good family who is bent on striving.' I sat down right there, *bhikkhus*, thinking: 'This is suitable for striving.'

> (M I.167.9:) O bhikkhus, being myself subject to birth, [but] understanding the danger in what is subject to birth, seeking the unborn, unsurpassed release from bondage that is *nibbāna*, I attained the unborn, unsurpassed release from bondage that is *nibbāna*.[59]

This last sentence is repeated a few times with minor changes to note that the goal of Nirvana is free from old age, illness, death, sorrow and defilement.[60] It is a description of liberation that is unique in the Suttapiṭaka, but an almost identical version of it appears in the Chinese Sarvāstivādin parallel to the APS.[61] This pericope is also an integral part of the APS and its Chinese Sarvāstivādin parallel: the same formula is found earlier in both texts to describe the Bodhisatta's reason for going forth from home to homelessness.[62] The account of the Bodhisatta's strivings in the original, pre-sectarian version of this text must have been structured around this formula. It is conceivable, then, that the account of the austerities and awakening found in the MSS *et al.* was excluded because of this narrative structure, for this structure makes the addition of the entire section on the austerities and awakening quite a tricky matter (M I.240.29–I.249.18 from the MSS *et al.* would have to appear at M I.167.8 of the APS). It would require the combination of two different accounts of the awakening – that from the APS cited above, plus the realization of the Four Noble Truths and destruction of the corruptions in the MSS *et al.* If these two different accounts of the awakening are put together, the account in the APS could be read as a sort of summary of the attainment of the liberating insight outlined in the MSS *et al.*, but the end result is awkward:

> (M I.249.4–18, from the MSS): When my mind was focused in this way, pure, cleansed, free from blemish and defilement, soft, workable, still and imperturbable, I directed it towards the knowledge of the destruction of the corruptions. I understood suffering, its origin, its cessation and the path leading to its cessation, as it really is; I understood the corruptions, their origin, their cessation and the path leading to their cessation, as it really is. Knowing and seeing in this way, my mind was freed from the corruptions of desire, becoming and ignorance. When my mind was released, there was the knowledge '[it is] released', and I understood: 'Birth is destroyed, the holy life has been lived, done is what had to be done, there is no more of this state'.[63]
>
> (M I.167.9ff, from the APS): O *bhikkhus*, being myself subject to birth, [but] understanding the danger in what is subject to birth, seeking the unborn, unsurpassed release from bondage that is *nibbāna*, I attained the unborn, unsurpassed release from bondage that is *nibbāna* . . . The knowledge and vision arose in me: 'Unshakeable is my release, this is my last birth, there is now no more rebecoming.'[64]

The combination of these two accounts creates the difficulty that two different pericopes describing the Buddha's knowledge of his awakening are juxtaposed, and this perhaps explains why the APS was closed to the account of liberating insight found in the MSS *et al*. But such a narrative consideration is not enough to explain the omission of the Bodhisatta's austerities from the APS. Surely the account of the austerities could have been combined, in some form, with the account of the strivings and awakening in the APS. This is seen in the *Mahāvastu*, where the austerities and the four *jhāna-s* are added to an account of the Bodhisattva's visit to the two teachers without describing the awakening in terms of the three knowledges.[65] There is nothing to prevent the APS having a similar form: the account of the austerities could have been added to it without also adding the account of the *jhāna-s* and three knowledges. We are forced to conclude that the peculiar narrative structure of the APS does not explain the absence of the austerities.

What could be the reason for the peculiar narrative structure of the APS, with its unique description of the awakening? As we have seen, the description of the awakening in the APS is unique in the early Buddhist literature. Indeed, the passage simply says that the Bodhisatta 'attained Nirvana'. The expression 'to attain *nibbāna*' (*nibbānam* + *adhi-√gam*) is not exclusive to the APS,[66] but there is no other similar description of the awakening.[67] This peculiarity may be due to the fact that the biographical account in the APS predates the development of a literary tradition, one in which the various pericopes describing the process of awakening had been standardized. Facts about the pericope that describe the Buddha's own knowledge of his awakening in the APS support this hypothesis. This pericope, as noted above, reads as follows:

> The knowledge (*ñāṇañ*) and vision (*dassanaṃ*) arose in me: 'Unshakeable is my release, this is the last birth, there is now no more rebecoming.'[68]

This 'simple liberation pericope' occurs a few more times in the Suttapiṭaka and is always applied to the Buddha's awakening,[69] in Suttas that are clearly later than the APS.[70] It is quite remarkable that this pericope is not used elsewhere in the Suttapiṭaka to describe the liberation of a *bhikkhu*. Indeed, some of the Suttas that include this pericope in the description of the Bodhisatta's awakening are followed by parallel Suttas describing the liberation of other people (*sattā*), and these parallel passages do not use the pericope.[71] The restriction of the pericope to accounts of the Bodhisatta's liberation alone seems to have been deliberate; the fact that outside the APS it is applied only to the Bodhisatta suggests that it was known to be a special sort of pericope, one that described the Buddha's attainment alone.[72] It seems, then, that the APS contains peculiar formulae that describe the awakening and the Buddha's recognition of it, as well as a limited account of the Bodhisatta's strivings. Both features support the hypothesis that it is the oldest account of these events. They are good reasons for supposing that the APS is an early composition that was hardly changed during its transmission, and so retained its archaic features.[73]

To summarize: the account of the APS is peculiar, both in its description of the awakening and the omission of the austerities and the *jhāna-s*. This omission could possibly be the result of an error in the text's transmission, although this is unlikely because the three other autobiographical texts in the *Majjhima Nikāya* (the MSS *et al.*) would have helped prevent such an error. Thus we must see the omission as a result of the editorial activity of the early redactors of the texts: the austerities and *jhāna-s* were most probably kept out on purpose. Such omissions could perhaps be due to the narrative structure of the pre-sectarian version of the text, but unlike the *Bhayabherava Sutta* and the *Dvedhāvitakka Sutta* (texts whose omission of the strivings can be explained on narrative grounds), the narrative in the APS is virtually identical to that in the MSS *et al.*, and the account of the austerities and the attainment of the *jhāna-s* (but not the realization of the Four Noble Truths) could have been added to it quite easily. Hence, there is no narrative reason that could explain this omission. Another reason for the form of the APS is suggested by the simplicity and uniqueness of the APS account of the awakening: both features suggest that it was a very early composition. Why, then, was this text preserved in its peculiar form along with its archaic features? Failing any other explanation for the text's peculiarities, the only other explanation is that it was closed early on because it was known to be the most ancient account of the awakening. If so, it is this account that is most likely to be historically authentic.

### *Polemic peculiarities*

Bronkhorst has recently claimed that the account of the Bodhisatta's visit to the two teachers is a polemic against non-Buddhist practices.[74] If this is correct, and the account does have such an ulterior motive, it would suggest that the account was not composed to record historical facts. But it seems to me that there is no clear evidence that this part of the APS is a polemic. The notion that the goals of the teachers are liberating is rejected, certainly, on the grounds that the meditative attainment of the spheres of 'nothingness' and 'neither perception nor non-perception' leads only to rebirth in these spheres.[75] But this is not a total condemnation of the teachers' meditative methods. Instead, when the Buddha wonders who would be the most worthy recipients of his new teaching later on in the text, the two teachers are depicted in a rather favourable manner:

> Āḷāra Kālāma is learned, intelligent, wise, [and] has long since possessed little in the way of defilement. Why don't I teach this doctrine to Āḷāra Kālāma first of all? He would understand it quickly.[76]

Uddaka Rāmaputta is considered in exactly the same terms. This generous appraisal of the teachers does not seem to reflect any polemic against them: if the account was a polemic, one would expect the denigration of the teachers' non-Buddhist practices to be much more obvious. Such is the critique of the ascetic practices outlined in the other autobiographical accounts, where the Bodhisatta considers that breathless meditation and emaciation are useless in the following terms:

> Whatever ascetics and Brahmins experienced violent, painful, sharp, piercing sensations in former times, [it was] only to this extent, [but] no more than this. Whatever ascetics and Brahmins will experience violent, painful, sharp, piercing sensations in future times, [it will be] only to this extent, [but] no more than this. Whatever ascetics and Brahmins experience violent, painful, sharp, piercing sensations nowadays, [it is] only to this extent, [but] no more than this. And yet through these piercing, difficult acts I have not attained a distinction of knowing and seeing, beyond human phenomena, which is suitable for the noble ones. Might there be another path to awakening?[77]

The first *jhāna* is sometimes said to be 'a distinction of knowing and seeing, beyond human phenomena, suitable for the noble ones',[78] and so it is implicit in the Bodhisatta's rejection of the ascetic practices that they did not get him as far as even the most basic meditative attainment.[79] This passage is therefore an unequivocal condemnation of the ascetic practices: it is made quite clear that the Bodhisatta had gone as far with asceticism as humanly possible, and yet did not attain any spiritual progress. The account in the APS, on the other hand, is not unequivocal: the teachers' meditative practices are not denigrated, and it is implied that they must be of some soteriological benefit for the Buddha is in no doubt as to the teachers' spiritual qualities.

If the tract is not obviously a polemic, the opposite could be argued, i.e. that positive features in the depiction of the teachers imply that it was really an attempt to legitimize their non-Buddhist practices in early Buddhist circles. This supposition would certainly explain the lack of an unqualified polemic in the account, as well as the complimentary description of the two teachers. The text, as it reads, seems to serve the purpose of legitimizing the Buddhist practice of the teachers' non-Buddhist methods. It is easy to imagine that it fostered the impression in the early *saṅgha* that the practices of the teachers were of some use, even if it was thought that they do not lead to *nibbāna*. Perhaps, then, the purpose of the account was 'inclusivistic',[80] i.e. a positive attempt to incorporate alien practices within the early Buddhist tradition.

This is by no means clear, however, even if the effect of the account may well have been to legitimize the two teachers' meditative practices. An inclusivist account should be critical, but not too critical, for the presence of derogatory elements would have weakened the legitimacy of alien practices within the Buddhist *saṅgha*. The denial that the teachers' goals lead to *nibbāna* is permissible for an inclusivist, provided that it is not an unequivocal condemnation of the teachers' meditative practices of the teachers. This seems to be the case in the APS: the denial that the goals of the teachers lead to *nibbāna* is not a total condemnation of non-Buddhist practices. However, the account also reports that the Bodhisatta left the teachers because he found their teachings unsatisfactory (*analaṅkaritvā*) and was 'disgusted' (*nibbijja*) with them.[81] This is hardly the statement of an inclusivist who wished to legitimize alien meditative techniques; its effect is wholly negative, and not conducive to the Buddhist acceptance of the practices.

The case against the argument for inclusivism is perhaps marginal, but important nevertheless. It seems to me that if the purpose of the account was to legitimize non-Buddhist practices, one would expect the efficacity of the practices to be clearly stated and the accounts to be lacking in negative features. This is not the case: the accounts are critical of the practices, and their efficacity is merely suggested. But the hypothesis of an inclusivistic polemic requires that the legitimacy of the practices is clearly articulated, rather than implied.

On the whole, it seems to me that the account of the visits to Āḷāra Kālāma and Uddaka Rāmaputta is equivocal: not obviously a polemic against non-Buddhist practices (as the account of the Bodhisatta's practice of breathless meditation and emaciation is), nor clearly an attempt to legitimize them in Buddhist circles (although this was probably the overall effect of the accounts). I doubt, therefore, that it was composed in order to promote a polemic or inclusivist agenda. The account is idiosyncratic. If so, is it not more likely to be a record of historical events rather than a composition with some sectarian axe to grind? The most likely reason for the composition of the account, as it seems to me, was to record the historical fact that the Bodhisatta really was taught by the two teachers.

Taken together, the philological, narrative and polemic peculiarities of the APS suggests that it contains the oldest account of the Bodhisatta's awakening. It contains episodes and facts that cannot have been invented, as well as an account of the awakening that is unique, simple, and lacking in any clear polemical purpose. There seems to be no reason to deny the historical authenticity of one of the most important episodes in the APS – that Āḷāra Kālāma and Uddaka Rāmaputta were teachers of the Bodhisatta.

## The APS as a description of the Buddha's awakening

At this point in my argument, it would be worth making a few more remarks on the simplicity of the account in the APS. Although simplicity is not necessarily an unambiguous sign of the historical authenicity of any Buddhist text, it seems to me that in this case it is likely. The simplicity in the account suggests the possibility that it is a description of liberating insight, i.e. 'an immediate verbalisation of (a conceptualisation of) an actual experience',[82] rather than a theory, i.e. 'a secondary transformation of such a primary verbalisation effected for logical, doctrinal or even tactical reasons'.[83] It is easy to understand the theoretical elaboration of a simple description of primary experience, but it is less easy to understand the simplification of a theoretical account. The latter course of events is conceivable – a movement might arise with the zeal to simplify that which is complex – in which case what appears to be a primary description might be a secondary theory, 'effected for logical, doctrinal or even tactical reasons'. But we can assume that the Buddha's own accounts of his awakening would have been 'immediate verbalisations of an actual experience', rather than secondary theories. If any trace of the original account of the Buddha's awakening is to be found in the early Buddhist sources, we should expect to find it in a simple description, and not a complex theory; the simpler the description the better.

Taking all these observations into consideration, the account of the awakening that is most likely to be the oldest, and which may even go back to the Buddha himself, is the one contained in the APS. This account is certainly not a theory (what doctrinal point does it make?), but a very simple description. It is the only account of the awakening that uses apophatic language; the account in the MSS *et al.* seems extremely complex and theoretical in comparison. It is quite possible that the MSS account is a theoretical elaboration of an earlier description of liberating insight, such as the description found in the APS. But there are no reasons for believing that the APS account is a theoretical simplification of the account in the MSS *et al.*

It is probable, then, that the simplicity of the account means that it is older than that contained in the MSS *et al.* Being older, its historical worth is greater. If this is correct, how are the other biographical episodes described in the MSS *et al.* and elsewhere to be explained? Did the Buddha really attempt severe austerities? This may be so, for we do not know, and perhaps never will, if the author(s) of the APS were comprehensive in their narrative, or if they included only what they considered to be the most relevant episodes. The matter is more complicated when it comes to the accounts of the Bodhisatta's liberation, rather than the practices leading to those accounts. The difference between the complex account in the MSS *et al.* and the simple account in the APS requires an explanation. It may be the case that the attainment of the four *jhāna-s* and three knowledges (in the MSS *et al.*) was a theoretical elaboration of the simple description in the APS. If so, it would mean that the content of the Buddha's discovery in the APS came to be formulated, by the Buddha or his immediate followers, as the four *jhāna-s* and the insight to which they lead. On the other hand, the complex account in the MSS *et al.* may represent a development of early Buddhist doctrine quite independent of the APS.

Whatever the case, the simplicity of the account contained in the APS implies that it is a description, whereas the same cannot be said of the account contained in the MSS *et al.*. It is more likely, therefore, that the APS contains the older account.

## The terms 'nothingness' and 'neither and perception nor non-perception' as epithets of liberation

It is likely that the terms used by Āḷāra Kālāma and Uddaka Rāmaputta to name their meditative goals were epithets of liberation. The Pāli account does not obviously suggest this, for the Bodhisatta's question to the two teachers ('you declare that you pass your time having realized this *dhamma* to what extent?')[84] can be interpreted in different ways, e.g. that the Bodhisatta wanted to know how far along the meditative path each teacher had progressed. Accordingly, because there is no declaration from the teachers that they had attained Nirvana, their answers might indicate only that they had gone as far as the 'sphere of nothingness' and the 'sphere of neither perception nor non-perception' respectively, without being liberated. However, in all sectarian accounts of the Bodhisatta's visits to the two teachers, it is clear that the Bodhisatta knows what meditative goal he is striving for in the beginning.[85] And the account only makes sense if the Bodhisatta is striving after what he imagined was liberation. The narrative implies, then, that the Bodhisatta thought that the teachers' goals to be liberating. Aśvaghoṣa certainly thought the teachers considered their goals to be liberating.[86] If this is not the case, the account of the Bodhisatta's disillusionment, upon attaining the teachers' goals and then realizing that they do not lead to Nirvana, would make no sense. The narrative works only if the Bodhisatta visits the two teachers because he thought that their goals were liberating.[87] And his disappointment shows that he thought he was striving after liberation.

If the two teachers taught what they thought were paths to liberation, a detail in the Sarvāstivādin account is unlikely to be true. According to Bareau,[88] in this account Udraka Rāmaputra taught that the 'sphere of neither perception nor non-perception' was to be attained by someone who had passed beyond the 'sphere of nothingness'. Are we to imagine that Uddaka Rāmaputta formulated his teaching in order to trump the goal of another teacher? This is possible, but I find it unlikely. And as the view of only one sect, it does not seem to be a representation of a common presectarian tradition. Instead, it is probably a reflection of the emergent Buddhist systematization of meditative schemes: in the meditative formulations of the early texts, the 'sphere of nothingness' always comes before the 'sphere of neither perception nor non-perception'. This was probably how the early Buddhists dealt with the pre-Buddhist heritage rather than a true representation of the teaching of Uddaka Rāmaputta. It probably crept into the Sarvāstivādin tract because of a scribe (or chanter) who was used to writing (or chanting) that the state of 'neither perception nor non-perception' was attained after passing beyond the state of 'nothingness'.

Another oddity is found in the account in the *Dharmaguptaka Vinaya*, although it might not reflect a later view. There, the goal of Udraka Rāmaputra is termed the 'meditative attainment of neither perception nor non-perception', i.e. *naivasaṃjñānāsaṃjñāsamāpatti*,[89] and not *naivasaṃjñānāsaṃjñāyatana*. This may not have been the terminology of the pre-sectarian biographical traditions, in which the word *āyatana* seems to have been the norm, but it does suggest that some sectarians thought that the word *āyatana* was not necessary to the formulation of the two teachers' goals. Aśvaghoṣa similarly knew the goals of the two teachers simply as *ākiṃcanya* and *asaṃjñānāsaṃjñā*.[90] If Johnston was correct in thinking that Aśvaghoṣa was a Bahuśrutika (a sect of the Mahāsāṅghikas) or 'an adherent of the school (the Kaulikas?) from which the Bahuśrutikas issued',[91] we can hypothesize that this terminology was not unusual in Mahāsāṅghika circles. Theravādin sources suggest the same thing: at Sn 1070, the Buddha teaches a Brahminic renouncer the meditative attainment of 'nothingness' (*ākiñcaññaṃ*), which the commentaries identify as *ākiñcaññāyatana*.[92] This suggests that the designation of the meditative goals of the two teachers without the word *āyatana* was an acceptable alternative in early Buddhist circles.

## Conclusion to Chapter 2

In this chapter I have argued that the original (or at least the earliest extant) biographical account of the Bodhisatta's awakening is found in the *Ariyapariyesana Sutta*. Its evidence suggests that Āḷāra Kālāma and Uddaka Rāmaputta were historical persons, as was Rāma, the teacher of Rāmaputta. They probably taught the Bodhisatta, although this does not mean that the Bodhisatta did not try other methods. I therefore accept that Āḷāra Kālāma was situated in the vicinity of Kapilavatthu in Kosala as stated in the *Bharaṇḍu-Kālāma Sutta*, and that the Bodhisatta's act of renunciation was to join Āḷāra Kālāma's hermitage. Uddaka Rāmaputta was based in Magadha, probably in or near to Rājagaha. The sources for these geographical locations (the *Bharaṇḍu-Kālāma Sutta* and the *Vassakāra Sutta*) are trustworthy because the information in them is incidental: they have no hidden agenda. The goals of the two teachers – *ākiñcañña*(*-āyatana*) and *nevasaññānāsaññā* (*-āyatana*) – were thought by the teachers to be liberating, but the Bodhisatta rejected this. If this analysis is correct, it means that we have a knowledge of some events that occurred in the early part of the Buddha's career. In the following two chapters, I will attempt to form an hypothesis about the intellectual development of the Buddha based on this historical understanding. In order to do this, it is important to establish the religious affiliation of the two teachers.

# 3

# FORMLESS MEDITATION AND EARLY BRAHMINISM

A strong case can be made for a Brahminic origin of formless meditation. The most convincing evidence for this consists of a number of early Upaniṣadic parallels to the goals of the two teachers. No less important is evidence connecting formless meditation to the tradition of early Brahminic meditation. This evidence consists of schemes of element meditation found in both the early Buddhist and Brahminic literature. In the early Brahminic literature, element meditation is based on the principle that the yogin who wishes to attain union with *brahman* must simulate the process of world dissolution in his meditative practice. Similar schemes of element meditation are found in the early Buddhist literature, and some of these include the formless spheres. Because there is no doctrinal background for these lists in the early Buddhist literature, it is more likely than not that they have been borrowed from an early Brahminic source. The early Upaniṣadic parallels to the goals of the two teachers suggest that the Brahminic source for these practices was the teachers themselves.

## Verses on meditation in the Mahābhārata and early Buddhist literature

That Buddhist and Brahminic meditators exchanged ideas and practices in early times is not in doubt. Similar verses on meditation, found in both the early Brahminic and Buddhist literature, seem to prove this. We can compare, for example, the following verses from the *Mokṣadharma* and *Theragāthā*:

> Mbh XII.180.28: *taṃ pūrvāpararātreṣu yuñjānaḥ satataṃ budhaḥ, laghvāhāro viśuddhātmā paśyaty ātmānam ātmani.*
>
> The wise man, constantly disciplining himself in the earlier and later parts of the night, taking little food, being pure, sees the self in the self. (28)[1]
>
> Th 415: *satthā hi vijesi maggam etaṃ saṅgā jātijarābhayā atītaṃ, pubbāpararattam appamatto anuyuñjassu daḷhaṃ karohi yogaṃ*

> The teacher has conquered this path which transcends attachment and the fear of birth and old-age. Being diligent, discipline [yourself] in the earlier and later parts of the night, make [your] practice firm.

Despite the fact that the word '*yoga*' is not found elsewhere in the Suttapiṭaka in a meditative context, the reference to the 'earlier and later parts of the night' and the verb *anu* + √*yuj* both indicate that this verse refers to meditative practice. We can conclude that meditation in the earlier and latter parts of the night was a common practice.[2] This hardly shows any significant connection between early Buddhist and Brahminic practices, but some sort of contact between the different traditions in early times cannot be denied. A few more verses indicate much the same thing, for example, the following verses from the Mahābhārata and *Dhammapada*:[3]

> Mbh I.74.2: *yaḥ samutpatitaṃ krodhaṃ nigṛhṇāti hayaṃ yathā, sa yantety ucyate sadbhir na yo raśmiṣu lambate.*
>
> Who restrains anger when it has arisen, just as [one would restrain] a mare, the good call him a 'restrainer', not the one who hangs onto the reins.

> Dhp 222: *yo ve uppatitaṃ kodhaṃ rathaṃ bhantaṃ va dhāraye, tam ahaṃ sārathiṃ brūmi rasmiggāho itaro jano.*
>
> Who would control anger when it has arisen, [just as one would control] a wandering chariot, I call him a charioteer, another person [merely] holds the reins.

It is notable that this *Dhammapada* verse also appears in the Gāndhārī Dharmapada,[4] which would seem to suggest that it dates to pre-Aśokan times.[5] If the verse was borrowed by Brahminic meditators, the date of the borrowing could not be determined – it could have occurred at any time before or after the Aśokan period from any one of a number of Buddhist sects. But if it was borrowed by Buddhists from Brahminic circles, for it to exist in both the Pāli *Dhammapada* as well as the *Gāndhārī Dhammapada* the borrowing would probably have occurred before the sectarian formation brought about by the Aśokan missions in the third century BC. If so, we can suppose that there was some sharing of meditative practices between early Buddhist and Brahminic groups within five or six generations of the Buddha's death. This scenario is more likely, in fact, for the widespread occurrence of the chariot metaphor in the early Brahminic literature suggests it has a Brahminic origin: in the early Brahminic literature, the chariot metaphor is not just an ethical exhortation to self-control, but is commonly applied to the meditative adept, e.g. Mbh III.202.20–21:

> The wise man who would control (*dhārayed*) the 'rays' of the six disciplined senses, the 'agitators', in himself – he is the supreme charioteer (*paramasārathiḥ*).
>
> The uncontrolled senses are like horses on a road. . .[6]

Even if a Brahminic origin of these chariot metaphors is likely, this cannot be established with absolute certainty. Another case is easier to determine. In an important early passage of the *Mokṣadharma* (Mbh XII.188), it is likely that early Brahminic meditators have borrowed Buddhist ideas, for Buddhist ideas and nomenclature are found in an incomplete form. Thus, at Mbh XII. 188.1 Bhīṣma informs Yudhiṣṭhira that he will teach him the 'fourfold discipline of meditation' (v. 1: *dhyānayogaṃ caturvidham*),[7] by which great sages attain Nirvana (v. 2: *nirvāṇagatamānasāḥ*). A further correspondence is found in v.15, where it is said that for the sage who has attained the first *dhyāna*, there is *vicāra*, *vitarka* and *viveka*.[8] The goal is again termed *nirvāṇa* in v. 22. This passage seems to have borrowed Buddhist ideas, and not vice versa, because the corresponding ideas (*dhyānayogaṃ caturvidham*, *vicāra*, *vitarka* and *viveka,* etc.) form part of a well-executed idea in the Buddhist scheme of four *jhāna-s*, [9] whereas in Mbh XII.188 an attempt is made to describe only the first *dhyāna*, after which the similarities disappear: there is no attempt to describe the second, third or fourth *dhyāna-s*. Mbh XII.188 is a sufficiently detailed account of meditation that appears to have survived with little or no corruption. If the four *dhyāna-s* were originally Brahminic, we should expect the only surviving passage on the subject – a reliable source, so it seems – to say something about each *dhyāna*. The incomplete description of the 'fourfold discipline of meditation' in Mbh XII.188 suggests that it is this passage that has borrowed Buddhist ideas.

That it is not possible to determine which passage is the source and which the borrower in the other cases does not matter. The correspondences allow us to suppose that there was meaningful contact between the two traditions in early times. The similar versions of the chariot metaphor in both the early Buddhist and Brahminic literatures even suggest that early Buddhism was influenced by the meditative ideas of early Brahminism. It is certainly possible that there were more substantial correspondences, and even that the practices taught by Āḷāra Kālāma and Uddaka Rāmaputta were related to early Brahminism. In fact, a closer relationship can be seen in corresponding schemes of element meditation outlined in the early literature of both religions.

## The elements and the formless spheres

The formless spheres are connected to the material elements of earth, water, fire and wind (*paṭhavī*, *āpo*, *tejo*, *vāyo*) in a number of lists of meditative objects in the Suttapiṭaka. This is seen in the *Samādhi Sutta*:

> Ānanda, it might be that there is the attainment of a concentration (*samādhipaṭilābho*) for a *bhikkhu* of such a kind that with regard to earth (*paṭhaviyaṃ*), he does not perceive the earth; with regard to water (*āpasmiṃ*), he does not perceive water; with regard to fire (*tejasmiṃ*), he does not perceive fire, with regard to wind (*vayasmiṃ*), he does not perceive wind; with regard to the sphere of the infinity of space (*ākāsānañcāyatane*), he does not perceive the sphere of the infinity of space; with regard to the sphere of the infinity of consciousness (*viññāṇañcāyatane*), he does not perceive the sphere of the infinity of consciousness; with regard to the sphere of nothingness (*ākiñcaññāyatane*), he does not perceive the sphere of nothingness; with regard to the sphere of neither perception nor non-perception (*nevasaññānāsaññāyatane*), he does not perceive the sphere of neither perception nor non-perception; with regard to this world (*idhaloke*) [or] the other world (*paraloke*) he does not perceive this world [or] the other world; and yet he is still conscious (*saññī*).[10]

The final item of which the *bhikkhu* is said to be unaware ('this world' and the 'other world') is not a proper object of meditation. Usually, rejection or acceptance of 'this world and the other world' forms part of the description of wrong or right view.[11] Perhaps, then, rather than being a straightforward list of meditative objects, this passage is an apophatic definition of a particular meditative state (*samādhipaṭilābho*): i.e. the *bhikkhu* attains such a meditative state that he is not aware of all the items mentioned, even 'this world' and 'the other world'. This meditative state is defined positively as a liberated or liberating state of consciousness:

> Here, O Ānanda, a *bhikkhu* may be conscious of the following: 'This is calm, this is supreme; namely, the calming of all mental constructions, the relinquishing of all attachment, the destruction of thirst; dispassion, cessation, *nibbāna*.'[12]

This pericope is found in a number of places in the Suttapiṭaka. As well as being an 'idea' that is the object of a concentration,[13] in a few places it forms the content of liberating insight.[14] However, in the *Sāriputta Sutta*,[15] which follows the *Samādhi Sutta* and repeats it almost verbatim, the pericope does not re-appear. Instead, Sāriputta (rather than the Buddha) tells Ānanda that at one time he was not aware of the same nine items mentioned (from earth to this world/the other world), but was aware (*saññī*) of the idea that 'the cessation of becoming is *nibbāna*, the cessation of becoming is *nibbāna*.'[16] The change in the final object[17] illustrates the fact that a core list consisting of the four elements and formless spheres was adapted to a similar but different end. The final object is noteworthy, since the pericope 'the cessation of becoming is *nibbāna*. . .' does not usually indicate a single meditative object.[18] This seems to support the notion that the lists in question are not lists of meditative objects. Further support for this idea is found in the next book of the *Aṅguttara Nikāya*, the 'Elevens' (*Ekādasakanipāta*, VII-X, *nissayavagga*), where the same sequence is repeated with minor differences.[19] Here, in order to extend the number of objects up to eleven, the final object of which the *bhikkhu* is unaware is said to be 'whatever is seen, heard, thought, cognized, attained, sought after [and] scrutinized by the mind.'[20] This item is not a proper object of meditation. One gets the impression that the composers of these Suttas extended the similar lists of the *Dasakanipāta* in order to present an even more apophatic definition of the liberated/liberating state of consciousness. The items in such a list need not be meditative objects.

Nevertheless, the essential items in all the lists appear to be objects of meditation. The point of all these Suttas is to describe the attainment of a meditative state (*samādhipaṭilābho*) in which the *bhikkhu* does not perceive certain objects. The context is meditation, and we should not be surprised if most of the objects of which the *bhikkhu* is unaware are objects of meditation, even if some are obviously not. Indeed, the four formless spheres are proper objects of meditation, and in the next section I will examine a list in which the elements also appear as objects of meditation. A more likely explanation for the lists of ten or eleven items is that they were initially based on a meditative sequence ending with the 'sphere of neither perception nor non-perception.'[21] This list was probably elaborated by the addition of two or three items in order that it could be included in the *Aṅguttara Nikāya's* book of 'Tens' and 'Elevens'. If so, it appears that meditation on the elements and formless spheres was an early Buddhist practice, and probably one that was thought to lead to liberation. We can conclude that in early Buddhism the practice of element meditation was thought to lead to states of abstract consciousness (the formless spheres) and finally liberation.

## The *kasiṇāyatana-s*

In addition to the above passages, another list of meditative objects in the Suttapiṭaka connects the formless spheres to the four elements. This is the list of ten 'spheres of totality' (*kasiṇāyatana-s*): the elements earth (*paṭhavī*), water (*āpo*), fire (*tejo*) and wind (*vāyo*); the colours dark blue (*nīla*), yellow (*pīta*), red (*lohita*) and white (*odāta*); and, finally, space (*ākāsa*) and consciousness (*viññāṇa*). The standard description of these ten objects in the Suttapiṭaka is as follows:

> The ten *kasiṇāyatana-s*: someone perceives (*sañjānāti*) the earth-*kasiṇa* (*paṭhavīkasiṇam*) above, below, across, without a second (*advayaṃ*), immeasurable (*apramāṇaṃ*).[22]

This is a description of a concentration on macrocosmic (*advayaṃ*, *appamāṇaṃ*) meditative objects. The fact that each object of meditation is said to be nondual suggests that the word *kasiṇa* is related to the Sanskrit adjective *kṛtsna* (MMW s.v: 'all, whole, entire'). DOP notes that the BHS form of the word is in fact *kṛtsna*.[23] It also states that it appears as an adjective and noun in Pāli texts: as an adjective it means 'all, whole, entire'; as a neuter noun it means 'the whole, totality', as well as:

> a meditational exercise of total and exclusive awareness of, or concentration on, one of four elements (earth, water, fire, wind) or one of four colours (dark-blue, yellow, red, white) or space or consciousness, leading to jhāna; one of ten objects or devices (the four elements or colours in a natural or specially contrived state, e.g. water in the sea or in a bowl, a restricted patch of light or of the sky) total and exclusive concentration on which is the first step to the attainment of jhāna; the meditational state brought about by this exercise and concentration.[24]

These definitions of *kasiṇa* vary between an adjectival form derived directly from Skt *kṛtsna* and a nominal form meaning something like 'meditative object', or the exercise of concentrating on this meditative object, or the state of meditation induced by such a practice. This final definition of *kasiṇa* as a noun is found also in DOP's definition of the compound *kasiṇāyatana* as 'a basis or source for total concentration'.[25] More or less the same range of meanings for *kasiṇa* are found in PED and CPD: both define it either as an adjective derived from Skt *kṛtsna*, or as a neuter noun meaning meditative object (PED: 'one of the aids to kamaṭṭhāna the practice by means of which mystic meditation [*bhāvana*, *jhāna*] may be attained';[26] CPD: 'totality [s.v. BHSD *kṛtsna*] denotes a category of ten subjects of meditation').[27]

These definitions do not make clear the exact form of the word *kasiṇa* in the above passage, however. Some derivation from *kṛtsna* is undeniable: *kasiṇa* must mean something like 'all, whole, entire', i.e. nondual. Such a derivation is also suggested by the close relationship between the formless spheres and *kasiṇāyatana-s*. The first two formless spheres are identical with the final two *kasiṇāyatana-s*; both are meditative states in which the objects are space and consciousness. Because the formless spheres of 'space' and 'consciousness' are said to be 'infinities' (*ānañca*), we should expect the 'space' and 'consciousness' *kasiṇa-s* to be the same. Thus the word *kasiṇa* must mean 'infinite' or 'nondual', and must therefore be related to Skt *kṛtsna*. But if so, it is hard to see how any of the dictionary definitions apply to the occurrences of *kasiṇa* in the passage from the *Dīgha Nikāya* cited above. The compounds *pathavīkasiṇa* etc. are objects of the verb 'to perceive' (*sañjānāti*). If so, the adjectival definition of *kasiṇa* as 'all, whole, entire' is unsuitable in this context, for one cannot perceive an adjective. In the compounds *paṭhavīkasiṇa* etc. the word *kasiṇa* must be a noun. The most suitable definition provided by the dictionaries for the word in this context is the noun 'object of meditation'. But the 'objects of meditation' in question are not just any objects – they are macrocosmic objects that are nondual. The nominal definition of *kasiṇa* as 'object of meditation' fails to take this into account; it gives no impression that the word *kasiṇa* must somehow be related to Skt *kṛtsna*. On the other hand, an adjectival definition of *kasiṇa* as 'all, whole, entire' is acceptable in the case of the compound *kasiṇāyatana*, for the compound surely means something like 'the spheres that are whole/total (i.e. nondual)'. The word *kasiṇa* in this compound can be taken as an adjective. However, it is preferable that the word *kasiṇa* is taken in the same sense in the two descriptive determinative (*karmadhāraya*) compounds that are, after all, adjacent; defining *kasiṇa* as an adjective in the compound *kasiṇāyatana* and then as a noun in the following compound *pathavīkasiṇa* is awkward.

If the word *kasiṇa* is taken similarly in both compounds (*dasa*) *kasiṇāyatanāni* and *paṭhavīkasiṇa* etc., and if the relationship with Skt *kṛtsna* is to be apparent, it must be taken as an abstract noun. DOP does in fact offer a definition of *kasiṇa* as 'wholeness, totality', although not in the context of the above passage on meditation. But this definition makes good sense in both compounds. In the case of (*dasa*) *kasiṇāyatanāni,* it gives the translation 'the (ten) spheres that are totalities' (hence CPD's translation of *kasiṇāyatana* as 'sphere of totality'), and in the case of *paṭhavīkasiṇa* etc. it gives a translation 'the totality that is earth'. If *kasiṇa* is taken in this way, i.e. as an abstract noun, a derivation from the Skt abstract noun *kārtsna* is most likely.[28] This hypothesis is supported by a further fact.

As pointed about above, the final two *kasiṇāyatana-s*, i.e. 'space' (*ākāsakasiṇa*) and 'consciousness' (*viññāṇakasina*), correspond to the first two formless spheres, i.e. the 'sphere of the infinity of space' and the 'sphere of the infinity of consciousness'. The compounds *ākāsakasiṇa/viññāṇakasiṇa* and *ākāsānañcāyatana/viññānañcāyatana* thus express the same meditative concepts, and must be more or less grammatically equivalent. The only obvious difference between the compounds is that *ākāsa/viññāṇa-kasiṇa* do not end in the word *āyatana*. But the passage on *kasiṇa* meditation is introduced as *dasa kasiṇāyatanāni.*[29] Thereafter, each individual meditative object is termed 'X-*kasiṇa*', e.g. *paṭhavīkasiṇa*. This surely indicates that each compound 'X-*kasiṇa*' is an abbreviation for 'X-*kasiṇāyatana*'. If so, *kasiṇa-* in the hypothetical compound X-*kasiṇāyatana* corresponds to the word *ānañca-* in the compound X-*ānañcāyatana*. The word *ānañca*, 'infinity', is an abstract noun formed from the adjective *ananta*, 'infinite, having no end'. If *kasiṇa* is grammatically parallel, it is most probably an abstract noun derived from the Sanskrit abstract noun *kārtsna*.

The list of 'spheres of totality' is thus made up of various macrocosmic items. The most important items in the list are the four elements (earth, water, fire, wind) plus 'space' and 'consciousness'. The significance of the colours is not clear, for there is no discussion of them in the early Buddhist literature. In the later Sinhalese work *The Yogāvacara's Manual of Indian Mysticism as Practised by Buddhists*,[30] element meditation is important and the attainment of each element is associated with various colours. But the colours do not correspond to the colours listed in the *kasiṇāyatana-s*, and even if they did, the text is late and has no bearing on the early Pāli literature.[31] In some late Upaniṣads and Tantric literature, such as the *Yogatattva Upaniṣad* and the *Śaṭcakranirūpaṇa*, element meditation usually involves the visualization of the element as a colour.[32] But these texts are much later than the early Pāli texts, and cannot be taken as evidence that the colours correspond to the elements in the list of 'spheres of totality'. Other evidence from the Suttapiṭaka is inconclusive. The same colours make up the final four of eight meditative objects in the list of 'spheres of mastery' (*abhibhāyatana*).[33] This may show that meditation on the colours was in some cases not related to the elements, but even this is questionable, for the significance of the colours in this list is far from clear. It is possible that they stand for the elements.

Whatever the significance of the colours is, a list of ten meditative objects that includes the four elements plus space and consciousness appears to be little more than a different elaboration of the similar schemes studied earlier (pp. 29–31). Underlying all the schemes, so it seems, is a doctrine of elements beginning with earth and ending with 'space' and 'consciousness'. From this perspective, the list of formless spheres (space, consciousness, nothingness and neither perception nor non-perception) appears in one sense to be an abbreviation of this list of six items, and in another to be an extension of it to include the goals of the two teachers.

## Element meditation and early Brahminism

A close conceptual relationship with early Brahminic thought is reflected in the list of *kasiṇāyatana-s*. In the early Brahminic literature, *kṛtsna* often means 'whole/total', and usually describes something that is infinite (the cosmos) or nondual (the self). The most significant early occurrence of the word *kṛtsna* is found at BU IV.5.13: a block of salt that is 'without an inner or outer, nothing but an entire (*kṛtsno*) mass of taste', is likened to the self that is 'without inner or outer, nothing but an entire (*kṛtsno*) mass of consciousness'.[34] In the *Bhagavadgītā*, *kṛtsna* is used adjectivally to indicate the 'total' sum of many parts,[35] or to refer to a nondual 'totality', e.g. the world (*loka*, *jagat*)[36] or *brahman*.[37] In the *Mokṣadharma*, *kṛtsna* is usually an adjective describing something that is nondual (e.g. the self),[38] or else it indicates the whole extent of something of enormous spatial dimensions (e.g. the earth, world or worlds, etc).[39] The word *kasiṇa*, applied to the elements in the early Pāli texts, suggests the possibility that element meditation was based on Brahminic notions of nonduality.

The list of colours in the *kasiṇāyatana-s* also seems to reflect Brahminic notions. Goudriaan has shown that the sequence 'dark blue → yellow → red → white' is found in early Sanskrit sources. At Mbh III.148, this sequence applies to the colour of Viṣṇu in the four world ages (*yuga-s*), each of which is more degenerate than the preceding. Thus in the *kṛta-yuga*, Viṣṇu is white; in the *tretā-yuga* he is red; in the *dvāpara-yuga* he is yellow, and in the degenerate *kali-yuga* he is dark blue.[40] In later literature the four colours are sometimes different or arranged in a different order, but according to Goudriaan 'in general one can say that the tradition is a consistent one',[41] i.e. it follows the order of Mbh III.148. Thus it seems that to the Brahminic mind the sequence 'dark blue → yellow → red → white' represented a transition from the gross to the subtle, although its exact significance in the list of *kasiṇāyatana-s* is unclear.

More important than these correspondences is the fact that the lists of elements studied in this chapter correspond to early Brahminic element doctrines. This is not to deny that lists of elements are common in the early Buddhist literature, and in general seem to have very little relationship with early Brahminic thought. The most basic list in the Suttapiṭaka is that of the four 'great elements' (*cattāri mahābhūtāni*: earth, water, fire and wind).[42] There are also a number of lists in which 'space' and/or 'consciousness' are added to this basic set of four elements to form lists of five or six 'strata' (*dhātu-s*). Apart from places where the *dhātu-s* are simply listed,[43] or listed without much additional comment,[44] in most places they occur in teachings where they form the objects of a detailed contemplation of the human person. The aim of such contemplations is to induce the correct understanding that the material derivatives of each *dhātu* are not one's self.[45] This sort of teaching can be seen in the *Mahā-Rāhulovāda Sutta*. After outlining those parts of the body that consist of a particular element, the Buddha teaches Rāhula that the element (and its derivatives) should not be considered as self:

> The internal earth element and the external earth element, they are [both] simply the earth element (*paṭhavīdhātur*). [Thinking] 'This is not mine, I am not this, this is not my self', one ought to see it [the earth element] as it really is with correct understanding. In doing so one becomes disillusioned with the earth element, one frees one's mind from passion for the earth element.[46]

In such teachings the five or six *dhātu-s* represent a convenient starting point for the division of the human body, and external reality, into its constituent parts in order to contemplate its true nature. This shows that a common early Buddhist assumption was that everything could be broken up into these five or six basic components. But why did the early Buddhists believe this? Was the division of everything into five or six elements a Buddhist innovation? Or was it a general early Indian understanding?

In order to answer these questions we must note that the same set of six items, without being termed *dhātu*, is used differently in the lists of element meditation (pp. 29–34). In a meditative context the focus is not on breaking up the world into its elemental parts. Instead, the objects of meditation are the elements themselves, in their unmanifest and undivided state or 'essence'. Moreover, the list of elements in these meditative schemes is arranged according to an increasing level of refinement, so that the meditator progresses from the relative grossness of earth and water to the more empyreal levels of fire, wind and space. The meditator, it seems, is traversing the higher levels of the cosmos in his meditative absorption. The notion that the cosmos is structured in this way is not, however, based on any Buddhist cosmology. But such cosmologies are common in the early Brahminic literature, e.g. the cosmogonies of TU II.1 and Mbh XII.195 (self → *ākāśa* → *vāyu* → *agni* → *āpas* → *pṛthivī*), and a similar cosmogony found at Mbh XII.224 (*brahman* → *manas* → *ākāśa* → *vāyus* → *jyotis* → *āpas* → *bhūmi*).[47] The Buddhist lists of element meditation appear to reflect this sort of cosmology. The essential part of the Buddhist lists of the elements as objects of meditation, i.e. the progression 'earth → water → fire → wind → space → consciousness', seems to be little more than an inversion of a cosmogony identical to that stated at Mbh XII.224.

From this perspective, the Buddhist lists of element meditation seem to reflect a Brahminic cosmogony in which the elements were created by the *ātman/brahman*. Why is this so? Why do these Buddhist lists of meditative objects correspond to the cosmogonic ideas of early Brahminism? How did an early Brahminic creation doctrine end up in a scheme of early Buddhist meditation? There are two possible answers. Either the early Buddhists borrowed such meditative practices from early Brahminism – where cosmology already had a meditative counterpart – or else they adapted an early Brahminic cosmology to a meditative end themselves. To find an answer to this dilemma, we must ask why ancient meditators would have used the elements as meditative objects. The first answer to that is that they believed that such a practice leads to liberation. But which meditators would have believed this? Probably only the early Brahmins who believed in their cosmologies, and accepted that that the ascension throught the elements leads to *brahman*, the source of creation and the religious goal. It is doubtful, however, that many early Buddhists believed anything like this. There is virtually no evidence, however, that early Buddhists accepted Brahminic cosmology and the religious goal of *brahman*: no cosmological texts on the six *dhātu-s* are found in the Pāli canon, and there is virtually no evidence for them in the post-canonical literature.[48] On balance, then, it is more likely that the relationship between cosmology and meditation originated in early Brahminic circles, and from there was borrowed by the early Buddhists. For it is more likely that the early Brahminic thinkers for whom the religious goal was the beginning and end of cosmological speculation believed that cosmology provided the path to liberation. Moreover, there is a widespread correspondence between meditation and cosmology in early Brahminic texts, and even some early Brahminic texts on element meditation itself. It seems that the ideology of early Brahminic meditation is provided by cosmology. If so, the notion that some early Buddhists innovated element meditation after borrowing a Brahminic cosmology is problematic, for it would require a Brahminic borrowing of a new practice based on the Brahminic ideology in turn. The theory of one borrowing – of element meditation by early Buddhists from a Brahminic source – is simpler and more likely.

## Element meditation in the *Mokṣadharma*

Evidence for the early Brahminic practice of element meditation is found in the *Mokṣadharma*. It is suggested at Mbh XII.247.13, where Bhīṣma advises Yudhiṣṭhira to 'be someone with a calm intellect, because of power over the elements'.[49] The practice of element meditation in early Brahminic circles is also implied in a very early passage in the *Mokṣadharma*. In Mbh XII.195, immediately after outlining the process of cosmic evolution (the sequence is the same as TU II.1: *akṣara* → *kha* → *vāyu* → *jyotis* → *jala* → *jagatī)*,[50] Manu states:

> Having gone to water with their bodies, from water [they go to] fire, [then successively to] wind and space. From space, those who are not capable (*na bhāvinaḥ*) return (*nivartanti*); those who are capable (*ye bhāvinaḥ*), they attain the supreme, (2) [which is] not hot or cold, soft or sharp, not sour, astringent, sweet or bitter; it has no sound, smell or visible form. [It is] the one whose own state is the ultimate (*paramasvabhāvam*). (3)[51]

This is a statement about how beings attain liberation: they regress through the cosmic elements and then escape from the manifest world. There is no mention of *yoga*, but the only soteriological method mentioned in the passage is *yoga*:

> The body knows touch, the tongue taste, the nose smells and the ears sounds; the eyes know forms. Men who do not know the higher self do not grasp what is beyond them. (4)
>
> Turning the tongue back from tastes, the nose from smells, the ears from sounds, the body from touch, the eye from objects that have the quality of visible form (*rūpaguṇāt*); then one sees the highest, one's own [true] state (*svaṃ svabhāvam*). (5)[52]

These two verses come immediately after the two verses that describe the path to liberation. It is unlikely that the close proximity of these four verses is insignificant: their juxtaposition implies a close relationship between meditation and the passage through the elements. They do not exactly suggest that the progression through the material elements of earth, water, fire, wind and space in v. 2–3 was the result of the meditative practice mentioned in v. 3–4. But they do suggest the possibility that early Brahminic meditators would have drawn the conclusion that to be 'capable' (*bhāvin*) of escaping the world, a yogin must be a meditative adept skilled in the progression through the elements. This evidence for element meditation is more convincing than that found at Mbh XII.247.13, but indisputable evidence is found in a few verses of Mbh XII.228:

> The person who, with speech suppressed, attains the seven absorptions (*dhāraṇāḥ*) of totality (*kṛtsnā*), and the other absorptions 'in the rear and on the flanks' (*pṛṣṭhataḥ pārśvataś*),[53] as many as there are, (13)
> Who gradually [attains the meditations on] earth and wind, and so space and water, [as well as] mastery (*aiśvaryaṃ*) over fire, the utterance 'I' (*ahaṃkārasya*) and intelligence (*buddhitaḥ*), (14)
> He attains, in due course, mastery over the unmanifest (*avyaktasya*), and possessing these powers, he practises in accordance with *yoga*. (15)[54]

The expression 'mastery over the unmanifest' (v. 15: *avyaktasya tathaiśvaryaṃ*) is the last term in the sequence, and so must refer to the attainment of liberation.[55] Supporting this idea is the fact that the tract is introduced in v. 12 as a method to attain liberation:

> I will explain the quick method for the person who intends to go (*gantumanasaḥ*) to the imperishable (*akṣaraṃ*), who is in a great hurry to yoke this chariot.[56]

It seems that the word *avyakta* ('unmanifest') is an epithet for *brahman*, and does not denote unmanifest matter. This is not immediately clear, for twenty-five items (*tattva-s*) are mentioned later in this passage (at v. 28), which must mean that this section of the passage knows unmanifest matter (the twenty-fourth) as a separate principle from *brahman* (the twenty-fifth). But it is likely that the section v. 27–32/36ff. is a later addition that does not have any relevance for the yogic scheme outlined in v. 13–15. The section after v. 27 mentions *sāṃkhya* and *yoga*-followers, and is introduced in v. 27 with a change of subject. The dialogue between Vyāsa and Śuka (Mbh XII.224–247) does not mention *sāṃkhya*-followers or schemes of twenty-five *tattva-s* before this, whereas after this point there is hardly any structure to the text. Furthermore, expressions such as 'hear from me' (*me śṛṇu*:

v. 21, v. 27, v. 28; *nibodha me*: v. 27) usually introduce didactic tracts in the *Mokṣadharma*, and often indicate the point at which separate sections have been added to a text. It appears, then, that the section after v. 21 is an addition or a separate stratum to Mbh XII.228. In the text before this, the description of element meditation is based on a cosmology in which the 'unmanifest' (*avyaktam*) was a designation of *brahman*.

The order of the objects of concentration (earth → wind → space → water → fire → *ahaṃkāra* → *buddhi* → *avyakta*) must be based on a doctrine of world creation from the unmanifest deity. This is not entirely clear, for there is no creation doctrine in the passage, and the usual cosmogonic order of material elements in the *Mokṣadharma* (space → wind → fire → water → earth) is not followed. But this peculiarity is relatively insignificant, since the elements are found in this order in a few of the *Mokṣadharma's* cosmogonies (e.g. Mbh XII.187.4). It seems that element meditation in early Brahminism, like element meditation in early Buddhism, was based on Brahminical cosmogonies which were thought to provide meditative 'maps' of the path to liberation. Element meditation, so we must understand, was thought to be the yogin's way of reversing the creation of the cosmos and attaining liberation.

The textual evidence shows that element meditation was practised in both Buddhist and Brahminic circles. Early Buddhist and Brahminic meditators, so it seems, believed that liberation was achieved by means of a meditative progression through the material elements and a few higher states of consciousness beyond them. The conceptual background to element meditation is provided by the cosmological thought of early Brahminism. There is no similar theoretical background to element meditation in the early Buddhist texts, where the elements appear simply as suitable objects of meditation. Moreover, it can be shown that cosmology provides the theoretical background to meditation in virtually all the early Brahminic tracts on meditation. If so, it would seem that cosmological speculation is integral to early Brahminic meditation, and that element meditation is but one aspect of this general theory of meditation.

## Cosmology and meditation in early Brahminism

The relationship between cosmology and meditation is made clear in all the detailed schemes of meditation in the *Mokṣadharma*. In Mbh XII.197, a passage in one of the most important early tracts in the *Mokṣadharma* (Mbh XII.194–199: *Manu-Bṛhaspati-saṃvāda*), a teaching on meditation is closely connected to cosmology:

> As one can see a form [reflected] in water, when it is calm, by means of the eye, so too the one who possesses calm sense faculties sees what can be known (*jñeyaṃ*) by knowledge (*jñānena*). (2)

> As one does not see a form when [the water] is disturbed, so too when the sense faculties have become agitated, one cannot see what ought to be known in knowledge (*jñāne na*). (3)
>
> Knowledge arises for men when bad *karman* is destroyed. Then one sees (*paśyaty*) the self in the self, when it is like the surface of a mirror. (8)
>
> One is unhappy (*duḥkhī*) when one's sense faculties are set free, happy (*sukhī*) when they are restrained. Therefore one should restrain the self from the objects of the senses (*indriyarūpebhyo*), by means of the self. (9)
>
> The mind (*manaḥ*) is beyond the senses, the intellect (*buddhi*) is beyond that. Beyond the intelligence is awareness (*jñāna*), [and] beyond awareness is the highest state (*paraṃ*). (10)
>
> Awareness (*jñānaṃ*) is emitted from the unmanifest (*avyaktāt*), from that [is emitted] the intelligence (*buddhis*), from that [is emitted] the mind (*manaḥ*). The mind, attached to the various sense faculties such as hearing, perceives (*paśyati*) the various sense objects, such as sounds, clearly. (11)
>
> The person who abandons the various sense objects, such as sounds, and so all that is manifest, he abandons all forms (*ākṛtigrāmāṃs*). After he has abandoned them (*tān muktvā*) he attains the immortal. (12)
>
> When the intelligence, free from the objects of sense activity (*karmaguṇair)* comes about in the mind, then one attains, right there, *brahman*, in its devolved state (*pralayaṃ gatam*). (17)
>
> He enters the highest essence (*sattvaṃ paraṃ*), which is without contact, hearing, taste, sight, smell and thought (*avitarkaṃ*). (18)[57]

The statement that the goal is *brahman* in its 'devolved state'(v. 8: *pralayaṃ gataṃ*) indicates that liberation was thought to be identification with the state of the cosmos, to be attained through the destruction of *karman* (v. 8). This implies that the reverse of the cosmogony (v. 11: *avyakta/para* → *jñāna* → *buddhi* → *manas* → *indriya-s*) is the path the yogin ought to take out of *saṃsāra*. In fact, exactly this scheme is alluded to later in the *Manu-Bṛhaspati-saṃvāda* at Mbh XII.199.25:

> Making the higher consciousness spotless through liberating knowledge (*jñānena*), and so the mind [spotless] through the higher consciousness, and the group of senses by the mind, he obtains the infinite. (25)[58]

The order of this progression is *manas* → *buddhi* → *jñāna* → *ananta*. This scheme and the scheme in Mbh XII.197, having two items in between the mind (*manas*) and the absolute (*brahman*), correspond roughly to the scheme outlined at Mbh XII.228, although nothing is said here about the elements. Another clear example of the relationship between meditation and cosmology is found in Mbh XII.304, where meditation is based on a cosmology of twenty-five items (*tattvas*):

> In the first period of the night, twelve yogic practices (*codanā*) are taught. Sleeping in the middle period, in the last period there are the same 12 yogic practices. (11)
>
> Thus the self ought to be disciplined by the one who is calm (*upaśāntena*), restrained, inclined towards lonely places, delighting in the self (*ātmārāmeṇa*) [and] awake; on that there is no doubt. (12)
>
> Warding off the fivefold faults of the five senses, i.e. sound, touch, visible forms, tastes and smells, (13)
>
> Repressing the appearance and disappearance [of the sense-objects], making the entire group of senses enter into the mind, (14)
>
> And thus establishing the mind in the self-consciousness (*āhaṃkāre*), the self-consciousness in higher consciousness (*buddhau*), and the higher consciousness in primordial matter (*prakṛtav*), (15)[59]
>
> Having reckoned (*parisaṃkhyāya*) in this way, he ought to meditate (*dhyāyeta*) on the absolute (*kevalam*), that which is spotless, sufficient, permanent, infinite, pure and woundless. (16)[60]

The last stages in meditation consist of the concentration on the higher cosmic levels – *ahaṃkāra*, *buddhi* and *prakṛti* – before finally reaching the absolute (*kevalam*). A similar relationship between meditation and cosmology is made quite clear in a number of other passages on meditation in the *Mokṣadharma* (e.g. Mbh XII.198.2–13, Mbh XII.238.3–13, Mbh XII.294.10–19). Thus, it seems that the most basic presupposition of the early Brahminic passages on meditation is that the creation of the world must be reversed, through a series of meditative states, by the yogin who seeks the realization of the self.

Given this widespread correspondence between meditation and cosmology in the *Mokṣadharma*, it is quite likely that element meditation originated in early Brahminic circles before it was borrowed and elaborated by the early Buddhists. Any other scenario is hardly likely. It is unlikely that a meditative practice originated in early Buddhism, but with a form corresponding to the early Brahminic cosmogonies. And it is even more unlikely that early Brahminic thinkers borrowed such a practice from Buddhists and structured their cosmogonic and/or yogic theories upon it. On the other hand, it is easy to imagine that Brahminic practices were borrowed and adapted by early Buddhists, with the original Brahminic ideology of the practices being discarded in the process. Moreover, a basic presupposition of early Brahminic thought is that there is a correspondence between man and cosmos. As Brereton has noted, the Upaniṣadic correspondence between microcosm and macrocosm

> implies that the world and the power that controls it are not outside, bearing down upon and threatening the individual. Rather, because the parts of the world are equivalent to the parts of the person, humans include everything within themselves.[61]

It is exactly this sort of thinking that underlies early Brahminic meditation. From this perspective, it is not surprising that meditative states of consciousness were thought to be identical to the subtle strata of the cosmos. In this sense, all early Brahminic meditation is in some sense cosmological, i.e. not only a practical elaboration of Brahminic beliefs about the origin and nature of the cosmos, but also an elaboration of the belief that man is identical to the world. The Brahminic background to element meditation seems indisputable. We can conclude that an item in the Buddhist texts that (i) corresponds to a similar item in Brahminic texts and (ii) follows Brahminic rather than Buddhist ideology is likely to be a non-original element in the Buddhist texts.[62]

If element meditation was borrowed from early Brahminism, the same must be true of formless meditation: as noted above (p. 34), the list of four formless spheres appears to be an abbreviation of a longer list of elements, for the first two formless spheres (infinite space and consciousness) are logically connected to a list of elements ending in 'space' and 'consciousness'. Indeed, these two spheres could easily be fitted into an early Brahminic cosmology. The evidence suggests, then, a Brahminic background to the two teachers of the Bodhisatta. Other passages in the early Upaniṣads support this claim.

## The goals of the two teachers: early Upaniṣadic parallels

The self (*ātman*) is conceptualized in terms similar to both 'nothingness' (*ākiñcañña*) and 'neither perception nor non-perception' (*nevasaññānāsaññā*) in the early Upaniṣads. The most obvious example of the latter is found in the *Māṇḍūkya Upaniṣad*, where the fourth quarter of *brahman* – the ultimate state of the self – is described as follows:

> Not one with awareness within (*nāntaḥprajñaṃ*), not one with awareness without (*na bahiḥprajñaṃ*), not one with awareness of both, not a mass of awareness (*prajñānaghanam*), not awareness nor non-awareness (*na prajñaṃ nāprajñam*). They consider the fourth quarter [of *brahman* thus]: unseen, supramundane, ungraspable, without characteristic, unthinkable, indescribable, whose

> essence is the perception of the one self, the stilling of the manifest world (*prapañcopaśamaṃ*), calm (*śāntaṃ*), auspicious, nondual (*advaitaṃ*). That is the self, that ought to be perceived.[63]

Thus, the goal of Uddaka Rāmaputta (*nevasaññānāsaññā-*) is virtually identical to the description of *brahman* in the *Māṇḍūkya Upaniṣad* (*na prajñaṃ nāprajñam*). Although the *Māṇḍūkya Upaniṣad* is almost certainly later than most of the early Buddhist literature, the use of the construction 'double negative (*na*+*a*) + negative (*na*)' in early Brahminic descriptions of the absolute reality is found in texts as old as the *Nāsadīyasūkta* (ṚV X 129.1: *nāsad āsīn nó sád āsīt tadānīm*). If such terminology goes back to the very beginnings of Brahminic philosophy, the *Māṇḍūkya Upaniṣad* is good enough evidence to suppose that the goal of Uddaka Rāmaputta (*nevasaññānāsaññā*) was, in fact, an early Brahminic conceptualization of the self.

Further evidence from the early Buddhist literature and the early Upaniṣads supports the notion that the goal of Uddaka Rāmaputta was a Brahminic one. In the *Pañcayattaya Sutta*, non-Buddhist ascetics and Brahmins are said to claim that the self after death is 'neither conscious nor unconscious' (*nevasaññiṃ nāsaññiṃ*), i.e. identical to the goal of Uddaka Rāmaputta (M II.228.16 ff: *neva saññī nāsaññī attā arogo parṃmaraṇati*). They argue that the self is neither consciousness (*saññā*)[64] nor unconsciousness (*asaññā*), the latter being defined as a state of 'bewilderment' or 'stupefaction' (*sammoho*).[65] Jayatilleke has pointed out that this corresponds to Yājñavalkya's definition of the self in his famous dialogue with Maitreyī in the *Bṛhadāraṇyaka Upaniṣad*.[66] In this passage, Yājñavalkya claims that after death there is no 'consciousness' (BU II.4.12/IV.5.13: *na pretya saṃjñāstīty are bravīmi*). He clarifies this statement by arguing that this state, although without 'consciousness' (*saṃjñā*), is not a state of 'bewilderment' (*mohaṃ*, i.e. stupefaction, non-awareness).[67] Thus, the evidence from Buddhist and Brahminic sources coincides: in both cases the self was thought to be neither perception/consciousness (*saññā*/*saṃjñā*) nor non-perception/unconsciousness (*asaññā* = [*sam*]*moha*).

There is a further correspondence. Yājñavalkya draws the logical conclusion of his arguments and states that the self that is neither conscious (*saṃjñā*) nor unconscious (*moha*) is a state of intransitive consciousness after death.[68] This is suggested earlier in the same dialogue when Yājñavalkya defines the self as a single mass of consciousness (Bu II.4.12/IV.5.13: *vijñānaghana*/*prajñānaghana*), i.e. consciousness that lacks an object. The Buddhist evidence suggests much the same thing for the state of 'neither perception nor non-perception'. In the Suttapiṭaka the attainment of this state is described in two important lists of meditative states, the eight 'releases' (*vimokha-s*: three form releases, plus the four formless spheres, and the 'cessation of perception and sensation', *saññāvedayitanirodha*)[69] and the nine 'gradual abidings' (*anupubbavihāra-s*: the four *jhāna-s* plus the four formless spheres and *saññāvedayitanirodha*).[70] In both lists the description of the attainment of the first three formless spheres is exactly the same. The sustained concentration on each object (e.g. *ākāsānañcāyatanaṃ upasampajja viharati*) is attained only after each object has been conceptualized in the mind (e.g. *ananto ākāso ti*). But the description of the attainment of the 'sphere of neither perception nor non-perception' says nothing about the prior conceptualization of it as a mental object. It simply states:

> Completely transcending the sphere of nothingness, one attains the sphere of neither perception nor non-perception.[71]

This must mean that the state is without an object of awareness. And yet it is not completely devoid of awareness, for this is a characteristic of the following meditative state, the 'cessation of perception and sensation'.[72] If the 'sphere of neither perception nor non-perception' is without an object of awareness but is not a state of unawareness, it follows that it must be a state of awareness without an object, i.e. a state of intransitive consciousness similar to that described by Yājñavalkya. The only difference between this state and Yājñavalkya's notion of the self is that the former is said to be attained by the meditative adept while he is alive, whereas the latter is said by Yājñavalkya to be realized after death. But this difference matters very little. The non-Buddhist ascetics and Brahmins of the *Pañcattaya Sutta* thought, like Yājñavalkya, that the self was neither conscious nor unconscious after death (M II.231.4: *nevasaññiṃnāsaññiṃ . . . paraṃmaraṇā*, and it is likely that the meditative goal of Uddaka Rāmaputta was also understood in this way.

It is likely that Uddaka Rāmaputta belonged to the pre-Buddhist tradition portrayed by these various Buddhist and Brahminic sources. His milieu was probably a Brahminic one in which the philosophical formulations of the early Upaniṣads were accepted. There is also early Upaniṣadic evidence suggesting that the goal of Āḷāra Kālāma was an early Brahminic conceptualization. For example, the first cosmogonic myth of the *Bṛhadāraṇyaka Upaniṣad* begins as follows: 'In the beginning there was nothing here at all' (BU I.2.1: *naiveha kiṃcanāgra āsīt*). It is plausible, on the basis of this evidence, to suppose that in early Brahminic circles the absolute reality (*ātman/brahman*) was known by the term *ākiñcanya*, the proposition of BU I.2.1 being turned into an abstract noun.[73] Similar evidence for the self being described as a sort of 'nothingness' or 'non-existence' is found in other Upaniṣads, e.g. CU VI.12.1, where Uddālaka Āruṇi questions Śvetaketu about what he can see when he cuts open the seeds of a banyan fruit:

'What do you see here?'
'Nothing → (*na kiṃcana*), sir.'[74]

Uddālaka Āruṇi then likens this 'nothing' to the self.[75] This evidence is perhaps not quite as good as BU I.2: the cosmogony of Uddālaka Āruṇi is, after all, based upon the idea that 'in the beginning this world was the existent alone, only one, without a second' (CU 6.2.1: *sad eva somyedam agra āsīd ekam evādvitīyam*). The pre-creative state in this tract, it seems, is not a 'nothingness' but exactly the opposite, i.e. a 'something', the 'existent'. Indeed, in CU VI.2.2–3 Uddālaka argues against the claim of some that the pre-creative state was one of non-existence (*asad* = the non-existent).[76] Nevertheless, the episode of splitting open the fruit is evidence for the *ātman/brahman* being thought of as a 'nothingness' in a figurative sense, even if this nothingness is termed 'the existent' (*sad*). And even if not, then the Brahminic opponents of Uddālaka – those who claimed that in the beginning there was the non-existent (*asad*) – show that some early Brahminic thinkers believed that the pre-creative state was a sort of non-existence, a 'nothingness'. Further evidence is found in the *Taittirīya Upaniṣad* (TU II.7.1):

> In the beginning, the world was non-existent; from it was born the existent.[77]

We might also cite TU II.6.1 ('He becomes non-existent, if he thinks that *brahman* is non-existent'),[78] which seems to be a polemic against those who thought that *brahman* is non-existent. And at CU III.19.1, the notion that the unmanifest state of the cosmos is 'non-existent' is connected to the idea that when it becomes manifest, it develops into a cosmic egg:

> In the beginning, this was simply non-existent (*asad*), the existent was that. Then it developed and turned into an egg.[79]

This must mean that some ancient Brahminic thinkers held the view that the unmanifest state of *brahman* was a sort of non-existence. The goal of Āḷāra Kālāma (*ākiñcañña*) can be understood as a formulation of this early philosophical tradition.

## The aphorism *passan na passati*

The notion that Uddaka Rāmaputta taught an early Brahminic goal is supported by further evidence in the early Buddhist literature. In the *Pāsādika Suttanta* (D no. 29) an aphorism attributed to Uddaka Rāmaputta is similar to a famous Upaniṣadic definition of the *ātman*. This aphorism occurs when the Buddha comments on a teaching of Uddaka Rāmaputta:

> Uddaka Rāmaputta, O Cunda, used to speak thus: 'Seeing one does not see (*passan na passati*).' Seeing what does one not see? One sees the blade of a well sharpened razor, but one does not see its edge. So, Cunda, it is said: 'Seeing one does not see.' But this, O Cunda, spoken by Uddaka Rāmaputta, is low, plebeian, mundane, ignoble, not connected with what is profitable; [it is] only about a razor. About whatever thing, when speaking correctly, he would say 'Seeing one does not see', it is about this alone that he would say 'Seeing one does not see' when speaking correctly. Seeing what does one not see? – The holy life that is well proclaimed [and] well illumined, successful in every way, complete in every way, not lacking, not surpassed, completely fulfilled: this one sees. With regard to this, one might remove [something from it thinking]: 'Thus it might be even purer'; but this one does not see. With regard to this, one might add [something to it thinking]: 'Thus it might be fulfilled'; but this one does not see. [So] it is said, O Cunda: 'Seeing one does not see.'[80]

The expression 'seeing one does not see' is obscure although some scholars have accepted its attribution to Uddaka Rāmaputta.[81] If it refers to the state of being aware ('seeing': *passan*) without being aware of anything in particular ('one does not see': *na passati*), it could be identified with the state of 'neither perception nor non-perception' (*nevasaññānāsaññā*), a state thought to be an awareness of nothing in particular. Indeed, the compound *nevasaññānāsaññā*, being made up of a negative and a double negative could be simplified along the lines *nāsaññā* = *sañjānāti* = *passan*, *nevasaññā* = *na sañjānāti* = *na passati*. If so, it is quite possible that the aphorism *passan na passati* was used by Uddaka Rāmaputta to elucidate his teaching of awareness without an object.

The simile used to explain the aphorism – being aware of the surface of a razor but not its edge – does not seem to suggest this, for it describes a state of awareness that has an object (the razor's surface). But if the simile was switched around so that it described an awareness of the razor's edge and not its surface, it would then indicate a state of awareness so subtle that it does not have a tangible object (seeing – *passan* – the imperceptible edge of the razor), which at the same time could be described as a sort of 'not seeing' because no corporeal object is perceived (not seeing – *na passati* – the blade's surface). If the aphorism *passan na passati* had been described by this simile, it would correspond closely to the state of 'neither perception nor non-perception', and there would be no reason to doubt its attribution to Uddaka Rāmaputta. Do we have any reason to believe that this was the case? Was the simile of seeing the blade's surface rather than its edge an inversion of a simile originally connected with the teaching of intransitive awareness?

There are reasonable grounds for believing this to be so. The first thing to note is the wording of the Pāli text. The simile about the blade and its edge are the Buddha's words, not Uddaka Rāmaputta's: only the aphorism 'seeing he does not see' is ascribed to Uddaka Rāmaputta (*passan na passatīti*). This raises the possibility that the simile as stated in the Pāli text was not originally related to the aphorism. Furthermore, the simile fits the Buddha's purpose rather well. To make his point the Buddha requires a simile in which someone sees that which is tangible and present (compared to the current state of the *saṅgha*), but does not see that which is abstract and intangible (compared to the hypothetical state of the *saṅgha* at any other point). The Buddha's explanation of *passan na passati* would not work if it were to be contrasted with an explanation in which someone is said to see the intangible (the razor's edge) and not the tangible (the blade's surface). The Buddha's explanation must be contrasted with a simile in which *passan na passati* refers to consciousness of a tangible object.

It is quite possible that by sleight of hand the original simile has been turned around. Richard Gombrich has written about how the Buddha 'twisted' the views of opponents by exercising his famed 'skill in means'.[82] For example, in the *Aggañña Sutta* the word *ajjhāyaka* ('reciter of the Veda') is explained by the Buddha to mean *a-jhāyaka* ('non-meditator').[83] This style of reinterpreting terminology perhaps explains the sort of method by which a simile used to explain *passan na passati* would have been turned around. It is possible that in order to demonstrate the fact that his teaching has been clearly revealed, and has been carried out by his followers, the Buddha has turned on its head a well-known simile illustrating a state of knowing without an object.[84] This sort of terminology-twisting is a bit more complicated than that found in the *Aggañña Sutta*. But to the audience aware of the original simile, such an interpretation of a well-known aphorism would have been seen as a striking critique of an old idea.

My argument can be put as follows. It is reasonable to suppose that the meditative states denoted by the expression *passan na passati* and *nevasaññānāsaññāyatana*, both being ascribed to Uddaka Rāmaputta, are identical. Although the simile that is used to illustrate *passan na passati* – seeing the razor's blade and not its edge – seems to disprove this, the punctuation shows that the simile is not directly attributed to Uddaka Rāmaputta. There is also a Buddhist motive for turning the simile around, as well as other episodes in the early Pāli literature where the terminology of opponents is twisted. Hence, I suggest that the expressions *passan na passati* and *nevasaññānāsaññā* indicate the same meditative state, and that the simile used to exemplify the former, even if it was similar to the one found in the Pāli text (possibly the same simile the wrong way around) was not the one originally used by Uddaka Rāmaputta. If the aphorism is taken in this sense, i.e. as referring to awareness without an object, it corresponds exactly to an important early Upaniṣadic conception of the self. In the *Bṛhadāraṇyaka Upaniṣad* (BU IV.3.23) the self's nondual state of awareness in deep sleep is described in language almost identical to *passan na passati*:[85]

> Verily, while he does not there see [with the eyes], he is verily seeing (*paśyan vai*), though he does not see (what is [usually] to be seen)[86] (*tan na paśyati*); for there is no cessation of the seeing of a seer, because of his imperishability [as a seer]. It is not, however, a second thing, other than himself and separate, that he may see.[87]

The important part of this statement is *paśyan vai tan na paśyati*. Olivelle translates *paśyan vai* as 'he is quite capable of seeing',[88] although it is not clear why he translates a present active participle as 'capable of doing' rather than 'doing'. One might suppose that the sense of 'capability' applies in this context because the subject of *paśyan vai* is in deep sleep, and therefore cannot be said to be seeing anything. The same reasoning would also apply for smelling, tasting, speaking, hearing, thinking, touching and perceiving – they cannot be said to be active because the subject is in deep sleep, although still 'capable' of each cognition. But this interpretation obscures the crucial point of the passage, which is that the subject continues to be conscious, although his sense functions have ceased to operate. The verbs of perception are applied to the subject metaphorically: the statement that he is 'verily seeing' (*paśyan vai*) indicates that he is still conscious, although he does not 'see' anything in particular. The present active participles are not meant literally, but highlight the fact that awareness has not totally disappeared. Thus, statements such as *paśyan vai* mean that there is still awareness, an awareness that will normally allow the cognition of a perceptible object, but which does not totally disappear (*na . . . viparilopo vidyate*) for the perceiver in the absence of an object.

The expression *paśyan vai tan na paśyati* is semantically and syntactically close to the Pāli aphorism *passan na passati*. It is quite possible that the original Sanskrit aphorism was abstracted from BU IV.3.23 and then used in meditative circles to indicate the goal of consciousness without an object. Such a scenario is suggested at the end of the passage in the statement 'He becomes the one ocean, the seer without a second' (BU IV.3.32: *salila eko draṣṭā 'dvaito bhavati*). Here the verb √*dṛś* is used to designate awareness in general rather than visual awareness alone.[89] It is quite likely that in a summary of this teaching the single verb used to cover the activity of all senses would have been √*dṛś*. Thus it is possible that the phrase *paśyan vai tan na paśyati* would have been used in early Brahminism to epitomize a state of intransitive consciousness. The occurrence of the phrase *paśyan api na paśyati* in the *Mokṣadharma* in a similar context seems to confirm this:

> One sees everything that is visible (*dṛśyaṃ*) by the eye connected to the mind. But when the mind is disturbed, although one sees it (*tad dhi paśyann api*), one does not see (*na paśyate*). (16)
>
> The person under the power of sleep does not see (*na paśyati*), speak, hear, smell or know a tactile impression or taste. (17)[90]

The author of this *Mokṣadharma* passage likens the state of being asleep and unaware of objects (*na paśyati*) to the state of being confused and hence unaware of objects (*na paśyati*), although still conscious in general (*tad dhi paśyann api*). It is likely that this theory of cognition was formed with the passage from BU IV.3.23 in mind, and it shows that the aphorism, originally coined about the state of the self in deep sleep, was adapted to make similar points about cognition. It was abstracted from its original context in the *Bṛhadāraṇyaka Upaniṣad* and used independently. It is quite possible that once abstracted in this way it was used by early practitioners of meditation to illustrate their belief in a meditative state of intransitive consciousness. The early Brahminic teachings on meditation certainly drew upon the nondualistic philosophy of the early Upaniṣads. The goal of yogic practice in some of the early Upaniṣads and the *Mokṣadharma* is to attain a state of consciousness not unlike deep sleep, a state of consciousness so attenuated that its attainer is said to be 'like a log of wood'.[91] The verb √*dṛś* is ubiquitous in these *Mokṣadharma* passages. It is easy to imagine that the maxim *paśyan vai tan na paśyati* was simplified and then used in early yogic circles influenced by Brahminic nondualism. It does not appear in the *Mokṣadharma* passages on *yoga*, although the occurrence of a similar idea in Mbh XII.180 is suggestive. In a Middle Indo-Aryan dialect similar to Pāli, *paśyan vai tan na paśyati* would have appeared as something like *passaṃ ve taṃ na passati*. It could easily have been simplified as the aphorism *passaṃ na passati*.

These observations suggest a Brahminic origin for the Pāli aphorism, and imply that Uddaka Rāmaputta was active in a yogic milieu familiar with the nondualistic teachings of the *Bṛhadāraṇyaka Upaniṣad*.

## Conclusion to Chapter 3

Element meditation is connected to formless meditation in the early Pāli texts, in lists where the two sets of objects are combined (pp. 29–31), and in the list of *kasiṇāyatana-s* (pp. 31–34) where the four elements are connected to the 'space' and 'consciousness' *kasiṇa-s* that are identical to the first two formless spheres. The doctrinal background to both lists is provided by the list of six 'strata' (*dhātu-s*: earth, water, fire, wind, space and consciousness), a list that appears to be based on the cosmological ideas of early Brahminism, such as the cosmogonies found at TU II.1/Mbh XII.195 (self → space → wind → fire → water → earth), and Mbh XII.224 (*brahman* → mind → space → wind → fire → water → earth). There is no similar doctrinal background to the list of elements in the early Buddhist literature. Moreover, early Brahminic cosmologies provide the doctrinal background to meditation in early Brahminism, and there is even evidence for element meditation in the early Brahminic literature. The basic presupposition of all these schemes of meditation is the early Brahminic identitification of man and cosmos. This suggests that element meditation and formless meditation originated in early Brahminic circles, a fact supported by a number of Upaniṣadic parallels to the goals of the two teachers. The simplest explanation of this evidence is that one (or both) of the two teachers of the Bodhisatta taught a scheme of element meditation as the path to the realization of the self.

The argument outlined in this chapter can be formulated as follows:

i) The Buddhist list of four formless spheres (space, consciousness, nothingness, neither perception nor non-perception) was inherited from the two teachers of the Bodhisatta.
ii) Formless meditation is related to element meditation.
iii) Therefore element meditation was borrowed from the same non-Buddhist source as was formless meditation, i.e. the milieu(x) of the two teachers.
iv) The doctrinal background to element meditation and formless meditation is provided by the list of six 'strata' (*dhātu-s*).
v) The list of six 'strata' is based on early Brahminic cosmogonies.
vi) Brahminic cosmogonies provide the doctrinal background to meditation in early Brahminism, the most basic presupposition of which is the early Brahminic identification of man and cosmos.
vii) Therefore, element meditation and formless meditation were borrowed from a Brahminic source in which meditation was the practical counterpart of cosmological speculation.
viii) The Brahminic source is probably the two teachers, a fact suggested by the Upaniṣadic correspondences to the goals of the teachers ('nothingness' and 'neither perception nor non-perception').

# 4

# THE PHILOSOPHY OF EARLY BRAHMINIC *YOGA*

The previous chapter has shown that there is a strong argument for a Brahminic origin of formless meditation. The most convincing for this, so it seems to me, are the Upaniṣadic parallels to the goals of the two teachers. Nevertheless, several objections could be raised against this theory. First, there is no convincing evidence for meditation in early Brahminic texts that are pre-Buddhist, and definitely no pre-Buddhist evidence for any sort of element meditation.[1] The only Brahminic text in which a scheme of element meditation is outlined – Mbh XII.228 – most probably dates to the early Buddhist period, and in any case does not correspond to the list of elements found in the early Buddhist literature. Moreover, the Buddhist evidence for element meditation is earlier and more abundant than that contained in the early Brahminic literature. If so, is it not illogical to argue that the practice was borrowed from early Brahminism? I think not. I argued in the last chapter that element meditation reflects Brahminic ideology, and that this supports the theory of a Brahminic origin. In this chapter I will develop this hypothesis. By studying some important cosmogonies in the early Brahminic texts, I will strengthen my argument that the relationship between meditation and cosmology was a Brahminic innovation. I will also argue that this development is rooted in speculation that goes back to the late Ṛg Vedic period. Indeed, some of the early texts of this speculative tradition seem to explain the sorts of element meditation found in the early Buddhist texts.

There are three parts to this chapter. First of all, I will investigate the philosophy of early Brahminic meditation in greater detail, by studying the cosmogonic background to the scheme of element meditation found at Mbh XII.228. This will show that the cosmogonic principles corresponding to this scheme of meditation pre-date Buddhism. Although this does not prove the existence of Brahminic sorts of meditation in pre-Buddhist times, the speculative tradition to which these texts belong can be traced back to the *Nāsadīyasūkta*. Following this, in the second part of my argument I will attempt to show that the *Nāsadīyasūkta* contains evidence for a contemplative tradition, even in the late Ṛg Vedic period. Finally, I will argue that a pre-Buddhist form of element meditation can be reconstructed from the early texts of this speculative tradition, and that this reconstruction explains the forms of element meditation and formless meditation outlined in the early Buddhist texts.

## Cosmogony in the *Vasiṣṭha-Karālajanakasaṃvādaḥ* (Mbh XII.291)

A detailed cosmogony, found in one of the most important philosophical tracts of the *Mokṣadharma* (the *Vasiṣṭha-Karālajanakasaṃvāda*, Mbh XII.291–96), corresponds to the scheme of element meditation contained in Mbh XII.228. It begins with a verse on the world ages (291.14, *yugadharma*), after which there is a detailed account of world creation:

> Know that an aeon (*kalpaṃ*) is fourfold (*caturguṇaṃ*), [and consists of] 12,000 *yuga-s*. A *brahmic* day lasts for 1000 aeons, and a night is this long, at the end of which [*brahman*] wakes up (*pratibudhyate*). (14)
>
> Śambhu, the self existent, minuteness (*aṇimā*) [and] lightness (*laghimā*), being formless in essence, emits (*sṛjati*) the one who possesses form, the great being, whose acts are infinite, the one born in the beginning: the world (*viśvaṃ*), the Lord (*īśānaṃ*), the imperishable radiance. (15)[2]
>
> Bounded by hands and feet on all sides, with eyes, heads and mouths everywhere, with ears everywhere, covering everything in the world, he [the first creation] abides. (16)
>
> This one, the one with a golden womb, the Blessed One, is traditionally known as 'intelligence' (*buddhir*). Among the *Yoga* followers he is known as 'the great' (*mahān*) or *Viriñca* (*brahmā*). (17)
>
> In the *sāṃkhya* instruction (*śāstre*), the one whose form is manifold is known by [many] names: 'the one whose form is diverse', 'the one whose self is everything' [and] 'the sole imperishable', according to tradition.(18)
>
> The self who covers the entire, manifold (*naikātmakaṃ*), triple world is traditionally known as 'the one whose form is everything', just because of his state of having many forms. (19)
>
> This one comes to a transformation (*vikriyāpannaḥ*), he emits (*sṛjati*) himself by means of himself (*ātmānam ātmanā*). The one of great splendour [emits] the utterance 'I' (*ahaṃkāra*) i.e. Prajāpati, the one who is formed by [the word] 'I' (*ahaṃkṛtaṃ*). (20)
>
> From the unmanifest (*avyaktād*) the manifest arose; they call that a creation of knowledge (*vidyāsargaṃ*). Self-consciousness (*ahaṃkāram)*, on the other hand, the great one (*mahāntaṃ*), is only a creation of ignorance (*avidyāsargaṃ*). (21)

> Knowledge and ignorance (*vidyāvidye*) are said by those who ponder the meaning of the Vedas and treatises to be that which is beyond the ritual law (*avidhiś*) and that which is the ritual law (*vidhiś*), [both] arisen (*samutpannau*) from the one (*tathaikataḥ*). (22)
>
> Know that the third [creation], the creation of the elements (*bhūtasargam*), is from the self-consciousness (*ahaṃkārat)*, O Pārthiva. Know that the fourth [creation] is what is modified (*vaikṛtaṃ*) from the elements which arose in the self-consciousness (*ahaṃkeṣu)*. (23)
>
> [The great elements are] Wind, fire, space, water and earth; [what is derived from them are the sense-objects] sound, touch, visible form, taste and smell. (24)
>
> Next (*evaṃ*), a set of ten arises simultaneously, on that there is no doubt; know this as the fifth creation that is material (*bhautikaṃ*), full of reality (*arthavat*). (25)
>
> Ears, skin, eyes, tongue, and the nose as the fifth; plus speech, hands, feet, anus and so the penis. (26)
>
> These are the faculties of cognition (*buddhīndriyāṇi*) and the faculties of action (*karmendriyāṇi*), arisen simultaneously along with the mind, O Pārthiva. (27)
>
> This twenty-fourth (*tattvacaturviṃśā*) exists in all forms, knowing which Brahmins, seers of the truth, do not grieve. (28)[3]

This account of creation seems to form part of the theoretical understanding of both Sāṃkhya and *Yoga*-followers (v. 17–18). It is based on twenty-four principles (*tattva-s*), the creative agent being the absolute *brahman*, which in v. 21 is called 'the unmanifest'. Creation is initiated by the awakening of *brahman* (v.14), the first creation being termed *hiraṇyagarbha*, *buddhi*, *mahān,* etc. (v. 15–19). The second creation, of the *ahaṃkāra* (or *prajāpati*) by the *hiraṇyagarbha/buddhi*, is outlined in v. 20. This process is summed up in v. 21 when it is stated that the first and second creations are creations of knowledge (*vidyā*) and ignorance (*avidyā*) respectively, i.e. *buddhi* is knowledge, and *ahaṃkāra* is ignorance. The third creation is termed *bhūtasargam* in v. 23, and although Edgerton translates *bhūta-* as 'existing beings' it is obvious that what is meant is the collection of five *mahābhūta-s*, the 'great' (i.e. macrocosmic) elements.[4] The expression *ahaṃkāreṣu bhūteṣu . . . vaikṛtaṃ*, referring to the fourth creation in v. 23cd), simply refers to the fact that the fourth creation – the creation of the different sense objects – are modifications of the great elements, themselves created from the *ahaṃkāra*.[5] I take it that *evaṃ* in the phrase 'Next (*evaṃ*), a set of ten arises simultaneously . . .' (v. 25ab), points forward rather than backwards, for the set of ten named in v. 24 (five elements plus their derivatives) are said in v. 23 to occupy two successive phases of creation (the third and fourth). Moreover, the set of ten items that constitute the fifth creation, i.e. the ten sense faculties named in v. 26,[6] are said in v. 27 to arise simultaneously along with the mind.[7] These must make up the set of ten that in v. 25ab are said to arise simultaneously.

The passage is a relatively straightforward creation tract, although this is not clear in Edgerton's translation, which for some reason only begins at v. 21.[8] It is clear that there is no principle of unmanifest matter (*prakṛti/avyakta*) different from the creator: *avyaktād* in v. 21a must refer to the deity. This fact is obscured when the subject of the passage changes in v. 29, at which point an extensive tract enumerating different classes of being in the cosmos is introduced with the phrase 'What is called "body" in the triple world'.[9] This passage has nothing to do with the earlier cosmogony, but is a separate tract added after it – the juxtaposition of different tracts in the same *Mokṣadharma* passage is hardly unusual. A further stratum is found towards the end of Mbh XII.291, where a different cosmological understanding is referred to (one with twenty-five *tattva-s*).[10] But this doctrine of twenty-five *tattva-s* does not interfere with the passage as far as v. 28, which is coherent and forms a unity.[11] The goal is the unmanifest *brahman*, the 'twenty-fourth'.

The basic principle in this tract is that world creation comes about when *brahman* awakens from his cosmic slumber. This event is followed by a vertical (i.e. sequential) pattern of world creation, each item being created from the item created before it. The vertical pattern applies to the phases *śambhu/brahman* → *buddhi/hiraṇyagarbha* → *ahaṃkāra/prajāpati*. After this the pattern is both vertical (sequential) and horizontal (i.e. collective): the collective creation of the five elements is followed by two successive phases in which the five objects of sense and then eleven organs (the ten faculties plus mind) are created collectively. The most striking feature of this cosmogony is that the awakening of *brahman* initiates world creation. The first creation is called *buddhi*, among other things, indicating the close relationship between the awakening of *brahman* and the first stage of creation. The verb √*budh* expresses the act of 'awakening', 'knowing' and 'understanding', etc., and so *buddhi* seems to be nothing more than the reification – or even the personification (as Viriñca/Brahmā) – of *brahman*'s state of consciousness upon awakening. The next creation is termed *ahaṃkāra* ('the utterance I') or *prajāpati* in v. 20. The latter term seems to suggest a personalistic understanding, although the *ahaṃkāra/prajāpati* is qualified by the adjective *mahāntaṃ* (v. 21), indicating that it is macrocosmic like the *buddhi/hiraṇyagarbha* (v. 17: *mahān*) and the 'great' elements (*mahābhūta-s*). It seems that although the verse on world ages positioned before the emanation tract is personalistic, the emanation tract itself contains features suggesting a more impersonalistic understanding. The use of the *ātmanepada* to describe the absolute's awakening in v. 14 (*pratibudhyate*), as well as the past passive participle to describe creative activity (v. 20: *vikriyāpannaḥ sṛjaty ātmānam ātmanā*; v. 21: *avyaktād vyaktam utpannaṃ*; v. 22: *samutpannau*), might even suggest creation without the divine will of a creator. Against this, the *parasmaipada* forms of the verb √*sṛj* in v. 15 and v. 20 might indicate the opposite. The exact understanding of the composers of the passage is hard to determine: in v. 20, the verb *sṛjati* occurs with the passive compound *vikriyāpannaḥ*. This suggests that there is nothing especially significant about the voice of the verbs. It seems that the distinction between personal and impersonal creation theories was not strictly observed by the ancient Vedāntic thinkers.[12]

Closely connected to the awakening of the deity is the emission of the *ahaṃkāra*. This term is significant: since it refers back to an old idea that the first utterance of the absolute upon awakening is the foundation for world-creation. This idea that world creation proceeds from the utterance 'I' is therefore closely related to the old Brahminic notion that verbal utterance and form are inseparable (*nāma=rūpa*). According to Van Buitenen, the idea of creation by naming is expressed in ancient myths where Prajāpati sends out 'speech' (*vāc*) to create the world,[13] and was old even in the period of the early Upaniṣads:[14] 'the difference between formulation and creation, obvious to us, does not really exist in this train of thought: formulation IS formation; name and form are inseparable.'[15] Although the ancient creation myths referred to by Van Buitenen are older than the occurrences of the term *ahaṃkāra* in the *Mokṣadharma*, he reckons that the two are connected:

> But considering the fact that when *ahaṃkāra* starts to occur again in the epic it brings along brahmanistic notions and carries mythological or theistic associations, I think it more probable that it had never been lost in circles which developed the upaniṣadic doctrines without broadcasting their views too widely at first.[16]

Van Buitenen interprets the term *ahaṃkāra*[17] as 'the cry, uttering or ejaculation *ahaṃ*!' and relates this to an important cosmogonic tract in the *Bṛhadāraṇyaka Upaniṣad* (BU I.4.1), where in the first stage of creation the self becomes self-conscious and then cries out 'I am!':[18]

> In the beginning, this world was the self alone (*ātmaivedam*), in the form of a man. He looked around ('*nuvīkṣya*) and did not see ('*paśyat*) anything else apart from himself. In the beginning he uttered 'I am!' ('*ham asmī*). From that the name 'I' came into existence.[19]

In this passage the process of world creation begins with the self-cognition ('*paśyat*) of the self, an event that is equivalent to the deity's awakening in Mbh XII.291. This is immediately followed by the utterance 'I am!', an event equivalent to the emission of the *ahaṃkāra* in Mbh XII.291. Thus, the cosmogony of Mbh XII.291 appears to be a sophisticated development of the creation myth of BU I.4.1, which is itself a reformulation of even older mythological notions. For our purposes, it is important to note that

Mbh XII.291 provides the philosophical background to the scheme of *yoga* found at Mbh XII.228.13–15. The meditative scheme *pṛthivī* → *vāyu* → *kha* → *payas* → *jyotis* → *ahaṃkāra* → *buddhi* → *avyakta* (Mbh XII.228.13–15) is a reversal of the cosmogony outlined in Mbh XII.291 (*brahman* → *buddhi* → *ahaṃkāra* → 5 elements, etc.). The only difference is that the elements are listed in a particular order in Mbh XII.228, whereas Mbh XII.291 knows only of their collective origin. But this is a relatively insignificant deviation.

There is no question of any outside influence in the cosmogony of Mbh XII.291. As we have seen, it is a logical development of ancient Brahminic ideas. The same could be said of the scheme of element meditation outlined at Mbh XII.228. As the meditative counterpart of Mbh XII.291, it is a logical development of early Brahminic ideas about the creation of the world. It seems, then, that the Buddhist schemes of element meditation studied in the last chapter presuppose some fundamental ideas of early Brahminic cosmogony. The meditation on 'intelligence' (*buddhi*) in these schemes reflects the Brahminic idea that world creation was triggered by the awakening/self-cognition of the absolute *brahman*. The key to liberation, according to early Brahminic thinking, is to reverse the creation of the cosmos through its successive stages until this primordial state of consciousness is realized in a meditative trance. This belief explains the progression from infinite space to infinite consciousness in the list of *kasiṇāyatana-s* and the formless spheres.

It seems clear that the speculative tradition providing the philosophical background to early Brahminic meditation is pre-Buddhist. This does not necessarily mean that the tradition of early Brahminic meditation was pre-Buddhist as well. The textual record – cosmogonic ideas that can be traced back to pre-Buddhist texts, but no pre-Buddhist texts on meditation – might suggest that the speculative tradition of early Brahminism only developed a corresponding contemplative tradition at a later date. Perhaps meditation originated in some other ascetic tradition of ancient India, and was elaborated into the cosmological sort of meditation we find outlined in the *Mokṣadharma* at a later date. Even if so, it is likely that the cosmological sort of meditation originated within the speculative circles of early Brahminism. Another possibility, however, is suggested by the peculiar nature of early Brahminic cosmogony. The notion that the world owes its creation to a state of consciousness – the state of consciousness of *brahman* upon awakening – is peculiar, and exactly the sort of theory likely to have been formulated by contemplatives. The idea of a creative state of consciousness could, of course, have been formulated by thinkers who did not have any mystical or contemplative inclinations. But it is more likely, perhaps, that such a theory was formulated in an early contemplative/speculative tradition on the basis of contemplative experiences. Some early evidence supports this claim. The *Nāsadīyasūkta*, one of the earliest and most important cosmogonic tracts in the early Brahminic literature, contains evidence suggesting it was closely related to a tradition of early Brahminic contemplation. A close reading of this text suggests that it was closely related to a tradition of early Brahminic contemplation. The poem may have been composed by contemplatives, but even if not, an argument can be made that it marks the beginning of the contemplative/meditative trend in Indian thought. If so, the roots of meditation in early Brahminism can be taken well back into the pre-Buddhist era.

## Cosmogony in the *Nāsadīyasūkta*

The *Nāsadīyasūkta* is only seven verses long, although the information packed into it is dense and obscure. Brereton has translated it as follows:[20]

> The non-existent did not exist, nor did the existent exist at that time.
> There existed neither the midspace nor the heaven beyond.
> What stirred? From where and in whose protection?
> Did water exist, a deep depth? (1)
>
> Death did not exist nor deathlessness then.
> There existed no sign of night nor of day.
> That One breathed without wind through its inherent force.
> There existed nothing else beyond that. (2)
>
> Darkness existed, hidden by darkness, in the beginning.
> All this was a signless ocean.
> When the thing coming into being was concealed by emptiness,
> then was the One born by the power of heat. (3)
>
> Then, in the beginning, from thought there developed desire,
> which existed as the primal semen.
> Searching in their hearts through inspired thinking,
> poets found the connection of the existent in the non-existent. (4)
>
> Their cord was stretched across:
> Did something exist below it? Did something exist above?
> There were placers of semen and there were powers.
> There was inherent force below, offering above. (5)
>
> Who really knows? Who shall here proclaim it?
> From where it was born, from where this creation?
> The gods are on this side of the creation of this world.
> So then who does know from where it came to be? (6)

This creation – from where it came to be,
 if it was produced or if not –
He who is the overseer of this world in the highest heaven,
 he surely knows. Or if he does not know . . .? (7) [21]

The hymn describes, in a most obscure way, the origin of the world. From mysterious beginnings to an unresolved conclusion, it almost seems to be a riddle posed by the ancient Vedic poets. The final verse, which lacks the correct number of syllables,[22] suggests that an answer to the origin of the world cannot be found. Verses one to four include most of the content that might provide an answer to the riddle, but they are ambiguous. They describe the process of creation, but all include adverbs such as *tadā́nīṃ* (v.1) and *tárhi* (v. 2), as well as nouns used adverbially (v. 3–4: *ágre*), indicating that the process of creation cannot be formulated into an exact temporal sequence. Time, it seems, is something that comes along with the creation of the world, and cannot be a measure of its beginning. The subject of creation is not even named until v. 2, when we are told that it is 'that One', i.e. the nondual source, which in v. 1 cannot even be described by the adjectives *sad* and *asad*. As Jurewicz has pointed out: 'That state is something so vague that it cannot be compared even to water which usually symbolizes – as it should be noticed – the first nameable form of the reality and not the state before the creation.'[23]

The apophatic style continues in v. 2, with the statement that the 'One' is neither death nor deathlessness, neither day nor night. As Brereton points out, the denial that it is neither death nor deathlessness (in 2a) 'mimics the negations of *ásat* and *sát'* (in 1a), whereas the denial that it is neither day nor night (in 2b) 'replace the spatial categories in which they exist, "midspace" and "heaven"' (of 1b).[24] According to Brereton, there has not yet been any progress in the hymn: 'The only real movement exists in the image created by the hymn, the more detailed and concrete knowledge of what is not there. The only real change is in the thinking of those hearing the hymn, not in the state of creation.'[25]

The ontological status of 'that One' changes in 2c, which, according to Brereton, is an answer to the question posed in 1c ('What stirred?'): we find out that it was the 'One' who 'breathed without wind through its inherent force'.[26] According to Jurewicz, 'That One executes the internally contradictory activity through its own power (*svadhā*). That word means – as it seems to me – the power of That One conceived not only as possibility or ability but also as freedom'.[27] In other words, it seems that in 2c the One is potent and active, but cannot be defined by the laws of the manifest world. And yet, at the start of v. 3, the process of creation is still said to be 'in the beginning' (3a: *ágre*, i.e. before time), when everything was still 'a signless ocean' (3b). However, an ontological change is suggested in *pāda-s* (a) and (c), which suggest the formation of some sort of rudimentary duality. In *pāda* (a) it is said that there was 'darkness . . . hidden by darkness', i.e. 'the thing coming into being was concealed by emptiness' (*pāda* c). According to Jurewicz, this 'describes a situation when That One, beyond which there is nothing else, begins to act on itself. The essence of this first creative change is constituted by the functional differentiation of the two spheres of the homogeneous reality: the covering and the covered spheres.'[28] This ambiguous situation is reflected in 3c by the indefinite term *ābhú*. According to Brereton, this word could derive from *a* + √*bhū* and mean 'not become', or *ā* + √*bhū* and mean 'come into being'. He comments: 'Thus the possibilities for interpreting *ābhú* as something "coming into being" and as something "empty" make this a word which embodies the ambiguous situation the verse describes, a state hovering between non-existence and existence.'[29] Brereton goes on:

> This core and the covering, described in 3a and 3c, further recall another image in 1c. There the poet asks 'in whose protection' lies the unidentified subject. Here again, the image is of something surrounded or covering something else. Over these first three verses, then, the hymn creates a trajectory in which the shape of core and a cover is first raised as a possibility (in 1c), then described paradoxically as a form whose outer and inner cannot be distinguished (in 3a, 'darkness hidden by darkness') and finally presented ambiguously as a form whose cover is imperceptible but whose core may carry the potential for existence (in 3c). As Thieme has rightly pointed out, this shape of core and cover describes the form of an egg.[30]

It seems that 3a–c describes the initial change in the One: as Jurewicz notes, 'That One' must have 'acted on itself'. A further change is suggested in 3d. This is indicated by the relative clause *yád/tán* in 3cd. Brereton takes *tán* in 3d as a correlative adverb 'then' and *yád* in 3c as the relative adverb 'when'. Thus, he translates 3cd as follows: 'When the thing coming into being was concealed by emptiness, then was the One born by the power of heat.' As Brereton points out: 'an egg carries with it the promise of further change'; this further change is, of course, the egg's incubation.[31] In other words, Brereton reckons that v. 3 implies a sequence: the division into what will become the world (*táma*, *ābhú*) and what will not (*támasā*, *tuchyéna*), outlined in 3a and 3c, is the necessary condition for the 'birth' of 'the One' (3d). And yet the duality is in such a rudimentary state that the poem assures us the primary unity of the One has not been violated: it is still homogeneous, a 'signless ocean' (3b).

According to Brereton, what is left unclear in v. 3 is the reflexive activity that separated the One into a rudimentary duality. Brereton has proposed a new solution to this problem. He reads *mánaso* in 4b as an ablative and construes it with (*ā́*)*dhi* of 4a,[32] translating the two *pāda-s*: 'Then, in the beginning, from thought there developed desire, which existed as the primal semen.' According to this interpretation, 'desire' (4a: *kā́mas*) originated from 'thought' (4b: *mánaso*). Brereton also notes that there is a connection between desire in 4a and heat (*tápasas*) in 3d.[33] If we identify the two, it must mean that the 'thought' or 'mind' of 4b preceded the 'heat' of 3d), and this places 'mind' at the very beginning of creation. This implies that 'mind' was the cognitive act that caused the separation of the One into cover and covered, the 'emptiness' and that which will become the world. Brereton seems to think something like this. Because 'thought' precedes desire/heat, he reckons that it must be identical with the One, the subject of v. 1–2 ,which neither exists nor does not exist:

> If desire corresponds to heat, then the One that precedes heat ought to correspond to the thought that precedes desire. And so it does, for *thought* is the 'One.' It is the hidden subject that dominates the first three verses. Thought is that which the first verse describes as neither non-existent or existent: it is not 'existent' because it is not a perceptible object, and it is not 'non-existent' because it is not absolutely nothing.[34]

But this interpretation of the *Nāsadīyasūkta* is not without problems. Given the complicated structure of the opening verses (which lack a positive definition of the One) and the final verse of the poem (which lacks a clear conclusion), it is questionable whether the composers of the poem would have revealed the One to be 'thought' as a sort of aside in v. 4. Moreover, I find Brereton's reasoning that thought 'is not "existent" because it is not a perceptible object, but not "non-existent" because it is not absolutely nothing' a simplistic interpretation of the opening stanza of the poem. He cites an ancient interpretation of the hymn to prove his point: ŚB X.5.3.2 states: 'for thought is in no way existent, (and) in no way is it non-existent.'[35] But at the same time he also observes: 'Inevitably, therefore, commentaries on *ṚV* 10.129 create a distinct picture of the origin of things, even though the poem itself resists such clarity and is even undermined by it.'[36] The same could be said of Brereton's interpretation.

Brereton's argument ultimately depends upon his interpretation of *mánaso* as an ablative. But this grammatical point is not entirely convincing. The attempt to construe (*ā́*)*dhi* of 4a with *mánaso* of 4b as an ablative is problematic, for it would be the only place in the poem where a syntactic unit crosses a *pāda* boundary. Furthermore, taking (*ā́*)*dhi* . . . *mánaso* as part of the predicate of *kā́mas* . . . *sám avartat*(*ā́*) ('desire developed from thought') leaves the word *tád* (in 4a) redundant. Brereton deals with this problem by taking *tád* as an adverb of time ('then'), but this would mean that two adverbs of time (*tád* + *ágre*) are adjacent, and such a construction is not found in the rest of the poem: in v. 1–3, the adverbs *tadā́nīṃ*, *tárhi*, and *ágre* occur alone. It seems more natural to take *tád* as a pronoun, and if so, it must be taken as the object of the verb in 4a, and must therefore be identical with 'That One' mentioned in 2c. But if 4a is read in such way, Brereton's interpretation of *(ā́)dhi . . . mánasaḥ* is implausible, for the resulting translation ('In the beginning desire came upon that [One], from thought') is awkward and unlikely. In fact, if *tád* is taken as a pronoun, the two *pāda-s* read better if the syntactic unit does not cross from *pāda* (a) into *pāda* (b), and a translation such as that proposed by Macdonell makes good sense: 'Desire in the beginning came upon that, (desire) that was the first seed of mind'.[37] According to this reading, desire arose from that One – or developed in it – and this desire was 'the first seed of mind'. The statement that 'desire' was 'the first seed of mind' is hardly clear, but the word *retas* ('semen' or 'seed') suggests that desire is the essence of 'thought' (or 'mind'), i.e. that which is its pure, undivided substance, which will develop into the mind. In other words, the desire that arose in the One was essentially a form of consciousness, a cognitive essence that would become mind.

Another problem with Brereton's interpretation concerns the interpretation of verse three. If thought (4b) – 'that One' – is taken as that which caused desire (4a) or heat (3d) to develop, the logical sequence is 'thought (nondual deity) → desire/heat → birth of the nondual deity'. However, Brereton takes *yád* in 3c and *tán* in 3d as a pair of relative adverbs with the temporal meaning 'when . . . then'. This suggests a temporal order in which the event described in 3c precedes the event described in 3d, i.e. the separation, in 3c, into 'cover' ('emptiness') and 'covered' ('the thing coming into being') spheres was temporally followed by the event described in 3d, i.e. the birth of the One from heat. But how does the separation of the One into cover and covered spheres fit into the sequence 'thought → desire/heat → birth of the nondual deity'? This is not clear in Brereton's analysis. Moreover, if the One has separated into cover and covered spheres, with one of these being termed 'the thing coming into being', it is not proper to speak in 3d of 'the One' (the nondual deity) being born, since the thing being born (the 'thing coming into being') is really a single part of 'that One'. These difficulties can all be avoided if the arising of 'desire' or 'heat' is taken as the seed of mind, rather than its product, as it must be if 'mind' in 4b is taken in the ablative case. According to such an interpretation, since mind in 4a is identical with heat in 3d, with both describing the first change in the One, the state of affairs described in 3d should precede that described in 3c. This means that the formation of 'cover' and 'covered' spheres described in 3c is subsequent to the birth of the One from heat in 3d. Such an interpretation only works if *yád* and *tán* are taken as pronouns qualifying *ābhú*. This would give a translation similar to Macdonell's: 'The thing coming into being which was covered by the Void, that one arose through the power of heat'.[38] In this reading, the 'One' of 3d is not the unnamed absolute of 2c, but is simply the thing 'coming into being' of 3c. This means, then, that the rudimentary duality into the 'thing coming into being' and the 'emptiness' was formed by 'heat'. The heat produced in the arising of desire caused the separation into cover and covered spheres, the rudimentary duality that formed in the One. As Jurewicz has pointed out, 'That One warms up in the self-cognitive act.'[39]

According to this interpretation, the cosmogony of the *Nāsadīyasūkta* ought to be read as follows:

that One → desire/heat → separation into existent and non-existent

The 'desire' that was the essence of 'mind' or 'thought' is therefore that which caused the separation into cover and covered, i.e. that which will remain void (*tuchya*) and that which will come into existence (*ābhu*), or that which will be termed the 'not-existent' (*asat*) and that which will be termed the 'existent' (*sat*). Hence the statement that the poets understood the connection of the existent (*sat*) in the non-existent (*asat*) by searching in their hearts through 'inspired thinking' (*manīṣā́*): if the seed or essence of mind was the connection between the two in the beginning, and indeed that which caused the two to separate from each other, it is also that by which this relationship can be understood. 'Mind', it seems, is indeed the solution to the poem.

The *Nāsadīyasūkta* is obscure. In particular, v. 3 and v. 4 leave room for many possible interpretations. The problem, as it seems to me, concerns not so much the interpretation of (*ā́*)*dhi . . . mánaso*, as Brereton thinks, but the confusion over the relative clauses in 3cd and 4ab. The relative/correlative construction *yád . . . tán* in 3cd may be pronominal or adverbial, and both possibilities suggest different cosmogonies. The problem is confused by the fact that *tán* in 3d agrees with (*e*)*kam*: this suggests that the subject of 3d may be identical with the subject of v. 1–2, named in 2c as *tád ékaṃ*. This identification is accepted by Brereton, but according to the alternative interpretation offered above, which generally agrees with Macdonell's translation, this is not so and the word *ekam* in 3d is a red herring. The same confusion surrounds the word *tád* in 4a – it could be either a pronoun or an adverb. Moreover, a confusion over the relative clause, similar to that found in 3cd, is again seen in 4b. Macdonell and Brereton think that *yád* in 4b picks up *kā́mas* of 4a, but it could be a relative pronoun agreeing with *tád* in 4a. If so, the subject qualified by *yád* in 4b would be the One, the unnamed absolute of 2c. And this may suggest that the One was 'mind', as suggested by Brereton, although the proposition of 4d ('which was the first seed of mind') again lacks clarity. The definitive interpretation of the *Nāsadīyasūkta* is hindered by what appears to be the intentional ambiguity of the Vedic poets.

What is clear is that 'thought' or 'mind' is intricately involved in the creation of the world. The reflexive act that initiated world creation is either 'thought' or closely related to it. The statement that the poets found the connection of the existent in the non-existent through inspired thinking (*manīṣā́*) indicates that the riddle of the universe is to be solved through the power of human thought. As Brereton states, the 'response [of the audience], their active mental engagement, mirrors the original power of creation, and their gradually developing understanding recapitulates the process of creation'.[40] From this perspective, the poem was not simply composed as a riddle about the origin of the world: it was also meant to provoke its audience to ponder the possibility that the answer to the origin of the world may be identical to the power of thought. Thus the final two verses question the possibility of ever knowing the origin of everything, but at the same time they incite the audience into further self-reflection. As Brereton comments on v. 5: 'Neither human knowledge nor speech, even if they are reflexes of the primal creative power, can capture that origin.'[41] If the state in the beginning was nondual, and thought arose 'afterwards' as the creative power, the implication is that thought cannot grasp the state beyond itself. That 'One' developed into the world because of the creative power of thought, but the process is barely thinkable, and the nature of the One remains a mystery beyond thought. Thus Brereton sums up the intention of the poem as follows:

> It does not offer a detailed picture of the origin of things nor describe the nature or agent of primordial thought, because to do so would defeat its own purposes. For if its function is to create thinking through questioning, then the poem must avoid a final resolution which would bring an end to questioning and an end to thought. Just as the poem begins with something between existent and non-existent, it must leave its readers between knowledge and ignorance. Thus the openness of the poem points to the process of thinking as an approximate answer to the unanswerable riddle about the origin of things.[42]

If the poem 'points to the process of thinking as an approximate answer to the unanswerable riddle about the origin of things', it seems inevitable that the speculation of the *Nāsadīyasūkta* eventually produced, or was indeed the product of, a tradition of early Brahminic mysticism. In fact 4cd seems to state that the poem was the work of contemplatives. The declaration that the poets found the connection between the existent and non-existent through 'inspired thinking' (*manīṣā*) is evidence for a tradition of contemplation/mysticism in Vedic times. The Vedic poets, it seems, came up with obscure creation poems through their 'inspired' inner contemplations. It is quite possible that the curious notion of a divine self-cognition being the cause of world creation was a theory of mystics or 'seers' who experimented with contemplative techniques. This is not to suggest that yogic or even proto-yogic practices were employed by the author(s) of the *Nāsadīyasūkta*. But it is easy to see how the poem set the agenda for the metaphysical and yogic speculation of the early philosophical period. Indeed, almost all the detailed yogic schemes of this period correspond to cosmogonies based on the fundamental principle of the *Nāsadīyasūkta*, i.e. that world creation depends upon the self-cognition of the unmanifest, nondual deity. It is hard to doubt that cosmogonic speculation provided the theoretical background to earlier schemes of meditation.

## Cosmogony in the *Śukānupraśnaḥ* (Mbh XII.224)

An important early cosmogony is found in the *Mokṣadharma* at Mbh XII.224. It appears to be a later philosophical formulation of the obscure thought of the *Nāsadīyasūkta*, but does not correspond to any scheme of *yoga* in the early Brahminic literature. However, the sequence of elements in it corresponds exactly to the six *dhātu-s* and so it seems to form the theoretical background to the forms of element meditation found in the early Buddhist literature. The cosmogony found in Mbh XII.224 begins at v. 11 with the introduction of the cosmic agent (*brahman*). Following this there are two short tracts on the divisions of time (v. 12–21) and the world periods (*yugadharmāḥ*, v. 22–27); these correspond to Manusmṛti I v. 64–70 and v. 81–86 respectively. There is another beginning to the cosmogony at Mbh XII.224.31, and this corresponds to the cosmogony that begins at Manu I v.74. It appears that both texts have drawn upon an ancient source, or even several old sources – one on the divisions of time, one on *yuga-s*, and one on cosmogony.[43] The *Mokṣadharma* cosmogony has one beginning at v. 11 and three more between v. 31 and v. 34. Thus it seems to juxtapose four different beginnings, a fact that probably indicates that the redactor has included different passages from different oral or manuscript traditions. This, according to Hacker, is 'a primitive method of redaction, caused by the desire of doing equal justice to different traditions'.[44] Hacker eliminates v. 31ab and v. 32–34, leaving us with an original tract of v. 11 → 31cd → 35–38:[45]

> Without beginning or end, unborn, divine, undecaying, fixed, immutable, unable to be examined or perceived, in the beginning *brahman* stirred, (11)
>
> . . . and emitted mind, the great being, [both] manifest and unmanifest in essence. (31cd)[46]
>
> Mind, being impelled by the desire to create, produced an emission. From it was born space; sound is thought to be its quality. (35)
>
> From space, modifying itself, was born the bearer of all smells, which is pure, i.e. wind, the powerful one; its quality is thought to be touch. (36)

> From wind, modifying itself, was born the element fire, the dispeller of darkness, the brilliant; visible form is said to be its quality. (37)
>
> And from fire, modifying itself, water came into being, its essence taste. From water, the earth [was born], its quality smell. This is said to be the creation [that took place] in the beginning (*pūrvaiṣā sṛṣṭir ucyate*). (38)[47]

If we follow Hacker's reading of the text including the variant for 31d,[48] the cosmogony is: *brahman* → *manas* (= *mahad bhūtaṃ*)→ *ākāśa* → *vāyus* → *jyotis* → *āpas* → *bhūmi*. If we do not accept Hacker's emendation to v. 31, we have a cosmogony *brahman* → *mahad bhūtam* → *manas*. However, another beginning to the cosmogony (v. 33) states that in the beginning when the absolute awoke (*vibuddhaḥ san*), he emitted the world, i.e. the great being (*mahābhūtaṃ*) or mind (*manas*), 'whose essence is the manifest' (*vyaktātmakaṃ*).[49] The equation of *manas* with *mahābhūtaṃ* and *vyaktātmakaṃ* in v. 33 suggests more or less the same understanding as that proposed by Hacker's emendation to v. 31d, indicating that *manas* and *mahad bhūtaṃ* are one and the same.

This cosmogonic tract, like the *Nāsadīyasūkta* and Mbh XII.291, is based on the idea that world creation begins with the self-cognition of *brahman*. There is no yogic tract that corresponds to it, in the way that Mbh XII.228 corresponds to Mbh XII.291. But it is likely, given the relationship between meditation and cosmology in early Brahminism, that there were schemes of meditation corresponding to important emanation tracts such as that found in Mbh XII.224. A hypothesized scheme of meditation based on the emanation tract of Mbh XII.224 would be almost identical to that found at Mbh XII.228. The philosophical presuppositions would be the same, the differences being due to minor differences in cosmogonic doctrine held by different thinkers (one stage between *brahman* and the elements, a different order of the elements, etc.). A scheme of meditation corresponding to the cosmogony at Mbh XII.224 would take the following form:

earth → water → fire → wind → space → consciousness → *brahman*

This reconstructed scheme belongs naturally to the stream of thought that goes back to the *Nāsadīyasūkta*. Although there is no evidence that Mbh XII.224 is pre-Buddhist, its vertical emanation of the elements is identical to an early cosmogony found at TU II.1.[50] It is reasonable to suppose that Brahminic schemes of element meditation such as this existed in pre-Buddhist times.

This hypothesized scheme of meditation corresponds exactly to the Buddhist list of six *dhātu-s* (earth, water, fire, wind, space, consciousness).

It can therefore explain the different Buddhist lists of element meditation, for the list of *kasiṇāyatana-s* (pp. 29-31), as well as the other lists of element meditation in the Pāli canon (pp. 31-34) are based on it. It seems, then, that some of the early Buddhists must have been influenced by the sort of meditative scheme related to the Brahminic cosmogony found in Mbh XII.224. If the goal of this hypothesized Brahminic element meditation – *brahman* – is replaced by its Upaniṣadic epithets, i.e. 'nothingness' or 'neither perception nor non-perception', this scheme has the following form:

earth → water → fire → wind → space → consciousness → 'nothingness'/ 'neither perception nor non-perception'

All the Buddhist lists of element and formless mediation seem to be elaborations of such a scheme of element meditation. If the tradition that the Bodhisatta first of all studied under Āḷāra Kālāma before Uddaka Rāmaputta is historically authentic, as I have claimed, and if they did teach element meditation as a path to *brahman*, it is easy to see that the above scheme of meditation would have been reformulated in early Buddhist circles as follows:

earth → water → fire → wind → space → consciousness → nothingness
↓
neither perception nor non-perception

The theory that one or both of the two teachers taught a sort of element meditation based on the cosmogony in Mbh XII.224 explains the Buddhist schemes of element meditation.

## Conclusion to Chapter 4

In the previous chapter I hypothesized that the schemes of element meditation in the early Buddhist texts are based on an early Brahminic ideology. I claimed that the notion of a meditation on macrocosmic elements has no philosophical basis in Buddhist thought, but does have such a basis in early Brahminic thought. This being the case, and given that a similar scheme of element meditation is found in an early Brahminic text, I argued that element meditation must have been absorbed from the meditative circles of early Brahminism. The most likely source for these practices was the two teachers, the religious goals of whom appear to be early Upaniṣadic formulations. In this chapter I have argued that despite the lack of any pre-Buddhist text on element meditation, its philosophical presuppositions are rooted firmly in the speculative tradition of early Brahminism. The relationship between cosmology and meditation, which is such a feature of meditation in the *Mokṣadharma*, seems to have its roots in the *Nāsadīyasūkta*. The basic idea of the *Nāsadīyasūkta* is that world creation was caused by the self-cognition of the unmanifest, nondual deity; this is also the basic presupposition of the early schemes of *yoga*. The *Nāsadīyasūkta* is a provocative and challenging poem that suggests that the riddle of cosmic creation can be solved by personal reflection. It states that the Vedic poets solved the mystery of cosmic creation through 'inspired thinking' (*manīṣā*). It seems, then, that this speculative tradition was related to an early sort of mysticism in which it was thought religious experience could explain the creation of the world. The presupposition that man and cosmos are identical paved the way for the elaboration of a cosmological sort of contemplation, on the material elements and higher strata of the cosmos. This tradition is the ultimate source of the yogic and cosmogonic speculations found in the *Mokṣadharma*.

The cosmogony that corresponds to the Buddhist list of six *dhātu-s* – and so to the various forms of element meditation found in the early Buddhist literature – is found in Mbh XII.224. The Buddhist schemes of element meditation must ultimately be due to this sort of Brahminic influence. If we have reason to believe that the two teachers were the source of the Brahminic influence on early Buddhism, it is likely that element meditation was one of their practices. Thus, the investigations of Chapter 3 and Chapter 4 allow us to form a theory about the Buddha's intellectual development. If the Bodhisatta was taught meditation by Āḷāra Kālāma and Uddaka Rāmaputta, he was probably well versed in the philosophical presuppositions of early Brahminic meditation and cosmology. This gives us some criteria by which the authenticity of early Buddhist teachings can be assessed.

## Appendix to Chapter 4: the early yogic doctrine of *karman*

In the following chapter I will analyse a few old passages from one of the oldest Buddhist texts, the *Suttanipāta*, and argue that the Buddha's teachings in them conform to the theory that he was taught in a Brahminic school of meditation. I will argue that the correct understanding of these dialogues depends on such a theory. To show this depends on proving that the Buddha knew some of the presuppositions of early Brahminic meditation.

The general early Brahminic understanding seems to have been that liberation is achieved by attaining union with the *ātman*/*brahman* by dissolving into it at death. It can, however, be anticipated in life through the realization of the self in a state of meditative absorption, a state that is thought to effect the destruction of the meditative adept's good and bad works (*karman*). Evidence for the notion that the realization of the self destroys *karman* is found as early as the *Muṇḍaka Upaniṣad* (MuU III.1.3):

> When the seer (*paśyaḥ*) sees (*paśyate*) the radiant one, the agent, the Lord, the person, the source of *brahman*,
>
> Then the wise man, having shaken off good and evil, being without blemish, attains the highest identity [with him] (*sāmyam*). (3) [51]

This belief in the destruction of *karman* by realizing the self is alluded to a couple of verses later:

> This self can always be attained by truth, by austerity, by correct knowledge [and] by constant chastity. [He lies] in the body, consisting of light, radiant, which ascetics see (*paśyanti*), their faults destroyed (*kṣīṇadośāḥ*). (5)[52]

The evidence for meditation in these verses is not obvious, although the verb √*dṛś* in the early verse Upaniṣads commonly refers to a sort of gnosis different from the early Upaniṣadic sort of magical knowledge, which is usually indicated by the verb *upa* + √*ās* ('veneration'). And in the *Mokṣadharma* the verb √*dṛś* is usually used to describe the cognitive act in *yoga*. In any case, other verses in the *Muṇḍaka Upaniṣad* show that its authors considered the realization of the self to be the result of *yoga*:

> The one on whom the veins converge, like spokes on the hub of a wheel, that one moves on the inside, becoming manifold. 'Oṃ': meditate (*dhyāyatha*) thus on the self; good luck to you, [as you go] to the far shore beyond darkness. (6)
>
> The one that consists of mind, the controller of the breaths and the body, who is established in food, having settled in the heart; with the perception of him by means of their intelligence, wise men see (*paripaśyanti*) it – the one whose form is bliss, the immortal which shines forth. (8)[53]

The use of √*dhyai* in v. 6 probably indicates a meditative method termed *dhyāna*, which was thought to produce a cognition described by the verb √*dṛś*. Further evidence for the destruction of *karman* through realizing the self is found in the *Mokṣadharma*:

> Mbh XII.180.28–29:
> The wise man, always disciplining (*yuñjānaḥ*) [himself] in the earlier and later parts of the night, taking little food, being pure – he sees the self in the self (*paśyaty ātmānam ātmani*). (28)
>
> Abandoning good and bad *karman* through the tranquilisation of thought (*cittasya prasādena*), the tranquil one (*prasannātmā*) establishes himself in the self, [and] attains imperishable bliss (*sukham akṣayam*). (29)[54]
>
> Mbh XII.197.8
> Knowledge arises for men when bad *karman* is destroyed, then one sees (*paśyaty*) the self in the self, when it is like the surface of a mirror. (8)[55]

> Mbh XII.238.10
> The ascetic abandons good and bad [*karman*] through the tranquilisation of thought (*cittaprasādena*); being tranquil (*prasannātmā*), having established [himself] in the self, he attains endless bliss.[56]

The other aspect of this meditative doctrine of *karma* is that liberation is only truly attained at death. This idea appears first in the *Kena Upaniṣad* (KeU II.5):

> If one has known it in this world, there is the real; if one has not realized it in this world, great is [your] destruction. Wise men, discerning it [*brahman*] (*vicitya*) among every being, having departed from this world, become immortal. (5)[57]

The nondual gnosis described here ('discerning it . . . among every being') seems to suggest a meditative gnosis, and one which leads to immortality at death. In KeU I.5 the liberating gnosis is differentiated from Upaniṣadic veneration (*nedaṃ yadidam upāsate*),[58] and is further described in KeU II.3 by a paradoxical description of the mental state of someone who perceives the *ātman*.[59] This illogical statement indicates an intuitive rather than intellectual understanding, one that seems more suited to a description of yogic practice. Further evidence for the notion of liberation at death is found in the *Muṇḍaka Upaniṣad* (MuU III.2.6, 8):

> Ascetics whose purpose is determined through the understanding of the Vedānta (*vedāntavijñāna-*), whose essence is purified through the discipline of renunciation (*saṃnyāsayogād*) – they are all released into the *brahma*-worlds at the time of death, and enjoy the highest nectar. (6)
> Just as flowing rivers sink into the ocean, abandoning name and form, so the wise man, released from name and form, reaches the divine person, beyond the beyond. (8)[60]

The metaphor of rivers running into the sea, indicating the final release from human existence (*nāmarūpād*), shows that liberation was thought to be attained at death. A few verses in the *Mokṣadharma* state the same belief:

> Mbh XII.231.18:
> The one who sees (*'nupaśyati*) the unmanifest (*avyaktaṃ*), the immortal residing in mortals whose bodies are manifest – when he dies (*pretya*), he is fit for the state of *brahman*. (18)[61]

> Mbh XII.289.35, 41:
> Thus the knower of truth, through *yoga*, disciplined in self-concentration, attains the place which is hard to attain, when he has abandoned the body (*hitvā deham*), O King. (35)

> With a spotless understanding, having quickly burnt away his good and bad *karman*, having practised the highest *yoga*, he is released if he so wishes. (41)[62]

The final verse suggests that the adept can choose to attain liberation when he likes, after he has realized the self and so destroyed his good and bad *karman*. In other words, liberation is conceived as something different from the yogic realization of the self. This must mean that liberation was thought to be a release from this worldly existence, i.e. a merging into *brahman* to be attained at death. A basic presupposition of early Brahminical *yoga*, so it seems, is that the one who realizes the self is not liberated until he dies and merges into the absolute. This is effectively a denial that the meditative realization of the self constitutes liberation. That the realization of *ātman/brahman* in a meditative trance was not thought to be identical with liberation is odd, but is, in fact, an inevitable consequence of the extremely pessimistic doctrine – typical of the ascetic religions of ancient India – that existence in the world is bondage, and liberation is an escape from it. J. A. B. Van Buitenen has commented on this idea as follows:

> Fundamental to Indian thought is the idea that the world and phenomena, being transitory, can never be an ultimately valid goal, that there is a lesser trueness in the creation than in that principle or person from whom creation originated, who is eternal, constant, reliable, free from changes and transformation, unalterable, and therefore truly real. Consequently, there is universal agreement that to seek communion with that ultimate is a higher purpose than to perpetuate one's existence in the world order. Let the world be, if you can do better.[63]

The notion that liberation is attained at death is the logical result of the idea that existence in the world is misery. Such a belief implies that the meditative realization of the self cannot be accepted as liberation itself, but is only a temporary anticipation of the yogin's final destiny.

It is not clear whether the notion of liberation at death, anticipated by the *karman*-destroying realization of the self in life, was a standard presupposition of all the meditative schools of early Brahminism. I would say, however, that the evidence for this idea comes from a wide selection of texts. Although the textual record is hardly complete, it is quite likely that the idea was widespread. Indeed it seems to me that this idea is the inevitable conclusion of the notion that the religious goal is the unmanifest *brahman*: if the goal is conceived to be union with the unmanifest source of the world, it cannot logically be something that occurs in life. It seems, then, that according to the most basic presupposition of early Brahminic meditation, the idea of liberation in life is an oxymoron.

The notion that liberation can only be achieved at death occurs in an early Buddhist dialogue on meditation between the Buddha and a Brahminic renouncer. I will study this dialogue, from the *Pāryanavagga* of the Sutta Nipāta, in the following chapter. I aim to show that the Buddha's teachings in this dialogue and others like it fit the theory of his intellectual background outlined in the last few chapters. One dialogue in particular, with the Brahminic renouncer Upasīva, seems to show a religious teacher familiar with the goal of one of his teachers – 'nothingness' of Āḷāra Kālāma – as well as the presuppositions of early Brahminic meditation, especially the notion that liberation is achieved at death. I will claim that if a discourse of the Buddha (i) refers to the teaching of one his former teachers and (ii) reflects the presuppositions of early Brahminic meditation, then we should take seriously (i) the texts' claim that the Bodhisatta studied under the teachers and (ii) the theory proposed in this book that the teachers belonged to early Brahminic milieu(x).

# 5

# MEDITATION IN THE *PĀRĀYANAVAGGA*

In the previous chapters I have argued that the Bodhisatta was taught a form of early Brahminic meditation. To what extent, then, were the teachings of the Buddha influenced by this Brahminic background? Perhaps the Buddha rejected the Brahminic methods of his teachers outright. If so, element meditation and formless meditation would be a 'non-authentic intrusion into the Buddhist texts', as claimed by Bronkhorst.[1] But it is also possible that the Buddha allowed, or even recommended, the practice of element meditation and formless meditation. The *Ariyapariyesana Sutta* suggests that the Buddha taught some sort of meditative practice to the first five disciples.[2] But there is no indication of the nature of this practice, and so this passage cannot be used as the criterion by which teachings in the early Buddhist literature could be ascribed to the Buddha. If, however, the Buddha was taught an early Brahminic sort of meditation, and if the early Buddhist literature is as old as I claim (pp. 4–7), then this theory of the Buddha's intellectual development can be tested on the early texts. We can analyse the teachings on meditation, particularly those that concern formless meditation, and consider if they might be proclamations of a teacher of such a background as we have hitherto suggested.

The texts in the *Pārāyanavagga* of the *Suttanipāta* depict the Buddha in dialogue with Brahmins on the subject of meditation. Three of these texts (Sn V.7: 'the Questions of Upasīva'; Sn V. 14: 'the Questions of Udaya'; Sn V. 14: 'the Questions of Posāla') are especially important. In particular, the questions of the Brahman Upasīva deserve a detailed examination, for they seem to show that the Buddha was familiar with the presuppositions of early Brahminic mediation, and that he recommended a reformulated practice of Āḷāra Kālāma's goal. This dialogue is quite unlike any other texts in the Suttapiṭaka; I will argue that it can only be explained if the theory elaborated in this book is correct. The dialogues with Udaya and Posāla are important for other reasons. In these texts the Buddha teaches a form of meditative practice and liberating insight concordant with the teachings given to Upasīva. They are, however, less historically significant than the dialogue with Upasīva since they do not make any reference to early Brahminic ideas. Their importance lies in their original teachings, which seem to formulate the ideas contained in the dialogue with Upasīva in an abstract, rather than an *ad hominem*, form.

## The antiquity of the *Pārāyanavagga*

The *Pārāyanavagga* is certainly very old. Along with the *Aṭṭhakavagga* (Sn IV) and the *Khaggavisāṇasutta* (Sn v. 35–75), it is commented on by the Niddesa, which is itself part of the Theravāda canon.[3] These three texts must have existed independently before they were incorporated into the *Suttanipāta*. Indeed, the *Suttanipāta* is not mentioned in the list of texts contained in the *Divyāvadāna*, although the *Arthavargīya* and *Pārāyana* are mentioned.[4] The evidence suggests, then, that the *Aṭṭhakavagga*, *Pārāyanavagga* and the *Khaggavisāṇa Sutta* were independent texts that were closed early in the pre-sectarian period before the formation of the Pāli *Suttanipāta*. The internal evidence of the Suttapiṭaka supports this conclusion. Norman has noted that substantial portions of Suttas from Sn I-III are found in other parts of the Suttapiṭaka. But there are no parallels in the rest of the Suttapiṭaka to portions of the *Aṭṭhakavagga* and *Pārāyanavagga*, and because of this Norman concludes: 'This would seem to imply that these two vaggas were regarded as a whole at the very earliest period of Buddhism, and had already been given a status of "original and indivisible".' [5] Moreover, only these two books are referred to by name in the Suttapiṭaka: there are three references to the *Aṭṭhakavagga* and four references to the *Pārāyanavagga*.[6] This is a sign that they were considered to be old even in the ancient period of canonical formation.

Although Norman comments that '[d]ating by metre is not particularly helpful', linguistic and metrical criteria also suggest that the *Aṭṭhakavagga* and *Pārāyanavagga* are very old:[7] Norman has noted that the core of *Aṭṭhakavagga* is in Triṣṭubh, which is generally thought to indicate an early date.[8] Of the three books from the *Pārāyanavagga* which I will consider here, the *Upasīvamāṇavapucchā* is in Triṣṭubh, whereas the *Udayamāṇavapucchā* and the *Posālamāṇavapucchā* are in Śloka. Perhaps of more importance than metrical considerations is the following stylistic peculiarity, found in both the *Aṭṭhakavagga* and *Pārāyanavagga*: the expression 'I have come with a question' (*atthi pañhena āgamaṃ/āgamiṃ*) occurs once in *Aṭṭhakavagga* and four times in the *Pārāyanavagga*; its only other occurrence in the Pāli Canon is in the late *Apadāna* (Ap II.488). It is likely that this peculiar style of introducing a Sutta was used in early times but soon became redundant.

It is also worth noting that the *Aṭṭhakavagga* and *Pārāyanavagga* include hardly any of the technical vocabulary found in the rest of the Suttapiṭaka. In the case of the *Pārāyanavagga,* this may be because it has preserved the Buddha's dialogue with non-Buddhists. In such cases the Buddha may well have adapted his vocabulary to suit the understanding of his interlocutors, using his 'skill in means'. But another explanation for the lack of typical

Buddhist vocabulary is that the *Aṭṭhakavagga* and *Pārāyanavagga* were composed at a very early date, before the composition of many of the prose passages of the four principle Nikāya-s. It is also possible that both explanations are true: in the Suttapiṭaka, there are no other teachings addressed to Brahmins quite like the teachings given to Upasīva and Posāla, and this may be because both texts have recorded dialogues with non-Buddhists from the earliest period, when the Buddha was still alive. In both explanations, the lack of technical terminology found in the two books points towards a very early date of composition. This is, of course, a version of the argument from silence, the application of which is debatable. However, the argument from silence can be a powerful tool when used to corroborate other evidence. In this chapter I will subject the dialogue with Upasīva to a literary and philological analysis, and bring to light many peculiarities that suggest its antiquity. In such circumstances the argument from silence is much more persuasive.

All these features support the idea that the texts collected in the *Pārāyanavagga* were composed at a very early date. How old exactly? Some of the Suttas of the *Suttanipāta* are mentioned in Aśoka's Bhairāṭ edict: what is there called *Munigāthā* is probably the *Munisutta* (Sn 207–21), whereas *Moneyasūte* is probably the second half of the *Nālakasutta* (Sn 699–723) and *Upatisapasine* is probably the *Sāriputtasutta* (Sn 955–75).[9] If these identifications are correct, and this material from the *Suttanipāta* is pre-Aśokan (*c*. late fourth/early third century BC), it is likely that the material in the *Pārāyanavagga* is at least as old but probably even older. Norman has noted that other Suttas from Sn I-III are found in the *Mahāvastu*,[10] and this means that they probably pre-date the first schism, which could have occurred at any point between the second council (*c*.60 AB/345 BC)[11] and the missions that occurred in the reign of Aśoka (*c*.154 AB/250 BC). This does not provide precise information about the date of pre-schismatic works, but if Frauwallner was correct in supposing that the old Skandhaka was composed shortly after the second council, and if he is also right in supposing that the author had access to an early version of the *Aṭṭhakavagga*,[12] then we can probably date it and the equally ancient *Pārāyanavagga* between the Buddha's life and *c*.50 AB (*c*.354 BC).

Not all scholars accept the antiquity of the *Pārāyanavagga* as a whole. Tilmann Vetter has argued that the *Pārāyanavagga* is made up of many different strata:

> we may be justified to call the Pārāyana a 'text' which was 'composed' by a person who wanted to mention as many tenets or methods as he knew and as many as were necessary to complete the solemn number of sixteen questions. All is related to the Buddha and, very likely, to the aim of overcoming rebirth. It may have been composed at a relatively early date, but to call it the oldest text of the Pali canon, as some scholars do, fails to convince me.[13]

According to this analysis, the meditative ideas of the *Pārāyanavagga* are diverse. Indeed, Vetter states that verses emphasizing the practice of mindfulness (*sati*) refer to 'a practice which seems to be . . . independent from Dhyāna-meditation except in one case (1107); in two (perhaps three) cases . . . it is combined with the method of discriminating insight (*paññā*).'[14] But this is an application of the argument from silence, and not even a very convincing one. It is not clear why verses mentioning mindfulness must refer to a practice independent from 'Dhyāna-meditation' simply because they do not mention the latter. I see no reason, for example, to suppose that a simple statement such as 'the *bhikkhu* should wander mindfully' (1039: *sato bhikkhu paribbaje*) implies a practice of mindfulness independent from 'Dhyāna-meditation'. One cannot be sure that Dhyāna-meditation is not assumed in the verses mentioned by Vetter. The same critique applies to verses where Vetter understands an intellectual rather than a 'mystical' meaning, simply because of the presence of the word *paññā*. According to him, this word indicates the method of 'discriminating insight', but the verses to which he refers hardly make such an intellectualist position clear.[15] For example, Vetter thinks that the statement 'destroying the belief in self' (*attānudiṭṭhiṃ ūhacca*) refers to an intellectual practice: 'The giving up of this seeing [belief] was very likely done by judging the constituents of a person as nonpermanent and therefore unsatisfactory and therefore non-self . . .'.[16] But there is no evidence to support this claim at all.

Whether or not the *Pārāyanavagga* is homogeneous and ancient as a whole is not an issue I will address here. Although I accept a very early date for it, I do not deny that different strata exist in it. My claim is simply that it contains some of the oldest Buddhist compositions. Just how old will become clear, I hope, from the internal evidence of the texts. In the course of this chapter I will propose an alternative interpretation of a few dialogues in the *Pārāyanavagga*. I will claim that the dialogues with Upasīva, Udaya and Posāla show that the Buddha taught a form of meditation similar to what Vetter calls 'Dhyāna-meditation', a meditative practice based on the goal of Āḷāra Kālāma that was thought to lead to a non-intellectual sort of insight.

## The *Upasīvamāṇavapucchā* (Sn 1069–76)

The *Upasīvamāṇavapucchā* is eight verses long:[17]

1069 *eko ahaṃ Sakka mahantam oghaṃ (iccāyasmā Upasīvo), anissito no visahāmi tārituṃ. ārammaṇaṃ brūhi samantacakkhu, yaṃ nissito ogham imaṃ tareyya.*

1070 *ākiñcaññaṃ pekkhamāno satīmā (Upasīvā ti Bhagavā), natthī ti nissāya tarassu oghaṃ. kāme pahāya virato kathāhi, taṇhakkhayaṃ nattam ahābhipassa.*

1071 *sabbesu kāmesu yo vītarāgo (iccāyasmā Upasīvo) ākiñcaññaṃ nissito hitva-m-aññaṃ, saññāvimokhe parame vimutto tiṭṭhe nu so tattha anānuyāyī?*

1072 *sabbesu kāmesu yo vītarāgo (Upasīvā ti Bhagavā), ākiñcaññaṃ nissito hitva-m-aññaṃ, saññāvimokhe parame vimutto tiṭṭheyya so tattha anānuyāyī.*

1073 *tiṭṭhe ce so tattha anānuyāyī pūgam pi vassānaṃ samantacakkhu, tatth' eva so sītisiyā vimutto cavetha*[18] *viññāṇaṃ tathāvidhassa?*

1074 *accī yathā vātavegena khitto (Upasīvā ti Bhagavā), atthaṃ paleti na upeti saṃkhaṃ, evaṃ munī nāmakāyā vimutto atthaṃ paleti na upeti saṃkhaṃ.*

1075 *atthaṅgato so uda vā so natthi, udāhu ve sassatiyā arogo? tam me munī sādhu viyākarohi, tathā hi te vidito esa dhammo.*

1076 *atthaṅgatassa na pamāṇam atthi (Upasīvā ti Bhagavā), yena naṃ vajju taṃ tassa natthi. sabbesu dhammesu samūhatesu, samūhatā vādapathā pi sabbe ti.*

K. R. Norman has translated it as follows:[19]

1069 'Alone (and) without support, Sakyan,' said the venerable Upasīva, 'I am not able to cross over the great flood. One with all-round vision, tell me an object (of meditation), supported by which I may cross over this flood.'

1070 'Having regard for (the state of) nothingness, possessing mindfulness, Upasīva,' said the Blessed One, 'supported by (the belief) "it does not exist", cross over the flood. Abandoning sensual pleasures, abstaining from (wrong) conversations, look for the destruction of craving day and night.'

1071 'He whose passion for all sensual pleasures has gone,' said the Venerable Upasīva, 'supported by the (state of) nothingness, having left the other (states) behind, being released in the highest release from perception, would he stay there not subject (to *saṃsāra*)?'

1072 'He whose passion for all sensual pleasures has gone, Upasīva,' said the Blessed One, 'supported by the (state of) nothingness, having left the other (states) behind, being released in the highest release from perception, he would stay there not subject (to *saṃsāra*).'

1073 'One with all-round vision, if he should remain there not subject (to *saṃsāra*), for a vast number of years, (and) being released in that very place were to become cold, would consciousness disappear for him in such a state?'

1074 'Just as a flame tossed about by the force of the wind, Upasīva,' said the Blessed One, 'goes out and no longer counts (as a flame), so a sage released from his mental body goes out and no longer counts (as a sage).'

1075 He (who) has gone out, does he not exist, or (does he remain) unimpaired for ever? Explain this to me well, sage, for thus is this doctrine known to you.'

1076 'There is no measuring of one who has gone out, Upasīva,' said the Blessed One. 'That no longer exists for him by which they might speak of him. When all phenomena have been removed, then all ways of speaking are also removed.'

Upasīva's first question concerns the object of meditation dependent on which he will be able to cross over the 'flood' (v. 1069: *ogham*, the flood of suffering).[20] The Buddha replies that he should mindfully observe 'nothingness' (*ākiñcaññam*; v. 1070). In the remaining verses Upasīva does not ask how this meditative practice leads to liberation, but instead questions the Buddha about the condition of the person who has attained the state of 'nothingness'.[21] Although the details concerning the process of attaining liberation from the state of 'nothingness' are not outlined in the *Upasīvamāṇavapucchā* (they are found in the *Posālamāṇavapucchā*), the dialogue reveals important facts about the meditative presuppositions of the Buddha and Upasīva. It has serious ramifications for the correct understanding of the early Buddhist dialogue with Brahminism, and thus for the origin of Buddhist meditation.

The first question and answer (v. 1069–70) are relatively straightforward. The following three questions and answers are more complicated, however. We can summarize Norman's translation of this interchange as follows:

1071–72 Upasīva asks the Buddha if the one who is 'released' having attained the highest release from perception (*saññāvimokkhe parame vimutto*) would stay 'there' without being subject to *saṃsāra* (*anānuyāyī*). The Buddha replies that he would.

1073–74 Upasīva asks the Buddha if this person's consciousness (*viññāṇaṃ*) would disappear if he should 'become cold' (*sītisiyā*) in that state.[22] The Buddha says that this person is released from his 'mental body', and like a flame gone out, he cannot be reckoned.

1075–76 Upasīva asks the Buddha if this person would be annihilated (*n'atthi*) or would exist eternally in a pleasant condition (*sassatiyā arogo*). The Buddha answers that the person has gone beyond the means by which one could determine this answer, i.e. because all 'phenomena' (*dhamma-s*) have been destroyed for him, all modes of speaking have been destroyed.

However, Norman's translations of the following terms are problematic: *vimutto* (1071c, 1072c), *anānuyāyī* (1071d, 1072d, 1073a), *sīti-siyā* (1073c) and *nāmakāyā* (1074c). A detailed study of these words will reveal much about the Buddha's adaptation of Brahminic ideas and metaphors, and the earliest Buddhist meditation.

## Sn 1071–72: *vimutto/ʿdhimutto*

Norman's translation of *vimutto* ('released') in v. 1071/72c implies that the person under discussion has attained liberation, in a state that is 'the highest release from perception' (*saññāvimokkhe*). He therefore reads *saññāvimokkhe* as a dependent determinative (*tatpuruṣa*) compound in the ablative case. Vetter also believes that *vimutto* means 'released' in the sense of liberated, and he translates the whole expression: 'released in the highest emancipation from apperception'.[23] He thinks that this idea is similar to some teachings found in the *Aṭṭhakavagga* where liberation is a state without apperception (*saññā*). However, both Norman and Vetter do not consider the fact that in v. 1071/72c there is the variant *ʿdhimutto* for *vimutto*. Norman's note on v. 1071–72 records that *ʿdhimutto* is the reading found in the European edition (i.e. the PTS edition) of the *Cūḷaniddesa* (Nidd II), the old commentary on the *Pārāyanavagga* and the *Khaggavisāṇasutta*.[24] This commentary is certainly old. As I noted above (p. 73, n. 3), in the Theravādin tradition it is classed as a canonical text. The variant *ʿdhimutto* is also attested in the Burmese VRI edition of Nidd II,[25] although the VRI edition of Sn 1071–72 contrastingly reads *vimutto*. Similarly, the Nālandā edition of the *Suttanipāta* reads *vimutto*[26] but its edition of Nidd II reads *ʿdhimutto*.[27] It is odd that these editions of Nidd II retain the reading *ʿdhimutto,* whereas their corresponding editions of the *Suttanipāta* read *vimutto*. The commentary on the *Suttanipāta*, the *Paramatthajotikā* (Pj II), does not quote either *vimutto* or *ʿdhimutto*, but its commentary on the *Upasīvamāṇavapucchā* follows that of Nidd II closely,[28] and its explanation of *anānuyāyī* in v. 1071–72d is almost identical to the explanation of this term in Nidd II.[29] This implies that it follows Nidd II in reading *ʿdhimutto*. Nidd II understands the word *ʿdhimutto* in v. 1071/72 as follows:

> *saññāvimokkhe parame ʿdhimutto*: the *saññāvimokkha-s* are said to be the seven attainments of [meditative states with] perception. The release that is the attainment of the sphere of nothingness is the tip, the best, superior, the foremost, highest, the choice of these seven attainments of [meditative states with] perception.
>
> *saññāvimokkhe parame ʿdhimutto* [means]: In the supreme, the tip, the best, the superior, the foremost, the highest, the choice [sphere of nothingness], he is concentrated (*adhimutto*) because of a release of conviction (*adhimuttivimokkhena*); [this means] he has the conviction with regard to that, he is concentrated on that, he has practised that, made much of it, that is valued by him, he inclines

towards that, he leans towards it, he slopes towards that, he is concentrated on that, he is guided by that.[30]

Nidd II therefore understands that *saññāvimokkhe* refers to the highest meditative state of perception, i.e. it takes the compound *saññāvimokkha* as a dependent determinative in the genitive case ('release of perception') and not an ablative dependent determinative compound as Norman and Vetter believe ('release from perception/apperception'). Pj II follows Nidd II and comments on *saññāvimokkhe parame* as follows: 'In the sphere of nothingness, the highest of the seven *saññāvimokkha-s*.'[31] Thus it understands that *saññāvimokkhe* refers to the meditative state of nothingness, indicating that the compound is a genitive and not an ablative dependent determinative. This makes it likely that Pj II also follows Nidd II in reading the word 'concentrated' (*°dhimutto*) rather than 'released' (*vimutto*). Whatever Pj II reads, the important point is that *°dhimutto/vimutto* in *pāda* (c) does not, according to the commentaries, refer to liberation.

The commentarial evidence is supported by the likelihood that the expression *saññāvimokkhe parame vi/dhi-mutto* (*pāda* c) is a gloss on *ākiñcaññaṃ nissito hitvā maññaṃ* (*pāda* b). This seems likely because there is nothing to indicate that there has been a change in state for the subject between *pāda-s* (b) and (c). If, however, one wishes to read *vimutto* as 'release/liberation' in *pāda* (c), one would expect some indication of this change of state, a change from being merely supported by the state of nothingness in *pāda* (b) to being liberated and so not dependent on it in *pāda* (c). This could be indicated by a verb in the optative mood, or a construction such as the locative absolute, or even the particle *ce*. But the past passive participle *nissito* in *pāda* (b) followed by the past participle *vimutto/°dhimutto* in *pāda* (c) does not indicate any such change in state.

It seems likely, then, that *pāda* (c) is a gloss on *pāda* (b), and if so, the subject in *pāda* (c) must be 'concentrated' rather than 'liberated', implying that *°dhimutto* is the correct reading. It is difficult to explain the reading *vimutto*, but the problem is more widespread than this occurrence in the *Pārāyanavagga*. In many other places in the Suttapiṭaka the verb *vi* + √*muc* is attested as a textual variant for *adhi* + √*muc*, and vice versa. In the places where the verbs are alternatives, they refer to a state of concentration rather than liberation.[32] One explanation for this is that early in the history of Buddhism *vi* + √*muc* arose as a variant on *adhi* + √*muc*, due to dialectical or orthographic changes. But it is also possible that *vi* + √*muc* had the technical sense of 'meditative release' and was used alongside *adhi* + √*muc* in early Buddhism.[33] Whatever the correct explanation is, the commentaries suggest that the compound *saññāvimokke* is a genitive dependent determinative and not an ablative compound as Norman and Vetter understand it. According to this interpretation, the person is not 'released in the highest release from perception' (Norman/Vetter) but is 'concentrated in the highest meditative release of perception'. Together with the fact that *pāda-s* (b) and (c) seem to be equivalent, it suggests that the correct reading is *°dhimutto*.[34] The subject of v. 1070–71 is concentrated, and not yet liberated.

## Sn 1071–72: *anānuyāyī*

The next problem in the dialogue concerns the translation of the word *anānuyāyī* in 1071/72d). Norman translates 1071d: 'would he stay there not subject (to *saṃsāra*)?' The meaning 'subject (to)' for *anuyāyin* is given in PED, CPD and more recently DOP, although it is not given as a meaning for the verb *anuyāti*. The agent noun *anuyāyī* is only found in one other place in the Suttapiṭaka, at Ja VI.310.6, where the meaning appears to be 'follower'. The meaning 'subject (to)' is not given for the verb *anu* + √*yā* or the agent noun *anuyāyin* in MMW. In these circumstances it is difficult to explain the definition of *anānuyāyi* as 'subject (to)'; the only plausible explanation is that it is based upon Rhys-Davids' and Stede's (the authors of the PED) interpretation of Sn 1071–72. Did they get it right? In this case, probably not. The first course of action ought to have been to attempt to derive an adequate meaning from the verb *anu* + √*yā*, 'to follow'. And a satisfactory meaning can be derived from the verb, for the translation 'not following' would simply refer to the fact that the subject of this verse has attained the state of nothingness and does not 'follow' or 'attain' other meditative states. This makes good sense, since in *pāda* (b) the person who has attained the state of nothingness is said to have abandoned 'another' (*hitvā m-aññaṃ*). Norman notes that *aññaṃ* could be an accusative plural that refers to meditative states other than *ākiñcaññaṃ*.[35] The translation of *anānuyāyī* as 'not following', determined according to the root meaning of *anu* + √*yā*, is in accordance with the meaning of *pāda* (b). It is also in close accord with the suggested reading *°dhimutto* in *pāda* (c).

It seems that Rhys-Davids and Stede took the word *vimutto* in *pāda* (c) to mean 'liberated', and were thus forced to take *pāda* (d) in a similar sense. Hence, they concluded that the word *anānuyāyī* must have the sense of 'being liberated' or 'not being subject (to *saṃsāra*)'.[36] But if *°dhimutto* is preferable in *pāda* (c), and if *pada* (c) is little more than a paraphrase of *pāda* (b), then the question posed in *pāda* (d) is straightforward and allows a simple rendering of *anānuyāyī* according to the root meaning of the verb. The question posed by Upasīva in 1071d (*tiṭṭhe nu so tattha anānuyāyī*) means: 'would he remain there not following (i.e. being unaware of) other meditative object(s)?' It seems that Upasīva wanted to know whether or not the person who has abandoned other states of meditation, and thus attained the state of nothingness, could sustain the state for an extended period of time without being aware of other states of consciousness.

This interpretation is in part supported by Nidd II and Pj II. Both understand that Upasīva, in using the word *anānuyāyī*, asks whether the person falls away from the state of nothingness. Nidd II comments on *tiṭṭhe nu so tattha anānuyāyī* in v. 1071d as follows:

> *Tiṭṭhe nu*: [this indicates] a question because of doubt, perplexity, uncertainty, indefiniteness. Thus [the expression] *tiṭṭhe nu* [is equivalent to], *evaṃ nu kho*, *nanu kho*, *kiṃ nu kho* [and] *kathaṃ nu kho*. *Tattha* means in the sphere of nothingness. *Anānuyāyī* means not leaving (*anānuyāyī*), not flinching,[37] not departing, not disappearing, not falling away, etc. Alternatively, [it means] not being excited, not being corrupted, not being bewildered, not being defiled.[38]

The basic meaning of this commentary is more or less the same as that proposed here. However, Nidd II on the Buddha's reply to Upasīva in v. 1072d – 'he would remain there not following' (*tiṭṭheyya so tattha anānunāyī*) – adds more information. It explains that the Buddha's reply 'he would stay (*tiṭṭheyya*)' means that he would stay for 60,000 aeons,[39] a view repeated in Nidd II on v. 1073a.[40] Although I agree with Nidd II that *anānuyāyī* concerns the continued attainment of the state of nothingness, it seems that at this point Nidd II is dealing with the dialogue in the terms of a later exegetical understanding, one that is not entirely suitable for an understanding of the original meaning of these early verses. This trait is already noticeable in its understanding of *ākiñcaññaṃ*, i.e. that it refers to the seventh *saññāvimokkha* (= *ākiñcaññāyatana*). Although I agree with its identification of the two terms as the same meditative attainment, it is not clear that *ākiñcaññaṃ* in v. 1069–70 refers to the seventh of nine attainments that in the Suttapiṭaka are usually termed 'gradual abidings' (*anupubbavihāra-s*: four *jhāna-s* + four formless spheres + *saññāvedayitanirodha*). In fact, there is no mention in the *Pārāyanavagga* of the four *jhāna-s*, the nine *anupubbavihāra-s*, or *saññāvedayitanirodha*. Thus Nidd II is almost certainly anachronistic on this point; its doctrinal understanding is based upon a later systematization of Buddhist thought.[41] Pj II follows Nidd II and is just as useless in this regard. Although it follows Nidd II in believing that *tiṭṭhe nu so tattha anānuyāyī* in 1071c refers to whether or not the person can remain in the sphere of nothingness without falling away from it, it states that *ākiñcaññāyatana* is a *brahmaloka* and that the Buddha's response was based on the understanding that the person could remain there for 60,000 aeons.[42] It seems that both commentaries understand the state of nothingness, in which the person described as *anānuyāyī* is stationed, as an eschatological destiny. But the idea of abiding in a formless sphere after death and from there attaining liberation is hardly mentioned in the Suttapiṭaka,[43] and no hint has been given that the discussion in these verses has moved on from issues concerning the attainment of 'nothingness' in this life to its continued attainment after death. Both commentaries have preserved the *Pārāyanavagga* verses, but their understanding of them accords with a later phase of Buddhist thought. This is not to deny Nidd II's value as an early textual source, possibly with earlier readings (e.g. *°dhimutto*) and preserving early traditions concerning difficult words (e.g. *anānuyāyī*). But it is likely that the discussion as far as Sn 1073 refers to somebody who has attained 'nothingness' and is still alive.

Thus far, I am more or less in agreement with the two commentaries. We agree that *saññāvimokkhe* is a dependent determinative compound in the genitive case; we agree that *°dhimutto/vimutto* means concentrated; and we agree that *anānuyāyī* refers to the subject not 'following' another state, i.e. not becoming aware of any state other than 'nothingness'. We are in disagreement over the length of time the person is said to 'not follow' another state. The commentaries think it can be sustained for sixty thousand aeons, whereas it seems to me that this understanding reflects the ideas of a later period of thought. However, I think that the rest of the dialogue makes it clear that for the Buddha at least, the length of time for which the person in question stays in the state of nothingness is confined to the person's lifespan. This will become clear in the Buddha's understanding of *sītisiyā* in v. 1074.

This explanation of v. 1071–72 has important ramifications for the meaning of the adjective *satīmā* in v. 1070. In v. 1070a the Buddha tells Upasīva to observe nothingness 'possessing mindfulness' (*satīmā*). The adjective *satimā* in the Suttapiṭaka is usually understood, as it seems to me, in a most vacuous way, as if it describes some vague sense of self-possession. Norman's translation of v. 1070a gives exactly this impression ('Having regard for (the state of nothingness), possessing mindfulness'). But this ignores the fact that in the early Buddhist texts, adjectives formed from √*smṛ*, e.g. *sato* and *satimā*, have a dynamic cognitive meaning. They usually indicate that the subject is aware of sense objects in a particular way, i.e. devoid of any emotional and/or intellectual content. If the adjective *satīmā* has this sense in v. 1070, it would seem that the Buddha is telling Upasīva to be aware of sense objects while he is in the meditative state of 'nothingness'.[44] If we understand that 'nothingness' is identical to the goal of Āḷāra Kālāma – as the commentaries understand it to be – it means that the Buddha has adapted a pre-Buddhist yogic practice to something quite different. Understood in the context of early Brahminic *yoga*, where the aim is to stop being aware of all objects, it is a radical departure. Thus, the word *satīmā* in this teaching seems to refer to the important difference between meditation in early Buddhism and Brahminism. Barnes has described this difference well:

> A vital difference is that [in early Buddhism] *sati* and *sampajañña* are virtues to be developed at all times, whereas for the yogin there is no such similar thing. He should not practice when defecating, but the bhikkhu should maintain awareness. This is due to the

> yogin's desire for a gnosis of an object outside the world; for the bhikkhu, sensual experience in the world is the object which only needs to be purified.[45]

If a Brahminic yogin such as Upasīva had encountered this new idea directly from the Buddha, in the statement that the meditator should be mindful as well as attain a high meditative state, we should expect him to question whether meditative states could be sustained during such a practice. This is exactly what Upasīva seems to ask in v. 1071. The combined force of the words *satimā* and *anānuyāyī* suggests that Upasīva wanted to know if it is possible to sustain the meditative state of 'nothingness' (*ākiñcañña*), given that the Buddha has also stated that the seeker of liberation should be 'mindful' (*satīmā*).

The only other possible explanation of the word *satimā* in v. 1070a is that it is equivalent to *pekkhamāno* ('regarding, observing'). If so, being a near-synonym of *pekkhamāno*, it would indeed be vacuous and we would have to translate v. 1070a as follows: 'Observing nothingness, being mindful [of it]'. This possibility cannot be ruled out, although it does not possess the same explanatory force of Upasīva's question in v. 1071. For, if *satīmā* is equivalent to *pekkhamāno* and simply refers to the awareness of 'nothingness', what is the point of Upasīva's question in v. 1071d? After asking about the correct meditative object, why should he then ask if the sustained awareness of it is possible? Surely this would indicate that Upasīva did not really believe that meditative states could be sustained for extended periods of time. In other words, it would imply that he had no knowledge of meditative matters at all. But this is impossible, for his initial question in v. 1069 shows that he did have such knowledge, and that he presupposed that sustained concentration on an object, a meditative 'support' (*ārammaṇaṃ*), was necessary in order to attain liberation. There must be something in the Buddha's reply in v. 1070 that led Upasīva to suppose that the prolonged experience of the state of 'nothingness' might not be possible according to the Buddha's teaching. It seems to me that this can only be the word *satīmā* referring to the awareness of other objects while in a state of meditative absorption.

To sum up: v. 1071c seems to be a paraphrase of v. 1071b, and both seem to refer to a person who experiences the meditative state of 'nothingness'. If so, the reading *'dhimutto* is preferable in v. 1071c, and the variant *vimutto* can be explained as a quite normal variant in the early Pāli texts for *adhimutto* (whatever the reasons for this variation are). It is highly unlikely that *anānuyāyī* means 'not subject (to)', for the meaning of *anu* + √*yā* in that sense is unattested elsewhere in the early Buddhist literature. But if v. 1071bc is read as suggested above, the meaning 'not following' for *anānuyāyī*, derived directly from *anu* + √*yā*, makes perfectly good sense. Upasīva, it seems, was asking if the meditative state of nothingness could be attained for an extended period of time. But this question is peculiar, for it is unlikely that Upasīva believed that meditative states could not be sustained, given his initial question in v. 1069. The question makes sense only if the Buddha had said something unexpected, something that suggested to Upasīva that the state of 'nothingness' could not be prolonged. And the only word in the Buddha's teaching that suggests such a sense is the adjective *satīmā* in v. 1070a.[46] It seems that the Buddha has stated his new teaching that meditative absorption should be combined with the practice of mindfulness.

## Sn 1073–74: *sītisiyā*

The next difficulty in interpretation is the compound *sītisiyā* ('would become cool'), which appears in Upasīva's third question in v. 1073. The correct understanding of this question depends upon the correct understanding of Upasīva's second question in v. 1071, for the four questions of Upasīva are based upon a temporal sequence of events. The first question concerns a suitable meditative object (v. 1069); the second concerns the sustained practice of it (v. 1071); and then the third and fourth (v. 1073, 1075) concern the fate of the person who has maintained the meditative state for a lengthy period of time. If the interpretation of v. 1071-72 offered here is correct, it means that Norman's translation of v. 1073 is unlikely to be correct, depending as it does on his different translation of v. 1071–72. In fact, it is not at all clear what he thinks the compound *sītisiyā* means. He translates 'becomes cool', and although this is literally correct, it does not explain the metaphor. There seem to be three possible explanations:

1 It is a metaphor for the liberation of the person who has sustained the meditative state of 'nothingness' for a prolonged period of time (*pūgam*).
2 It is a metaphor for the death of that person.
3 It refers to both of these events occurring simultaneously, i.e. death and liberation in one go. In other words, Upasīva is asking something about what happens when, from the state of being not liberated when alive, someone dies and achieves liberation. If so, it would mean that Upasīva accepted the fundamental idea of early Brahminical *yoga*, i.e. that liberation is the attainment of liberation (*brahman*) at death, a union already anticipated in a meditative trance in life. This is different from what is referred to in the Buddhist commentarial texts by the term *parinibbāna* – the final emancipation attained at death of the person who had previously attained liberation when alive – for the concept of *parinibbāna* presupposes the notion of liberation in life, which is not possible according to early Brahminic meditation.

For Norman, the first and third possibilities are ruled out because he thinks that liberation has already been described in v. 1071–72, before the term *sītisiyā* is introduced into the passage. It seems, then, that he must take *sītisiyā* either as a metaphor for the death of the liberated person, i.e. option two, or as a reference to the Buddhist theory of the death/final liberation (*parinibbāna*) of the already liberated person, although this is unlikely, for it is the Brahmin Upasīva who introduces the concept into the conversation. If, however, we have seen that the discussion thus far has been about meditative attainment and not liberation, then liberation must somehow be involved in the meaning of *sītisiyā*. Thus *sītisiyā* cannot refer to death alone, and option two is unlikely to be correct. Indeed, the presence of the word *vimutto* in v. 1073c seems to indicate that *sītisiyā* is synonymous with liberation (*tattheva so sītisiyā vimutto*). Norman translates this phrase '(and) being released in that very place were to become cool'. But this translation inverts the order of the words *sītisiyā* and *vimutto*, suggesting that the event of 'becoming cool' comes after the event of 'being released', as if the two events occur in sequence. Norman must translate in this way because he has already understood *vimutto* to mean liberated in v. 1071–72. But it is significant that there is no variant reading *ᶜdhimutto* for *vimutto* in 1073c, and that Nidd II and Pj II both read *vimutto* in 1073c in contrast to *ᶜdhimutto* in 1071–72. This suggests that the word *vimutto* in 1073c indicates a change of state as much as does the compound *sītisiyā*. I therefore think that the words *sītisiyā* and *vimutto* are near synonyms, a suggestion that is supported by the tendency in early Pāli literature to string lists of near synonyms together.[47] According to this interpretation, Upasīva wants to know if consciousness remains when the person has 'become cool' or liberated (*sītisiyā* = *vimutto*). Since liberation at death appears to have been a standard belief in early Brahminic meditation, option three – liberation at death – is the most likely explanation. So is there any suggestion in Upasīva's question that the liberation of the subject coincides with death?

The commentarial tradition on v. 1073 is confusing and of little use. Nidd II interprets both 1073c and 1073d as two possible answers to an 'if' clause posed in 1073ab, as if the answer to 1073ab can be either 1073c or 1073d. Thus, it takes both *tatth ᶜeva sītisiyā vimutto* (1073c) and *cavetha viññāṇaṃ tathāvidhassa* (1073d) as alternative eventualities for the person who has attained the 'sphere of nothingness' (*ākiñcaññāyatana*) for a number of years, and proposes two possible explanations for each expression:

> *tatth' eva sītisiyā vimutto, cavetha viññāṇaṃ tathāvidhassā ti*: would the person have attained the cool state of right there [in the sphere of nothingness, i.e.] would he remain permanent, fixed, eternal, not subject to change, exactly the same for ever and ever? Or (*atha vā*) would his consciousness fall away (*caveyya*), [i.e. *cavetha* in the sense of:] be cut off, perish, be destroyed [i.e.] become non-existent?[48] [Summary:] He asks about eternalism or annihilation of

the one who has attained the sphere of nothingness.

Alternatively (*udāhu*), would the person attain final emancipation into the *nibbāna*-realm without remainder (*anupādisesāya nibbānadhātuyā parinibbāyeyya*) right there [in the sphere of nothingness]? Or would his consciousness fall away [i.e. *cavetha* in the sense of:] would a re-connecting consciousness be produced in the realm of sensual pleasures, the realm of form, or the realm without form? [Summary:] He asks about the final emancipation or connection to [re-becoming] of the one who has attained the sphere of nothingness.[49]

In these two explanations *sītisiyā* is interpreted as 'become eternal' (*sassato*) or 'final emancipation' (*parinibbāna*) respectively. In both cases the concept of 'becoming cool' seems to refer to the death of the person who is in the sphere of nothingness. But these explanations are unacceptable: *pāda* (d) is not an alternative to *pāda* (c), but a question based upon the condition expressed in *pāda* (c); this is how Norman understands it, and on this point he is surely correct. The explanation of Pj II is just as confusing. At the end of its explanation it comments:

> Then the Blessed One, not admitting [the possible explanations of] annihilation or eternalism for him, explaining the final emancipation (*parinibbānaṃ*) without clinging of the noble disciple, spoke the verse beginning 'As a flame . . .' [v. 1074].[50]

This means that for Pj II, 1073cd has presented a trilemma from which the Buddha has chosen one alternative, the final emancipation (*parinibbānaṃ*) of the adept. The three options understood to be presented to the Buddha by Upasīva for the attainer of nothingness in v. 1073 are annihilation, eternalism or final emancipation (*parinibbānaṃ*), and the Buddha chooses the latter. This summary comes at the end of a discussion of 1073cd, which presents the same three options, the first being the option stated in 1073c:

> *tatth' eva so sītisiyā vimutto ti*. The meaning is 'Would that person be released from various sufferings right there in the sphere of nothingness, [i.e.] would he have attained the cool state; the meaning is: being one who has attained *nibbāna*, would he exist for ever?'[51]

The compound *sītisiyā* is understood to indicate the attaining of *nibbāna*, which apparently coincides with death, because the commentary understands it to be a question about becoming eternal. Following this, Pj II understands that v. 1073d presents two alternatives – annihilation or the connection to rebirth – to the possibility stated in 1073c. However, it is odd that the possibility of annihilation seems to be identified with the attainment of final emancipation (*parinibbāna*):

> *cavetha viññāṇaṃ tathāvidhassā ti*. Alternatively (*udāhu*), he asks about annihilation (*ucchedaṃ*): 'Does the consciousness of the one who is like that (*tathāvidhassa*) attain final emancipation without remainder (*anupādāya parinibbāyeyyāti*)?' Or (*vāpi*), he asks about the connection to rebirth (*paṭisandhim*): 'For the sake of grasping reconnection, does it (consciousness) disappear (*vibhaveyya*)?'[52]

Thus, we see the two alternatives of annihilation and rebirth are indicated by the words *uccheda* and *paṭisandhi*, reasonable enough explanations of the phrase *cavetha viññāṇaṃ* in 1073d. But the identification of annihilation with the attainment of *parinibbāna* is peculiar, and seems to be at odds with the differentiation of *parinibbāna* from annihilation and eternalism at Pj II.594.20.

It is clear that the commentarial tradition on Sn 1073 is confused. Pj II seems to understand that 1073cd presents at least three possibilities for the fate of the attainer of 'nothingness', the two possible meanings of *pāda* (d) being alternatives to the possibility stated in *pāda* (c). Nidd II gives two alternative interpretations for 1073cd: in both, *pāda* (d) is understood to present an alternative possibility to (c). But these commentarial passages are not much help in understanding the original meaning of the verse, for at least two reasons. First, the issue of the eternality of the person under discussion does not enter the dialogue until v. 1075: the commentaries are too eager, and wrong, to bring it into their discussion of v. 1073. Second, 1073c and 1073d cannot be two alternative questions about the state of the person who in 1073ab is said to have attained 'nothingness' for a vast number of years. There is nothing to indicate that (c) and (d) are alternatives, and surely the particle *vā* or some other indicator would be found. The only possibility is that *pāda* (d) expresses an outcome based upon the condition expressed in *pāda* (c), i.e. would the *viññāṇa* fall away if the person becomes cool/liberated? At least we can say that the two commentaries presuppose the death of the person in 1073cd, which implies that for them *sītisiyā* was thought to involve death. But the commentaries are far-fetched and offer no meaningful information for the original meaning of *sītisiyā*.

To come to a more satisfactory answer to the problem of *sīti-siyā* there are three other courses of investigation. First, we should see what Upasīva says in the remainder of the dialogue, for there may be clues indicating what he meant by the term *sītisiyā* in v. 1073. Second, we should note that Upasīva, a Brahmin, introduces the concept of *sītisiyā* into the discussion. We should therefore look for occurrences of forms based on *śītī-√bhū* as a metaphor for liberation in the early Brahminic literature. If such examples can be found, Upasīva's use of this metaphor might be more easy to understand. And finally, we can attempt to understand the term *sītisiyā* based upon its occurrences in the Suttapiṭaka. This might not explain Upasīva's use of the term, but it might be able to explain what the term meant for the Buddha and the early Buddhists.

Upasīva's question in v. 1075 makes it clear that for him *sītisyā* refers to death and liberation at the same time. In v. 1075 we must understand that Upasīva is still talking about the person who was described in v. 1073 as *sītisiyā vimutto*, for in v. 1074 (the Buddha's answer to v. 1073) the state of the subject of the dialogue (the hypothetical meditator) has not changed, with the Buddha only saying something about the person to whom the verb *sīti* + √*bhū* has been applied. To be more precise, the Buddha uses another metaphor to describe the person who has 'become cool': he says that he has 'gone out' (*attha*ṃ *paleti*). It seems that for the Buddha, the metaphor of 'going out' is equivalent to the metaphor of 'becoming cool'. In response to this, in v. 1075 Upasīva asks: 'When he has gone out (*atthaṃ gato so*), does he not exist, or is he without disease eternally (*sassatiyā arogo*)?'.[53] This question is revealing. In the early Pāli literature the question of the liberated person existing eternally or not is an eschatological question. In the *Brahmajāla Sutta*, thirty-two of the forty-four ways of declaring opinions about the future concern the existence of the self, in its various modes, as existing without disease (*arogo*) after death (*paraṃ maranā*).[54] All these questions are said to be held by non-Buddhist ascetics and Brahmins. It is likely that with the question beginning *atthaṃ gato* in v. 1075, Upasīva was asking about what happens to the liberated person after death. It follows that he must have used the phrase *sītisiyā vimutto* to describe the liberation achieved at death for the person who had sustained the attainment of 'nothingness' for a long period of time. Thus the question in v. 1073 seems to presuppose that liberation is attained at death, having been anticipated by a meditative attainment in life. This understanding seems to agree with the basic presupposition of the yogic passages in the early verse Upaniṣads and *Mokṣadharma*, in which *brahman* is thought to be attained finally at death after the meditative anticipation of it in life. Moreover, the early Brahminic literature contains evidence showing that the metaphor 'becoming cool' refers to the attainment of liberation at death, an event preceded by its yogic anticipation in life.

No forms of *śītī*-√*bhū* are found in the early Upaniṣads, although the past passive participle *śītībhūto* is found in one *Mokṣadharma* verse (Mbh XII.192.122) where it describes the state of the liberated 'mumbler' (*jāpaka*: a reciter of Vedic mantras, a meditator of sorts):[55]

> The reciter of the Vedas attains *brahman*, the highest state. Alternatively, he unites with fire or he enters the sun. (118)
>
> If he attains delight there with that fiery state of being, bewildered by desire he assumes the qualities [of fire or the sun] (119)
>
> Thus it is with regard to the moon or wind, or else he attains a body [made of] earth or space. He dwells full of passion for these states (*tatra*), practising their qualities. (120)

> But when he becomes tired of these things, he doubts their worth; seeking the highest once again, which is without decay, he enters right into it. (121)
>
> Having become cool (*śītībhūto*), having become *brahma* (*brahmabhūtaḥ*), [being] beyond duality, blissful, peaceful, without disease, without a body (*nirātmavān*)[56] [and] immortal, he attains the immortal.[57] (122)
>
> He attains the condition of *brahman*, from which there is no return, which is singular and called 'the imperishable', the calm state which is without suffering and decay. (123)[58]

The section in which this verse is found (Mbh XII.192.117–127) is the conclusion of the description of a *jāpaka's* attainments. The attainment of *brahman* is described in v. 118ab, although a few other attainments are listed between v. 118cd and v. 120, which seem to be supernatural attainments that are optional for the *jāpaka* if he so desires them. Verse 121ab returns to the *jāpaka*'s attainment of liberation, which is introduced in contrast to the supernatural attainments with the statement that the *jāpaka* then becomes without desire (*tatra virāgī*) for the supernatural states of being listed from v. 118cd–120. I take it that *nirātmavān* in v. 122b indicates that liberation occurs when the person leaves the body, i.e. at death. This suggestion is supported in v. 120b: one of the supernatural attainments for the *jāpaka* is that 'he attains (*-gaḥ*: "goes to") a body of earth or space' (*bhūmyākāśaśarīragaḥ*). It seems that *nirātmavān* indicates that the attainment of final liberation occurs when the adept leaves the body at death and unites with *brahman*, whereas the attainment of magical powers occurs when the adept possesses a body. Thus the difference between a supernatural type of attainment and the attainment of 'becoming cool' is that the former is to be attained when one is alive, whereas the latter occurs when one does not desire supernatural attainments and leaves the body, i.e. dies. This means that *śītī-√bhū* in this passage is a metaphor for the state of liberation achieved at death.

Although it would be wrong to read too much into this one occurrence of *śītī* +√*bhū*,[59] it is striking that the term *śītībhūta* is found in the early Sanskrit sources with the same sense as the term *sītisiyā* at Sn 1073. This correspondence suggests that Upasīva held the standard early yogic view that liberation is attained at death. It would seem, then, that Upasīva was knowledgeable about the sort of *yoga* that was later described in the early verse Upaniṣads and *Mokṣadharma*. Moreover, when viewed in the light of the early Brahminic background, it is clear why Upasīva would have asked if the *viññāṇa* existed after death: the view that the self is an unchanging 'consciousness' is well attested in early Brahminic texts. As I noted above,[60] this opinion is associated with Yājñavalkya in the *Bṛhadāraṇyaka Upaniṣad*. There is even evidence of this opinion being held by some early Buddhists. In the *Mahātaṇhāsaṅkhaya Sutta* (M no. 38) the *bhikkhu* Sāti believes that the *viññāṇa* is an unchanging, transmigrating entity.[61] It seems, however, that this view is not that of the passages on early Brahminic meditation studied in Chapter 3, which follow the cosmogonic tradition stemming from the *Nāsadīyasūkta*; according to this tradition, the *ātman/brahman* was thought to be beyond consciousness (*buddhi*, *manas*, etc.). We can understand why Upasīva, a Brahminic renouncer, may have had doubts about the matter: different views must have been current in early Brahminic circles. Some postulated a self that was consciousness, whereas others believed the self to be beyond consciousness. Upasīva, it seems, sought an answer to this difficult question from a renowned sage.

To summarize: v. 1075 suggests that in v. 1073 the Brahminic renouncer Upasīva introduced the concept of *sītisiyā* in order to ask a question about the death/liberation of the attainer of 'nothingness'. Mbh XII.192 suggests that *śītī-√bhū* was indeed a metaphor used to denote the early Brahminic notion of liberation at death. Thus it seems reasonable to assume that Upasīva was an adherent of a Brahminic group familiar with the yogic ideas recorded in the early Upaniṣads and *Mokṣadharma*. He seems to have believed that the Buddha, speaking about someone maintaining awareness of 'nothingness', was talking about the meditative 'anticipation', in life, of liberation that he believed – according to the standard view – was attained at death. The interpretation offered here of v. 1070 suggests that the Buddha was not talking along such lines: the phrase 'observing nothingness, possessing mindfulness' (*ākiñcaññaṃ pekkhamāno satimā*) in v. 1070 seems to refer to a practice that allows an awareness of objects, and is not an anticipation of a liberation to be achieved later on.

## Sn 1073–76: the metaphors 'becoming cool' (*sīti* +√*bhū*) and 'going out' (*atthaṃ* + √*gam*)

In the Buddha's response in v. 1074 to Upasīva's question in v. 1073, it seems that the metaphor of 'going out' (and therefore the metaphor of 'becoming cool') has the sense of liberation in life:

> Just like a flame blown with the force of the wind goes out [and] cannot be reckoned, so the *muni* released from the category name (*nāmakāyā vimutto*) 'goes out' (*atthaṃ paleti*), he cannot be reckoned. (1074)

I understand *nāmakāyā* as a descriptive determinative compound (*karmadhāraya*) in the ablative singular case, based on the definition of *kāya* as 'group', 'assemblage' or 'collection'.[62] Norman also takes the compound as a *karmadhāraya*, although he takes the word *nāma* as an adjective (he translates the compound as 'mental body'). Alternatively, despite the fact that the word *kāyā* is in the ablative singular case, it is possible that *nāmakāyā* is a co-ordinative compound (*dvandva*), for the similar co-ordinative compound 'name and form' (*nāmarūpa*) is usually declined in singular cases.[63] This would mean that the word *kāya* in *nāmakāyā* is equivalent to the neuter noun *rūpa* in *nāmarūpa*, giving *nāmakāyā vimutto* the sense 'released from name and form'. But other canonical evidence does not suggest that the compound is co-ordinative. In the *Mahānidāna Sutta*, the only other place in the Suttapiṭaka where the compound *nāmakāya* is found, the co-ordinative compound *nāmarūpa* is split into the descriptive determinative compounds *nāmakāya* and *rūpakāya*.[64] In this case it is clear that *kāya* means 'category' or 'group', and the compound is found in para-canonical works with exactly the same sense.[65] The lack of any evidence to the contrary suggests that the compound *nāmakāyā* in Sn 1074 should be taken as a descriptive determinative rather than a co-ordinative compound. If so it means that the *muni*, being released from name alone, is liberated in life, for if the metaphor of 'going out' were to refer to the liberation achieved at death, then the 'going out' of the flame should be analogous to the release from name and form (*nāmarūpā*, which could easily have occurred in place of *nāmakāyā*).

This interpretation tallies well with the only other occurrence of the metaphor of 'going out' in the Suttapiṭaka (i.e. *attham* plus a verb meaning 'to go'), which describes the state of a person liberated in life:

> For whomever passion, aversion and ignorance have faded away, he has crossed over this ocean with its crocodiles [and] demons, with its dangerous waves, which is hard to cross over. He has overcome attachment, conquered death, and is without acquisitions; he has abandoned suffering, for the sake of no further rebecoming. 'Gone out' (*atthaṅgato*). He cannot be defined (*na pamāṇam eti*), and has confused the King of death, I say.[66]

The statement 'gone out, he cannot be defined' (*atthaṅgato so na pamāṇam eti*) is almost identical to the Buddha's at Sn 1074d: 'Going out, he cannot be reckoned' (*atthaṃ paleti na upeti saṃkhaṃ*). It is not clear if these two passages are of the same antiquity, but it is likely that the metaphors in both passages follow a common early tradition and refer to the same phenomenon, i.e. liberation in life. In much the same way, the Suttapiṭaka evidence shows that *sīti/siti-√bhū* was a metaphor used by the early Buddhists to refer to the liberation of a person in life. For example, the following pericope is repeated a number of times:

> (A person) passes his time in this very life (*diṭṭhe va dhamma*) being without cravings, satiated, having become cool (*sītibhūto*), experiencing bliss, having himself become *brahma* (*brahmabhūtena attanā*).[67]

In this context *sītibhūto* refers to the blissful state of a person who is liberated in this life (*diṭṭhe va dhamma*). The compound *sītibhūto* is also used repeatedly in verse composition, especially as part of an individual's declaration of liberation. In this sense, it is found in the Buddha's declaration of liberation in the *Ariyapariyesana Sutta*:

> For I am an *arahant* in the world, I am the unsurpassed teacher,
> I alone am completely awakened, having become cool (*sītibhūto*),
> being satiated (*nibbuto*).[68]

The refrain *sītibhūto 'smi nibbuto* is found in a few Theragātha verses, as part of certain *bhikkhus*' declaration of liberation;[69] in a few other verses, *sītibhūto* qualifies a living, liberated being.[70] It is absolutely clear that all the early Buddhist uses of *sīti* +√*bhū* refer to the liberation thought to be attained in life: it does not refer to the liberated state achieved at death. There are a few occurrences where the metaphor refers to the extinction of feelings (*vedanā*) at death, but they hardly seem to be relevant:

> Feeling a feeling the limit of which is the body (*kāyapariyantikaṃ*), he understands 'I am feeling a feeling the limit of which is the body.' Feeling a feeling the limit of which is life (*jīvitapariyantikaṃ*), he understands 'I am feeling a feeling the limit of which is life.' He understands: 'After the break up of the body, beyond the exhaustion of life, right here, all feelings, not being delighted in, will become cool (*sītibhavissanti*).'[71]

In this case, the metaphor of 'becoming cool' is used to describe how the feelings (*vedanā*) cease at death for a liberated person, a condition differentiated from how this person experiences feelings in life – mindful and aware, without clinging.[72] But this does not matter for the interpretation of Sn 1073. When the verb *sīti-bhū* is used to describe liberation in the early Pāli literature, its subject is the person liberated in life. This does not explain its usage at v. 1073, which seems to reflect non-Buddhist terminology. It does, however, explain the Buddha's interpretation of it in v. 1074. In his answer to Upasīva, the simile of 'going out' refers to the state of the liberated, living person.

This brings to light a peculiar but crucial point of the dialogue. Upasīva seems to be talking about liberation coinciding with death (v. 1073, v. 1075), whereas for the Buddha the liberated person is alive (v. 1074), an understanding that he seems to maintain in v. 1076. It seems, then, that the Buddha and Upasīva are speaking at cross-purposes. To be more accurate, the Buddha interprets Upasīva's question about 'becoming cool' (v. 1073) as a question about the state of the person liberated in life; the Buddha simply assumes that liberation occurs in life (v. 1074). Upasīva does not grasp this, and continues to speak about the person liberated at death (1075). In response to this, in the final verse of the dialogue (1076) the Buddha uses the metaphor of 'going out' to explain the state of the person who is liberated in life. He begins: 'There is not a measure for the one who has gone out' (*atthaṅgatassa na pamāṇam atthi*), language which is almost identical to v. 1074 (*atthaṃ paleti na upeti saṃkhaṃ*).[73] The teaching is concluded with the statement: 'when all *dhamma-s* are removed, then all modes of speaking are removed' (*sabbesu dhammesu samūhatesu, samūhatā vādapathā pi sabbe pi*).[74] If the word *dhamma* here refers to mental phenomena, then the Buddha must still be talking about a living person. If, however, it means phenomena in general (Norman's translation is 'phenomena'), then we might suppose that it includes physical phenomena, the destruction of which would mean death. The understanding of the word *dhamma* is a complicated and unresolved problem in the study of early Buddhism, and a protracted discussion is beyond this study. But I will at least comment on the meanings of *dhamma* in the *Pārāyanavagga*.[75]

In most places it simply means 'teaching' or 'subject matter'.[76] In one place it is an adjective meaning 'nature' in the sense of the main characteristic of a thing,[77] and in another place it means 'righteousness'.[78] Variants on the idiom *diṭṭha-dhamma* are found in four places, which Norman always translates as 'in the world of phenomena'.[79] It seems that Norman relates this idiom to the expression *diṭṭhe va dhamme*, for he translates the latter in exactly the same way.[80] I am not sure of the exact meaning of this difficult expression, and although in this case Norman translates *dhamma* as 'phenomena', it is probably not relevant to the occurrence of *dhamma* in v. 1076. There are only seven more occurrences of *dhamma* in the *Pārāyanavagga*, but all of them have a direct bearing on the meaning of word in v. 1076; in virtually all of these occurrences, Norman translates *dhamma* as 'phenomena'.

Three of these occurrences occur in the expression 'gone to the far shores of all *dhamma-s*' (*sabbadhammāna pāragū*), an expression which describes the Buddha in Sn 992, 1105, 1112. Here, it is doubtful that the meaning of the word *dhamma* is 'phenomena' in general: if so, it would suggest that the Buddha had gone to the far shore of all phenomena, physical as well as mental phenomena, in which case he would be dead. In fact in two of these verses in which the expression 'gone to the far shores of all *dhamma-s*' is found, it occurs among a group of adjectives that describe the mental state of the Buddha: in v. 1105 the Buddha is described as a meditator (*jhāyiṃ*) who is without passion (*virajaṃ*) or corruption (*anāsavaṃ*), and in v. 1112 he is described as without desires (*anejo*), the one who has cut off doubt (*chinnasaṃsayo*). It makes better sense to suppose that the expression 'gone to the far shores of all *dhamma-s*' in this context refers to the Buddha's elevated mental state, i.e. that he is a meditator 'gone to the far shore of all mental states/phenomena'. This must be true in the only other verse where the expression is found. In v. 992 the Buddha is said to 'have vision into all *dhamma-s*' (*sabbadhammacakkhumā*) and to 'have attained the destruction of all *dhamma-s*' (*sabbadhammakkhayaṃ patto*). In the latter expression *dhamma* cannot refer to physical phenomena, for then the verse would be a eulogy of a dead person; the word *dhamma* throughout this verse must refer to mental phenomena. Moreover, the compound *sabbadhammacakkhumā* is similar to the phrase *kusalo sabbadhammānaṃ* (v. 1039), which Norman translates as 'skilful in all mental states'. They must have more or less the same meaning, i.e. that the Buddha is knowledgeable about the workings of the mind. The occurrences of *dhamma* in v. 992, which include the expression *sabbadhammāna pāragū*, must all refer to 'mental phenomena'. This suggests that the word similarly means 'mental phenomena' in v. 1105 and v. 1112, as argued above for different reasons. The only other occurrence of *dhamma* is in the phrase *upekhāsatisaṃsuddhaṃ dhammatakkapurejavaṃ* (1107), which Norman translates as 'purified by indifference and mindfulness, preceded by examination of mental states'. The word here could just as easily mean 'doctrine', i.e. 'preceded by an examination of the doctrine'.[81] It is even possible that the word has shades of both meanings; at least we can be quite sure that it does not refer to physical phenomena.

It seems that the word *dhamma* in the *Pārāyanavagga* – excluding, perhaps, the idiom *diṭṭhe va dhamme* – does not refer to physical phenomenon. Thus it is most likely that the radical statement 'when all *dhamma-s* are removed' (or 'abolished': *samūhatesu*) refers to the removal of mental phenomena. Exactly what mental phenomena are meant is not made clear. Given the meditative context of this discussion in the *Upasīvamāṇavapucchā*, it is possible that the word *dhamma* is a technical term for meditative objects. This usage is attested in the accounts of the Bodhisatta's training under Āḷāra Kālāma and Uddaka Rāmaputta, where the meditative states of *ākiñcaññāyatana* and *nevasaññānāsaññāyatana* are termed *dhammaṃ*.[82] It is certainly possible that the usage of the word *dhamma* at Sn 992, 1039, 1076, 1105, 1107 and 1112 reflects the technical vocabulary of pre-Buddhist yogic circles. But this would seem to limit the scope of the word *dhamma* excessively: surely the verse does not mean that one cannot speak about the sage because only meditative states have been transcended. Moreover, Sn 1076 suggests a wider frame of reference: it explains that the destruction of all *dhamma*-s prevents all ways of speaking about the sage. This suggests that *dhamma* refers to the mental states or conditions upon which language depends. This suggestion is supported by Sn 1074, where it is stated that the sage cannot be reckoned (literally 'does not approach any [act of] reckoning') because he is freed from the category (*kāya*) 'name', or, more generally, concepts (Sn 174b: *atthaṃ paleti na upeti saṅkhaṃ*). It seems that *nāma* in Sn 1074 is loosely equivalent to *dhamma* in Sn 1076: the absence of both precludes the possibility of reckoning or articulating a state of affairs; both must refer loosely to the concepts or apperceptions that make propositions possible.

## The indefinability of the sage

The Buddha's point in Sn 1074 and 1076 is that because the sage is freed from concepts or language, he is therefore indefinable, like an extinguished flame. The metaphor of the extinguished flame is also used in a similar fashion in the *Aggi-Vacchagotta Sutta* (M no. 72), where the Buddha declares that it is not possible to reckon the state of the Tathāgata, since he is like a flame gone out. In other words, the metaphor is used just as it is in Sn 1074. The important part of the Sutta reads as follows:

> 'If, O Vaccha, [someone] were to ask you: "When this fire in front of you is blown out, in which direction does it go from here – to the East, West, North or South?" Being questioned thus, how would you explain it?'
>
> '[The issue] does not arise, O Gotama. For the fire burnt dependent upon its fuel of grass or firewood (*tiṇakaṭṭhupādānaṃ*), and when it (the fuel) has been consumed, and no more is provided, being without fuel it is reckoned (*saṅkhaṃ gacchati*) as "blown out" (*nibbuto*).'
>
> 'In just the same way, O Vaccha, the form [feeling, apperception, volitions and consciousness] by means of which someone might designate the Tathāgata has been abandoned, uprooted, extirpated, annihilated, [and] not liable to arise in the future for the Tathāgata. The Tathāgata, O Vaccha, is released from that which is reckoned as "form" (*rūpasaḥkhā-vimutto*), he is deep, immeasurable, unfathomable, just like a great ocean. [The proposition] "he is reborn" is inapplicable, [the proposition] "he is not reborn" is inapplicable, [the proposition] "he is both reborn and not reborn" is inapplicable, [the proposition] "he is neither reborn nor not reborn" is inapplicable.[83]

The purport of this passage is more or less identical to Sn 1074–76 of the *Upasīvamāṇavapucchā*. In both cases, the sage who is liberated and alive is said to be beyond reckoning or conceptual categorization (*saṅkhā*). The *Aggi-Vacchagotta Sutta* is not nihilistic, despite the metaphor of the fire having gone out, and despite the statement that the Tathāgata has 'uprooted' and 'annihilated' the five aggregates (*rūpa*, *vedanā*, *saññā*, *saṅkhārā*, *viññāṇa*), for it is clear that the Buddha is the subject to whom the metaphor of going out is applied, and it is the Buddha who has 'annihilated' the five aggregates while he is alive. It seems that the 'annihilation' (*anabhāvaṃkataṃ*) of the five aggregates is equivalent to being released from the act of reckoning or apprehending them (e.g. *rūpa-saḥkhā-vimutto*). Being free from reckoning (*saṅkhā*) means that the ways in which one would usually designate somebody (*saṅkhaṃ gacchati*) do not apply to the

Tathāgata: he cannot be said to reborn or not (or both 'reborn and not reborn' and 'neither reborn nor not reborn'); such concepts have no applicability for him.

The *Aggi-Vacchagotta Sutta* allows us greater insight into the fire metaphor employed by the Buddha in the dialogue with Upasīva. In the *Aggi-Vacchagotta Sutta* the Tathāgata is compared to the extinguished flame – both are indefinable because they have gone beyond the criteria necessary for them to be defined. The flame can only be defined by referring to its supply of fuel (grass or firewood); upon its exhaustion, the flame can only be reckoned as 'extinguished', and nothing positive can be said about it. By analogy, the fuel that has been exhausted by the Tathāgata is the five aggregates. Released from the act of reckoning or apprehending them, which is equivalent to their exhaustion or destruction, the Tathāgata cannot be defined. In the light of this Sutta it is no surprise that the five aggregates are usually termed *upādāna-kkhandha*. This compound is usually translated as 'aggregates of attachment', although taken literally it means 'bundles of fuel', a translation that makes good sense in the context of the *Aggi-Vacchagotta Sutta*. The term *upādāna* is not applied to each of the five aggregates in the *Aggi-Vacchagotta Sutta*, but the implication is clear: just as the flame goes out when its fuel (*upādāna*) is consumed, so the *bhikkhu* is released when the fuel that is the five *khandhas* is transcended. The five aggregates (*khandha*) that define the phenomenal person are the fuel (*upādāna*) necessary for the continuation of his phenomenal experience. The appellation *upādāna* applied to the five groups into which the phenomenal person is analysed was probably not intended to indicate that the five items were forms of attachment. Instead, it is likely that the appellation was originally intended in a metaphorical sense: the analysis focused on the five aspects of the phenomenal person that acted as the fuel for the flame of phenomenal existence. The compound *upādāna-kkhandha* is a metaphor; a more suitable translation of it would be 'bundles of fuel'.[84]

The fire metaphor used in the *Aggi-Vacchagotta Sutta* and the *Upasīva-māṇavapucchā* is a radical way of making the point that the liberated sage is beyond phenomenal experience. It also makes the additional point that this indefinable, transcendent state is the sage's state even during life. This idea goes against the early Brahminic notion of liberation at death, an idea that Upasīva seems to accept in Sn 1073. It seems, then, that the Buddha used old Brahminic metaphors to articulate his new teaching.[85] Upasīva's use of the metaphor 'become cool' in Sn 1073, and its occurrence at Mbh XII.192.22, show that the similes originally referred to the adept's attainment of union with *brahman* at death. And it makes good sense to suppose that this metaphor and that of 'going out' were originally Brahminic. Early Brahminic householder religion was centred around the sacred fire (*agni*): the fire was both a deity and a symbol of the continuation of life in the world. But early renunciant Brahminism rejected the aims of the social religion as well as its most important symbol, the sacred fire. The metaphor of 'becoming cool' likened the liberated person to the fire gone out, and so emphasized his otherworldly condition by contrasting it to the symbol of worldly life. The metaphor would have been shocking to a Brahmin devoted to the maintenance of the sacred fire. But, along with the metaphor of 'going out', it was the perfect metaphor to use. Both drew upon the belief that when a fire is extinguished it is not destroyed, but returns to the essence whence it came. This idea is articulated in an important early dialogue of the *Mokṣadharma* (contained in the *Bhṛgu-Bharadvāja-saṃvāda*):

> Bhṛgu said:
> 'The soul (*jīvas*) which rests in the body is not destroyed when [the body] is destroyed, just as fire is not destroyed when its kindling wood is burnt.' (2)
> Bharadvāja said:
> 'As it is for fire, so it is [for the soul, i.e.] perhaps (*yadi*) there is no destruction. But at the end of the use of the kindling wood, the fire is not perceived – (3)
> '[so] I think that the fire which is extinguished (*śāntaṃ*), being without kindling wood, is destroyed; for its[86] course, or measure, or shape, is not seen.' (4)
> Bhṛgu said:
> 'When the kindling wood is used up, the fire really exists [but] is not seen, because it has entered the ether (*ākāśānugatatvād*); certainly, it is hard to grasp, being without a support. (5)
> 'So when the body is abandoned, the soul (*jīvo*), being just like space, persists. Undoubtedly it is not grasped because of its subtlety, just like fire.' (6)[87]

This argument about the post-mortem existence of the soul shows that fire was not thought to cease when it goes out: it was thought to re-enter the ether whence it came. In other words, it was thought to return to its unmanifest source. It is easy to imagine that this belief was drawn upon by the early Brahminic renouncers who formulated the metaphor of 'becoming cool'. They used it to point out that their aim was similarly a return to the source, *brahman*, and not a non-existence. 'Becoming cool' was therefore the desirable opposite of mainstream Brahminism. Such were the intricacies of the metaphor, which contrasted the yogic goal with the cult of fire worship, and portrayed the aim of returning to the source in a positive manner. One must imagine that the Buddha's description of the liberated person as 'having become cool (*sītibhūto*), experiencing bliss, himself having become *brahma* (*brahmabhūtena attanā*)' would have been a bold and striking declaration of his teaching in contrast to the old yogic view that liberation – merging into *brahman* – was thought to occur at death.[88] The metaphor, and the world of beliefs upon which it was based, was radically subverted by the Buddha. One becomes *brahman*, so to speak, in this very life (*diṭṭhe va dhamme*), not in death.

If we return to the dialogue between the Buddha and Upasīva, it seems that in Sn 1076 the Buddha has once again brought the discussion back to the living, liberated person, despite the eschatological implications of Upasīva's question in v. 1075. Perhaps the eschatological tone of the question was not so obvious in v. 1073, but it is unavoidable in v. 1075. Thus it seems that for the Buddha the concepts of life and death, existence and non-existence, and even whether a person is conscious or not, do not apply to the liberated person. Perhaps this is not too different from the perspective of a Brahminic ascetic steeped in the philosophy of the *Nāsadīyasūkta*, for whom the state of the nondual source (*brahman*) was thought to be beyond the dualities of life and death, existence and non-existence, eternality and impermanence, and consciousness. But the Buddha's teaching in this dialogue is distinguished from the thought of the *Nāsadīyasūkta* by virtue of the fact that ontological categories are not taken at face value, but are seen merely as concepts that do not apply to the liberated sage during his life.

## The historical significance of the *Upasīvamāṇavapucchā*

The dialogue with Upasīva can be summed up as follows:

1069–70 Upasīva asks what meditative object one should practise in order to escape suffering. The Buddha answers that one should observe 'nothingness' mindfully; the word *satimā* appears to mean that this practice combines meditative absorption with the practice of mindfulness.

1071–72 Upasīva asks if this state of meditation can be sustained without falling away from it, probably because he was surprised to hear that one must observe 'nothingness' and practise mindfulness at the same time. The Buddha answers that this state of meditation can be sustained without falling away from it.

1073–74 Upasīva asks if consciousness disappears for the one who, after sustaining this state of meditation for some time, attains liberation at death ('becomes cool'). For the Buddha, the issue is not in question because the state of the living liberated person cannot be reckoned.

1075–76 Upasīva asks if the one who is liberated/dead exists in a state of eternal bliss, or ceases to exist. The Buddha again denies the possibility of answering this question, because all modes of speaking do not apply to this living person. The conceptual framework upon which the dichotomies of existence and non-

> existence are based has ceased to function for the sage, even when he is alive.

The dialogue with Upasīva depicts an interaction between a religious teacher with new ideas and an adherent of an existing religion. It is a spectacular example of the Buddha's famed 'skill in means', showing how the ideas and metaphors of the old religion were revolutionized. For half the dialogue (v. 1069–72) the Buddha and Upasīva are almost speaking on the same level. Upasīva has difficulty understanding the combination of meditation and mindfulness in the Buddha's teaching, but at least recognizes the problem it creates in the context of early Brahminic meditation. But in the latter half of the dialogue Upasīva does not seem to grasp the meaning of the Buddha's words, and continues to speak as a Brahmin conditioned by the Brahminic ideas of his time. The Buddha, we can assume, has a knowledge of Upasīva's ideas and knows exactly what he is doing. In this way, the new teaching is expertly introduced into the framework of the old.

The historical worth of this document cannot be underestimated. The composers/redactors of this passage have recorded a quite remarkable interchange in which two individuals speak at cross-purposes. The words of T. W. Rhys-Davids, originally the *Kassapasīhanāda Sutta* in the *Dīgha Nikāya*, are equally applicable here:

> Gotama puts himself as far as possible in the mental position of the questioner. He attacks none of his cherished convictions. He accepts as the starting point of his own exposition the desirability of the act or condition prized by his opponent . . . He even adopts the very phraseology of his questioner. And then, partly by putting a new and (from the Buddhist point of view) a higher meaning into the words; partly by an appeal to such ethical conceptions as are common ground between them; he gradually leads his opponent up to his conclusion. This is of course Arahatship . . .
>
> There is both courtesy and dignity in the method employed. But no little dialectic skill, and an easy mastery of the ethical points involved, are required to bring about the result . . .
>
> On the hypothesis that he was an historical person, of that training and character he is represented in the Piṭakas to have had, the method is precisely that which it is most likely he would have actually followed.
>
> Whoever put the Dialogues together may have had a sufficiently clear memory of the way he conversed, may well have even remembered particular occasions and persons . . .
>
> However this may be, the method followed in all these Dialogues has one disadvantage. In accepting the position of the adversary, and adopting his language, the authors compel us, in order to follow

> what they give us as Gotama's view, to read a good deal between the lines. The *argumentum ad hominem* can never be the same as a statement of opinion given without reference to any particular person. That is strikingly the case with our present Sutta.[89]

It is, of course, strikingly the case with the *Upasīvamāṇavapucchā* too, whose correct understanding requires that we read 'a good deal between the lines'. Indeed, the nuances of the passage show that the authors must have had a clear memory of a particular dialogue of the Buddha. For if the interpretation offered here is correct, the exchange is far too intricate to have been fabricated at a later date. Earlier on, I pointed out that Richard Gombrich asked whether committees compose jokes. In the same way, we can ask if they author teachings in which the Buddha and his interlocutor speak at cross-purposes. The answer to both questions is that they generally do not. Thus the dialogue must be based on events that really happened, composed by persons with 'a sufficiently clear memory of the way [the Buddha] conversed,' and who 'may well have even remembered particular occasions and persons.' I therefore take the *Upasīvamāṇavapucchā* to be an accurate record of a historical event that has preserved the teaching, and possibly even the words, of the Buddha.

There are two more passages in the *Pārāyanavagga* that are important for the understanding of early Buddhist meditation (the *Udayamāṇavapucchā* and the *Posālamāṇavapucchā*).

## The *Udayamāṇavapucchā* (Sn 1105–11)

In the dialogue with Upasīva, the Buddha is depicted as a teacher engaged in the adaptation of Brahminic practices and metaphors. The principles of the Buddha's teaching can be deduced from this dialogue (the necessity of mindfulness, liberation in life, the indefinability of the sage, etc.), although there is no simple statement about the stages to liberation or a description of liberation itself. The dialogues with Udaya and Posāla cover both these points. The former is an elaboration of what the Buddhist path comprises, whereas the latter is a detailed statement of how liberation comes about for an advanced practitioner of meditation. Within the *Pārāyanavagga* the dialogue with Udaya is placed just before the dialogue with Posāla. It consists of seven verses, and like the dialogue with Upasīva it is a catechism:

> 'I have come with the desire [to ask] a question to the seated meditator who is without passion, who has done what has to be done, is without taint (*anāsavaṃ*), [and] has gone to the far shore of all *dhamma-s*. Proclaim the release through understanding (*aññāvimokham*), the destruction of ignorance.' [1105]
>
> 'The abandoning of both desire (*kāmacchandānaṃ*) and depression (*domanassāna*), O Udaya,' said the Blessed One, 'the dispelling

of sloth (*thīnassa*) and the warding away of perplexities (*kukkuccānaṃ*), [1106]

'Purified by equanimity and mindfulness (*upekhāsatisaṃsuddhaṃ*), preceded by the investigation of mental phenomena, I say, is the release through understanding (*aññāvimokham*), the destruction of ignorance.' [1107][90]

'What is the world's fetter, what is its doubt (*vicāraṇā*)? With the abandoning of what [is there that which] is called Nirvana?' [1108][91]

'The world is fettered by delight (*nandī*), investigation (*vitakka*) is its doubt. With the abandoning of craving [is there that which] is called Nirvana.' [1109]

'How is consciousness (*viññāṇaṃ*) stopped (*uparujjhati*) for one who wanders mindfully? We have come to ask the Blessed One [this, and] will listen to your teaching.' [1110]

'For the one who does not delight in sensation, both internally and externally, for the one who wanders mindfully in this way, consciousness is stopped.' [1111][92]

The Buddha's definition of the 'release through understanding' (1107: *aññāvimokham*) is a summary of the path to liberation. A general progression is implied, beginning with the overcoming of those factors that hinder the religious life (desire, depression, sloth, perplexity), followed by an investigation of states of mind or teachings (1007: *dhamma*) and the attainment of a state of pure equanimity and mindfulness. This summary of the path to liberation is, of course, elaborated in greater detail in the scheme of the four stages on meditation (the four *jhāna-s*, on which see p. 122ff.). This is apparent even at the beginning of the summary, where the items that ought to be abandoned according to the Buddha in Sn 1106 correspond to the hindrances in the classical scheme of four *jhāna-s*. The five hindrances to the four *jhāna-s* are longing (*abhijjhā*), malice (*vyāpāda*), sloth (*thīnamiddha*), excitement (*uddhaccakukkucca*) and perplexity (*vicikicchā*).[93] Two of these terms are identical with those mentioned in Sn 1106 (*thīna*, *kukkucca*), and one of them is equivalent (*kāmacchanda* = *abhijjhā*). There are a few other parallels. The fourth *jhāna*, the highest state of meditation in this scheme, is described as 'the complete purification of mindfulness and equanimity' (*upekhāsatipārisuddhiṃ*).[94] This is equivalent to the statement in Sn 1107 that the 'release through understanding' is 'purified by mindfulness and equanimity' (1107: *upekhāsatisaṃsuddhaṃ*).

If the analogy with the four *jhāna-s* is extended, it is possible that the phrase *dhamma-takka-purejavaṃ* in v. 1107b) is equivalent to the definition of the first *jhāna* as 'possessing *vitakka* and *vicāra*' (*sa-vitakkaṃ sa-vicāraṃ*). This has been suggested by Brough: 'Thus *dhamma-takka-purejavaṃ* means simply that the latter stages of the trance are "preceded by (or start from) the first *jhāna*". A more literal rendering would be "preceded by an examination of the *dhamma-s*".'[95] This is likely, although the verse is too vague to be certain.[96] It is also possible that this expression refers to a contemplation of the Buddha's teachings before any meditation has taken place at all.

Another allusion to one of the principle features of the *jhāna-s* is clearer. In v. 1109b), the Buddha declares that the world's 'doubt' (*vicāraṇā*) is 'investigation' (*vitakka*). This implies that investigation has to be overcome or abandoned in order for liberation to be attained, a principle that is elaborated in the second *jhāna*.[97] Verse 1109 is important for other reasons. The statement that the world is fettered by delight (*nandī*) is consistent with the principle that craving is the cause of suffering, i.e. the second Noble Truth. This suggests that the way to liberation is facilitated by comprehening the fact that delight or craving is the cause of one's suffering. This is similar to the Buddha's proclamation in the following dialogue with Posāla, i.e. that liberating insight consists of the comprehension that delight (*nandī*) is the cause of the meditative experience of nothingness (Sn 1115). The understanding and abandoning of desire is therefore a major feature of the dialogues with Upasīva (Sn 1070), Udaya (Sn 1109) and Posāla (Sn 1115).

The final two verses of the *Udayamāṇavapucchā* indicate the important role of mindfulness in early Buddhist meditation. Not delighting in sensation, both internally and externally, most probably refers not to the mindfulness of one's own sensations (*ajjhatañ*) as well as those of others (*bahiddhā*), but to the observation of one's sensations that occur within (*ajjhatañ*) or which come from without (*bahiddhā*), i.e. sensations caused by internal and external objects. Of considerable difficulty is the question posed by Udaya in v. 1110ab, however. Asking how 'consciousness' is 'stopped' must be equivalent to asking how liberation is attained, although the exact significance of the verb *upa* + √*rudh* is not clear. If it is taken in a strong sense to mean 'cessation', then the Buddha in Sn 1111 appears to accept that consciousness disappears in liberation. This is different from the teaching given at Sn 1073–74 to Upasīva, where the Buddha denies that one can answer whether the liberated person's consciousness 'falls away' (√*cu*). There are various solutions to this problem. First of all, it is possible that the word *viññāṇa* in both dialogues is used in a different sense. Second, it is possible that the verbs used in both dialogues have a different sense (√*cu* in Sn 1073, *upa* + √*rudh* in Sn 1110). Third, it is possible that this dialogue is different from the dialogue with Upasīva because the passages were composed at different times by people who believed different things. And finally, it is possible that there is no difference in meaning, and that the apparent difference is due to poetic licence.

It is not clear which of these answers might be correct. On the whole, I think that the difference between the two dialogues is not significant and is just a matter of poetic licence. The general tenor of the questions about consciousness in both dialogues is different – the concern is abstract and metaphysical in the dialogue with Upasīva, whereas it is practical and meditative in the dialogue with Udaya. It may even be the case that the exchange with Udaya concerning the 'stopping' of consciousness is an example of the Buddha's skill in means. Udaya's question in Sn 1110 is a question about liberation – he presupposes it comes about when consciousness is 'stopped'. In order to state the means of attaining liberation, the Buddha may have accepted this formulation without any acceptance of its philosophical implications. But even if the Buddha accepted the stopping of the *viññāṇa* in liberation, this is not a denial that the liberated person is insentient, for liberation is said to be attained by desisting from delighting in sensation, i.e. it presupposes the person is conscious. Perhaps, then, the translation of *viññāṇa* as 'consciousness' is incorrect. Although it seems to refer to sentience in general in the dialogue with Upasīva, it must be something more specific, i.e. a particular way of perceiving something, in the dialogue with Udaya. And perhaps these different understandings of the *viññāṇa* are indicated by the different verbs used: √*cu* in the dialogue with Upasīva seems to imply a metaphysical question about the cessation of *viññāṇa*, i.e. its existence or non-existence, whereas *upa* + √*rudh* seems to imply a temporal stopping or transcendence of the normal workings of consciousness.

The historical importance of the *Udayamāṇavapucchā* is not as obvious as that of the *Upasīvamāṇavapucchā*; it is an abstract statement of what meditation is, according to the Buddha, and does not depend on a subtle adaptation of Brahminic metaphysics and metaphors. As such, it is devoid of features that suggest that it is an authentic teaching of the Buddha. Rather, it is a fairly straightforward statement of the principles of the Buddhist path. It may go back to the Buddha. Indeed I think this most likely, for it is generally concordant with the *Upasīvamāṇavapucchā*. Moreover, its connection with the following dialogue, the *Posālamāṇavapucchā*, is quite obvious, and this latter dialogue is little more than a continuation of the *Upasīvamāṇavapucchā*. All three dialogues seem to outline different aspects of the same meditative teaching.

## The *Posālamāṇavapucchā* (Sn 1112–15)

This short passage, consisting of four verses (one question and one answer), expands upon the teachings of the *Upasīvamāṇavapucchā*. It indicates how liberation is attained from the meditative state of nothingness, and shows how the Buddha's meditative teaching differed from the standard Brahminic method. Inner concentration is said to be insufficient. Understanding, which requires cognition and is therefore the opposite of the Brahminic goal of cognitive inactivity, is essential:[98]

'I have come with the desire [to ask] a question,' said the venerable Posāla, 'to the one who has gone to the far shore of all mental phenomena, who without desire and with doubt cut off, teaches about the one who is released (*atītaṃ*).' (1112)

'I ask, Sakyan, about the knowledge of one whose perception of forms has disappeared,[99] who has abandoned all corporeality, who sees (*passato*) [both] internally and externally that nothing exists. How is such a person to be led [further] (*neyyo*)?'[100] (1113)

'The Tathāgata, O Posāla,' said the Blessed One, 'understanding all stations of consciousness, knows that [person as he] is stationed [there in the state of nothingness], concentrated [on it], intent on it.'[101] (1114)[102]

'Knowing that the origin of nothingness is the fetter "delight" (*nandīsaṃyojanaṃ*), understanding it thus, he then has insight into it. This is the true knowledge of the liberated Brahmin.'[103] (1115)[104]

This discussion picks up where the dialogue with Upasīva left off, the subject being the person who has attained the meditative state of 'nothingness'. I assume that *sabbakāyapahāyino* (v. 1113) refers to the mental state of a meditator, and that *viññāṇaṭṭhitiyo* (v. 1114) refers to the meditative states of consciousness that can be attained by a living human being. It is perhaps possible that the compounds *sabbakāyapahāyino* and *viññāṇaṭṭhitiyo* refer to a non-human deity who exists in the sphere of nothingness, one of the cosmological realities termed *viññāṇaññhitiyo*. But *sabbakāyapahāyino* is synonymous with *vibhūtarūpasaññissa* which immediately precedes it in v.1113. And *viññāṇaṭṭhitiyo* can just as easily refer to meditative stations of consciousness rather than eschatological realms.[105] Moreover, Posāla is asking for personal religious guidance rather than theoretical discussion. He wants to know how he himself can progress beyond the attainment of 'nothingness', and the Buddha is giving such guidance; his answer must show Posāla how he might attain liberating insight himself. That the subject of the dialogue is a human practitioner of meditation seems to be confirmed in v. 1115, where the words *brāhmaṇassa vusīmato* must refer to a human being.

The most important verse is Sn 1115, but Sn 1113 already indicates the orientation of the Buddha's teaching. Posāla understands that one must observe (*passato*) 'that nothing exists' both 'internally and externally' (*ajjhattañ ca bahiddhā*). This is a reference to the practice of mindfulness, which in this case implies the careful observation of the perceiving subject and perceived object based on a particular concentrative attainment. I noted earlier that this idea seemed strange to Upasīva. Here, however, and also in the dialogue with Udaya (Sn 1111), it seems to be presupposed; it is almost as if Udaya and Posāla have heard the Buddha's dialogue with Upasīva, as well as others contained in the *Pārāyanavagga*. The ideas in

Sn 1113 therefore correspond to the Buddha's teaching to Upasīva in Sn 1070, and to a lesser extent to those given to Udaya in Sn 1111:

| Sn 1070 | | Sn 1113 |
|---|---|---|
| *ākiñcaññaṃ/natthīti* | = | *natthi kiñcīti* |
| *pekkhamāno* | = | *passato* (Sn 1111 = *satassa*) |
| *satimā* | = | *ajjhattañ ca bahiddhā ca* (= Sn 1111) |

A general correspondence between these passages is undeniable; there is also a correspondence between *nandīsaṃyojanaṃ* in Sn 1109 and Sn 1115. In verse 1115 the Buddha teaches what must be done in order to attain release, although the exact meaning of the Buddha's words – the description of liberating insight – is far from clear. I take it that *pāda* (b) (*nandīsaṃyojanaṃ iti*) spells out what is declared in *pāda* (a) (*ākiñcaññasambhavaṃ ñatvā*), meaning that the origin of nothingness is delight, delight being a fetter or that which fetters a person.[106] *Pāda* (c) is a gloss on the process described in *pāda-s* (a-b): *etaṃ* probably qualifies *-sambhavaṃ*, which would give a meaning 'understanding it [the fetter that is the origin of nothingness] thus [i.e. as delight]'. *Pāda* (d), I presume, describes the state of insight (*vipassati*) that arises after one has grasped that delight is the origin of the state of nothingness. The passage thus states that someone who has attained the meditative state of nothingness, and has applied his meditative state of mind to the practice of mindfulness, must understand something about the meditative state, namely, that its existence in one's experience depends upon desire. When this is grasped (*abhiññāya*), then one 'sees' (*vipassati*) into it (*tattha*) and becomes a 'liberated Brahmin'. The difference between this teaching and the *yoga* prescribed in early Brahminic texts is striking. Meditative states alone are not an end, for even the highest meditative state is not liberating. Instead of attaining a complete cessation of thought, some sort of mental activity must take place: a liberating cognition, based on the practice of mindful awareness.

Why are these questions not included in the *Upasīvamāṇavapucchā*? One would expect that redactors or reciters would have constructed the *Pārāyanavagga* as logically as possible, connecting all related points in the same passage. This is especially true of the oral Pāli literature, in which the transmission of verses without writing was sometimes aided by listing verses on similar topics together, a good example being the *Dhammapada*. Why, then, are the questions of Upasīva and Posāla not placed together in one passage? Surely, it is because the questions were asked by two different people called Upasīva and Posāla, both of whom visited the Buddha together. If so, the dialogue with Posāla, like the dialogue with Upasīva, probably records a historical event. It is even possible that the close relationship between the teaching given to Posāla in v. 1113 and the Buddha's teaching to Upasīva in v. 1070 is due to the fact that Posāla heard the teaching given to Upasīva.

Indeed, as I have noted on the previous page, the ideas running through the dialogues with Upasīva, Udaya and Posāla cohere. An even stronger resemblance is shown in the vocabulary used in each dialogue, even in the compound *nandīsaṃyojana* used by the Buddha in the dialogues with Udaya (Sn 1109) and Posāla (Sn 1115). The question of *Posāla* reads almost as if he had heard the Buddha's dialogue with Udaya and the dialogue with Upasīva before it.

## Conclusion to Chapter 5

The dialogues with Upasīva, Udaya and Posāla contain important teachings on meditation. The dialogues with Upasīva and Posāla are two of the most peculiar early Buddhist texts; the former in particular is of the utmost historical importance. The Brahmin Upasīva betrays an awareness of the philosophy of early Brahminic meditation, which must be a tradition of which he had first-hand knowledge. To him the Buddha teaches an adapted form of the meditative exercise of Āḷāra Kālāma. To do this, the Buddha must be fully conversant with the ideas and terminology of this stream of thought (e.g. *sītī-√bhū*, *viññāṇaṃ* etc.), as well as the teaching of Āḷāra Kālāma. The Buddha is represented as someone with a new teaching, one that he was able to introduce to Upasīva using the old terminology and metaphors. The structure of the dialogue is so intricate, and the interchange between the two men so subtle, that it could hardly be a fabrication. It has probably recorded a historical event, i.e. a particular instance of the Buddha's teaching to a person.

These observations agree well with the hypothesis of earlier chapters, i.e., that the Buddha really was taught an early Brahminic form of meditation by Āḷāra Kālāma and Uddaka Rāmaputta. The interchange with Upasīva suggests that the Buddha was well informed about early Brahminic thought. Moreover, because the Buddha not only understands the Brahminic thought of Upasīva but also teaches an adapted form of Āḷāra Kālāma's meditative practice to him, it is likely that he gained this understanding of early Brahminic thought under Āḷāra Kālāma. If a teaching of the Buddha reflects the presuppositions of early Brahminic meditation, and refers to the teaching of one of his supposed teachers, then we should take seriously both the early texts' claim that the Bodhisatta was a pupil of these teachers and the theory that the teachers belonged to an early Brahminic milieu. Other explanations of the evidence are, of course, possible. It is conceivable, for example, that the Buddha acquired a working knowledge of the goals of the two teachers and early Brahminic meditation through dialogues with his disciples who had converted from these traditions. Other scenarios can be imagined. It is even possible that the dialogue in the *Pārāyanavagga* was fabricated in order to integrate a Brahminic tradition into the early Buddhist *saṅgha*. What counts against these objections, however, is that the evidence in the *Ariyapariyesana Sutta* and *Upasīvamāṇavapucchā* is circumstantial.

As I have noted elsewhere:

> circumstantial evidence is the indirect, unintentional evidence that affords a certain presumption. In the context of the early Buddhist literature, circumstantial evidence is not the direct evidence contained in the Buddhist texts, e.g. that the Buddha said such and such a thing on such and such an occasion (which may be true or false), but consists of the indirect facts from which other facts can be inferred.[107]

The *Ariyapariyesana Sutta* and *Upasīvamāṇavapucchā* contain this sort of indirect evidence, i.e. evidence that is besides the main points being made in these texts. It is difficult, a priori, to accept the claim of the *Ariyapariyesana Sutta* that the Bodhisatta studied under the two teachers. However, from the various philological, narrative and polemic peculiarities – the text's circumstantial evidence – we can infer that it is very early and contains historical facts; it is hard to establish any reason for its composition other than to record historical fact. The same can be said of the dialogue with Upasīva. At first, it appears to be an account of a meeting and conversation that cannot be verified. But further investigation shows that it contains peculiarities, i.e. unintentional evidence (such as that the Buddha and Upasīva are speaking at cross-purposes) that affords the presumption that the dialogue cannot have been faked. This suggests, therefore, that there is no reason for its composition other than to record historical fact. Without a deeper reflection on the verses, it is, of course, impossible to accept that the Buddha 'said such and such a thing on such and such an occasion' to Upasīva. But this objection applies only in so far as the context of the teaching is a straightforward description of Buddhist norms. But it is not. The interchange is highly unusual and much too intricate to have been fabricated or doctored. Texts such as these are never invented. The best explanation is that it is a record of a historical event. And the best explanation for the Buddha's knowledge of the early Brahminic ideas and the goal of Ālāra Kālāma is that the *Ariyapariyesana Sutta* is historically authentic.

# 6

# CONCLUSION

## The origin of Buddhist meditation and early Buddhism

Āḷāra Kālāma and Uddaka Rāmaputta were religious teachers in northern India in the fifth century BC. They taught the meditative practices of early Brahminism, the goal of which was thought to be a nondual state of meditation identical to the unmanifest state of *brahman*. In early Brahminical *yoga*, liberation was thought to be anticipated in a meditative trance that has passed beyond the possibility of cognition, a state in which the subject/object division has been dissolved. This means, of course, that true liberation is only realized after death, when there is no longer any possibility of cognizing an object. The adept, through his meditative trance, was thought to anticipate in life what he will realize at death – the nondual source of creation. Āḷāra Kālāma and Uddaka Rāmaputta termed this nondual goal 'nothingness' (*ākiñcañña*) and 'neither perception nor non-perception' (*nevasaññānāsaññā*) respectively, terminology that ought to be understood according to the early speculative tradition rooted in the *Nāsadīyasūkta* (ṚV X 129). The early verse Upaniṣads and *Mokṣadharma* show that the practice of *yoga* flourished in this speculative tradition in the last few centuries BC. Āḷāra Kālāma and Uddaka Rāmaputta were figures in their tradition at an earlier date, their teachings representing an earlier phase of yogic practice and thought. The Bodhisatta was taught by them, but rejected their goals, which he did not think were liberating. He set out to strive for liberation alone and claimed to have awakened to a different truth. His awakening came to be conceptualized in early Buddhist circles in terms of the attainment of the four *jhāna-s* and the liberating insight to which they lead. If the early biographies have any relevance to historical events, it means that the new path and goal discovered by the Buddha consisted of the adaptation of the old yogic techniques to the practice of mindfulness and attainment of insight. The yogic practices, when thus adapted towards the inculcation of mindful awareness (*sati*), were, of course, radically transformed.

The Buddha's adaptation of the old yogic techniques and ideology can be seen in the dialogues with the Brahmins Upasīva, Udaya and Posāla. These dialogues tell us that not only did the Buddha consider that the state of 'nothingness' was not liberating but also that it was no longer to be thought of as a state of 'enstasy'. Instead, the Buddha taught that it was a meditative state to be retained in the practice of mindful awareness, day and night, for lengthy periods of time. Liberation is achieved through this state of meditation, and results from understanding something about the meditative experience, namely, that it owes its origin to joy or pleasure (*nandī*). What the Buddha means by this is obscure: exactly what liberating insight was considered to be and how it came about are not made clear in the dialogue with Posāla (Sn 1115). At least we can say that liberation, according to the Buddha, was not simply a meditative experience but an insight into meditative experience. The Buddha taught that meditation must be accompanied by a careful attention to the basis of one's experience – the sensations caused by internal and external objects – and eventually an insight into the nature of this meditative experience. The idea that liberation requires a cognitive act of insight went against the grain of Brahminic meditation, where it was thought that the yogin must be without any mental activity at all, 'like a log of wood'.[1] The idea of liberation in life is just as strange for the Brahminic yogin, for whom liberation was thought to be the realization at death of the nondual meditative state anticipated in life. Indeed, old Brahminic metaphors for the liberation at death of the yogic adept ('becoming cool' and 'going out') were reinvested with a new meaning by the Buddha; their point of reference became the sage who is liberated in life.

Both the Buddha's conception of the liberated person and the goal of early Brahminic *yoga* can be defined as nondual in different ways. The nondual goal in early Brahminism was conceived in ontological terms as that into which one merges after death, a state lacking the ontological duality necessary for the perceiving subject's cognition of an object. But for the Buddha, liberation is achieved without dissolving the ontological duality between the subject and object, and indeed depends upon this duality, for liberation is an insight into the subject's (meditative) experience. Nevertheless, this state of insight is nondual in another, more radical, sense. This is made clear in the dialogue with Upasīva, where the liberated sage is defined as someone who has passed beyond conceptual dualities. Concepts that might have some meaning in ordinary discourse, such as consciousness or the lack of it, existence and non-existence, etc., do not apply to the sage. For the Buddha, propositions are not applicable to the liberated person, because language and concepts (Sn 1076: *vādapathā*, *dhammā*), as well as any sort of intellectual reckoning (*saṅkhā*), do not apply to the liberated sage. If it is correct to read the Buddha's dialogues with Upasīva and Posāla together, then we can conclude that the insight advocated by the Buddha to the latter must have been non-intellectual.

The veracity of this theory depends upon my interpretation of a few important pieces of textual evidence. The starting point is my interpretation of the *Ariyapariyesana Sutta*. Any critique of my position must argue that the peculiarities of this Sutta do not give good enough reason for believing that it is the earliest account of the Bodhisatta's strivings, an authentic text according to which Āḷāra Kālāma and Uddaka Rāmaputta taught the Bodhisatta. It must also assert that the more artificial and theoretical biography of the *Mahā-Saccaka Sutta et al.* does not necessarily mean that it is later. I argued that there is no reason to be sceptical about the historical worth of the biographical account in the APS, as Bareau has led us to believe. The anomalous philological forms (*hupeyya* and *tuvaṃ*), the simple and unique description of liberating insight, the use of the 'simple liberation pericope', the peculiar incident of the meeting with Upaka, and deviations in the usual oral repetition in order to differentiate Uddaka Rāmaputta and Rāma: all this suggests that the text is old and contains much authentic information. If so, I would argue that the Bodhisatta was taught by the two teachers, an impression enhanced by the respectful treatment of the teachers (who are considered to be the most worthy recipients of the Buddha's teaching) and the lack of any unqualified polemic against their methods. Thus I believe that the peculiarities of the text contain compelling historical evidence. Corroborating evidence for the idea that the Bodhisatta trained under Āḷāra Kālāma is found in the *Upasīvamāṇavapucchā*, the peculiarities of which suggest that it is very old. The *Upasīvamāṇavapucchā* and the *Ariyapariyesana Sutta* suggest a religious teacher knowledgeable about particular meditative practices. If the former is a true reflection of the Buddha's meditative teaching, as it seems to be – for it is hard to explain it in any other way – we must assume that the Buddha would not have taught the state of nothingness had he not had some experience of it. He must have been taught this practice, and if the texts tell us he was taught it by Āḷāra Kālāma, we should take them seriously.

Vital to my argument are certain deductions I have made about the meditative goals of Āḷāra Kālāma and Uddaka Rāmaputta. A critic of my position must argue that the evidence is not explicit enough to conclude a Brahminic origin for these goals. For example, Frauwallner and Nakamura argued that the goals of these teachers were found in early Jainism,[2] and although they do not present any textual evidence to support this claim, perhaps their opinions cast some doubt on my attempt to localize the vague terms *ākiñcañña* and *nevasaññānāsaññā*. Moreover, it could also be argued that my hypothesis that element meditation was related to the teachings of the two teachers in pre-Buddhist times is dubious, there being not enough evidence to suppose the wider existence of element meditation in early Brahminism, and thus little reason to think that the Buddhist sort of element meditation can have been absorbed from early Brahminism. Have I not conflated different aspects of early Buddhist meditation theory (element meditation and formless meditation) and projected them back to a pre-Buddhist period? Moreover, the elements of the meditative practice at Mbh XII.228 are listed in an order different from the order in which they are found in the Suttapiṭaka. Is it not mistaken to relate meditative lists with some important differences?

The Buddhist evidence suggests otherwise. Formless meditation and element meditation are connected a number of times, and logically belong together: a concentration on infinite space naturally follows concentrations on the material elements (before it) and precedes the formless spheres (after it); the lists of *dhātu-s* and *kasiṇāyatana-s* show that element meditation and formless meditation belong together. Moreover, the elements logically belong to the conceptual world of early Brahminism. Lists including formless meditation and element meditation in the Suttapiṭaka resemble the list of element meditation at Mbh XII.228, as well as some of the other early Brahminic cosmogonies. They therefore follow the philosophical presupposition of early Brahminic meditation, i.e. that inner concentration is a means of reversing the process of cosmic creation in one's mind. Formless meditation and element meditation must have been borrowed from a Brahminic source. Such a Brahminic source is suggested by the correspondences between the early Brahminic evidence and the goals of Āḷāra Kālāma and Uddaka Rāmaputta. The goal of Āḷāra Kālāma (*ākiñcañña*) corresponds to the Brahminic notion that the unmanifest *brahman* is a state of 'non-existence' (*asat*: CU III.19.1, CU VI.2.1, TU II.1; *naiveha kiṃcana*: BU I.2), the goal of Uddaka Rāmaputta (*nevasaññānāsaññā*) corresponds to the description of the unmanifest state of the cosmos in the *Nāsadīyasūkta* (ṚV X 129.1: *nā́sad āsīn nó sád āsīt tadā́nīm*) and the ultimate state of the self in the *Māṇḍūkya Upaniṣad* (MāU 7: *na prajñaṃ nāprajñam*), and the aphorism *passaṃ na passati* (D III.126) corresponds to *paśyan vai tan na paśyati* used at BU IV.3.23 to describe the nondual state of the *ātman*. Such a comprehensive correspondence is difficult to explain away. The evidence strongly suggests that the two men's teachings were influenced by early Brahminic thought. If so, is it a mere coincidence that element meditation existed in the early Brahminic tradition to which I suppose these two men belonged, as well as the Buddhist stream of meditation connected to their meditative goals? I think not. We can explain the evidence as follows. It is only to be expected that the practices related to Āḷāra Kālāma and Uddaka Rāmaputta continued to be practised not only in early Buddhism, but also in the non-Buddhist milieu(x). And, finally, I think that the evidence of the *Upasīvamāṇavapucchā* is conclusive: if a very old source tells us that the Buddha taught a modified form of Āḷāra Kālāma's practice to a Brahmin renouncer, it suggests that the practice of Āḷāra Kālāma was known in Brahminic circles. All this evidence is far too compelling to be dismissed. A critic should consider if a different theory could be formulated to explain the evidence better. At present, I see no better way of interpreting the evidence.

But there have been different interpretations of this evidence. In particular, Johannes Bronkhorst, in his seminal work *The Two Traditions of Meditation in Ancient India*, has supposed that formless meditation was borrowed from early Jainism. In the same work, Bronkhorst also considered some of the early Brahminic evidence for *yoga* (Chapter IV: 'Meditation as part of asceticism in early Hindu scriptures') and concluded that the yogic ideas of Mbh XII.294.13–18, KaU III.6 and VI.10–11, ŚU II.8–9 and Mbh XII.304.8–10, i.e. texts that contain important evidence on the early tradition of Brahminic meditation, show that 'meditation is only one aspect of a more general process in which all bodily and mental activities are stopped.'[3] However, it seems to me that this opinion understates the role of meditation in early Brahminism and creates a quite misleading impression: the goal of these passages is the cessation of mental activity, to which end the cessation of bodily activity is merely a support. Bronkhorst's estimation of early Brahminic meditation clearly applies to the other texts that he considers: the ideas about ascetic observance he quotes from Mbh I.86.14–16 and Mbh I.81.10–16, as well as the *Maitrāyaṇīya Upaniṣad*, *Viṣṇusmṛti*, *Mahā Upaniṣad*, *Muktikā Upaniṣad*, *Triśikhabrāhmaṇa Upaniṣad*, *Yājñavalkyasmṛti* and the *Āpastamba Dharma Sūtra* all stress some kind of painful asceticism that corresponds to the Jaina sort of observances.[4] But these texts are concerned with practices very different from the *yoga* practices described in the early Brahminic texts on meditation.

The problem I have with Bronkhorst's theory is that it seems to conflate the evidence from different texts. He does not recognize the differences between texts that do not include any reference to extreme asceticism (e.g. Mbh XII.294.13–18, KaU VI.10–11 and III.6, ŚU II.8–9 and Mbh XII.304.8–10) and those that do. The ideal of fasting to death described in Mbh I.81.10–16, *Yājñavalkyasmṛti* II.3.50–55 and *Āpastamba Dharma Sūtra* II.9.31.1–2 is not found in any of the early Brahminic texts on meditation such as those studied earlier in Chapter 3. Moreover, the passages on *yoga* in the early Brahminic texts do not mention the ideals of emaciation (Mbh I.86.14.16)[5] or painful breath restraint. In other words, the texts tell us that there were different streams of early Brahminic asceticism in which different soteriological practices were valued. It seems to me that a tradition of meditation alone is consistently described in the early verse Upaniṣads and throughout the *Mokṣadharma*, a tradition in which *yoga* was thought to be a pleasurable activity. But Bronkhorst considers some of this evidence from the early Upaniṣads and *Mokṣadharma* alongside evidence found in other early Brahminic texts that profess very different ideas. Thus, he is able to claim: 'There can be no doubt that the early Jaina and Hindu scriptures describe forms of meditation which belong to the same tradition.'[6] My own understanding is that the forms of meditation described in the early verse Upaniṣads and *Mokṣadharma* did not belong to the same tradition as that described in the Jaina scriptures.

The early Jaina, Brahminic and Buddhist schools were important traditions in a diverse ascetic scene. Although we can identify some common features in the scriptures of these different schools, it does not mean that we can reduce large amounts of the early textual evidence to the same meditative tradition. For example, breath restraint (*prāṇāyāma*) is attested in a number of different early Brahminic texts, and is perhaps the only practice that connects some of the diverse texts gathered together by Bronkhorst in Chapter 4 of his work. This might lead us to believe that these texts mentioning *prāṇāyāma* profess the same ascetic practices. But this is not the case. Important differences are found in the different texts on *prāṇāyāma*: in the *Śvetāśvatara Upaniṣad*, breath restraint is not total for the adept is said to continue breathing through the nose (ŚU II.9: *nāsikayocchvasīta*); in the *Maitrāyaṇīya Upaniṣad*, the practitioner is supposed to restrain speech, mind and breath by squeezing the tip of the tongue against the palate (Mai U VI.20: *tālurasanāgranipīḍanāt*);[7] other Brahminic texts noted by Bronkhorst advocate the grinding together of the teeth;[8] whereas breath restraint, and *Mokṣadharma* passages is not said to be painful.[9] These important differences show only a superficial agreement between the texts on breath restraint, and do not prove that the scriptures belonged to the same tradition of meditation.

Contrary to Bronkhorst, I think it is clear that extreme physical asceticism played no more than a superficial role in the tradition of meditation recorded in the early Upaniṣads and *Mokṣadharma*. There is no suggestion that practices such as starving to death were valued in this early yogic tradition, which I think can be called the 'meditative mainstream' of early Brahminic asceticism. Bronkhorst does show that there must have been some tradition of extreme asceticism in early Brahminism, i.e. an ascetic tradition quite similar to early Jainism. But the aim of the meditative mainstream was to achieve freedom from *karman* by attaining the realization of the *ātman*. Emaciation and other painful methods were practised by some, but according to the most important Brahminic texts, these practices were marginal. Towards the end of his treatment of the Brahminic evidence, Bronkhorst admits that meditation apart from physical austerities became a way to the knowledge of the self in early Brahminism.[10] But it seems to me that the vast majority of early Brahminic texts suggest that this was the fundamental idea of the meditative mainstream of early Brahminism.

## The relationship between early Buddhism and Brahminism

This theory of a Brahminic origin of Buddhist meditation allows us to reassess some of the problems in the study of early Buddhism. One of these problems is the existence of Brahminic views in early Buddhist texts. According to Stanislaw Schayer and A. B. Keith, these views are evidence for a 'precanonical' form of Buddhism different from the form of Buddhism attested in most of the early texts. This view has recently been stated by Christian Lindtner as follows:

> The Pāli Canon shows several clear traces of precanonical Buddhism. This kind of early Buddhism was based on a belief in the six *dhātus* and was thus a kind of natural philosophy. At the peak of existence (*bhūtakoṭi*) we found Nirvāṇa. Like the spirit, which may have stopped breathing there, it was considered permanent and blissful, but one had to pass through *ākāśa* and *vijñāna* to get there. One could[11] actually attain it by some sort of yogic method. It was a yogi's paradise, hardly a place for the common herd. The world of the senses was considered impermanent and full of suffering.
>
> Canonical Buddhism, on the other hand, was a reaction to this view. Now everything was considered impermanent. Nirvāṇa was now rather a state of mind, not a place at the top of the universe. Not only was canonical Buddhism a reaction against early Buddhism, or certain trends in early Buddhism, but also against the absolutist tendencies in Jainism and the Upaniṣads.[12]

According to Lindtner, in this early or 'precanonical' form of Buddhism ideas flourished that were similar to those that formed the theoretical background to *yoga* in early Brahminism. Some time after this, there was a reaction to these old ideas, and Buddhism in this reactionary form became the mainstream, canonized religion, with most of the early Pāli texts being composed by Buddhists of this 'canonical' period. In other words, canonical Buddhism is something quite like the Theravāda Buddhism that has existed in South and South-east Asia for some millennia, whereas precanonical Buddhism was more akin to the early Vedānta. The evidence for this view consists of the odd fragment in the Suttapiṭaka that reflects early Brahminic ideology. Schayer[13] referred to Suttapiṭaka passages in which 'consciousness' (*viññāṇa*) seems to be the ultimate reality or substratum (e.g. A I.10) 14 as well as the *Ṣaḍdhātu Sūtra*, which is not found in any canonical source but is cited in other Buddhist texts – it states that the personality (*pudgala*) consists of the six elements (*dhātu*) of earth, water, fire, wind, space and consciousness; Schayer noted that it related to other ancient Indian ideas.[15] Keith's argument is also based on the *Ṣaḍdhātu Sūtra*,[16] as well as 'passages where we have explanations of Nirvāṇa which echo the ideas of the Upaniṣads regarding the ultimate reality.'[17] He also refers to the Mahāsāṅghika doctrine of 'a consciousness, originally pure, defiled by adventitious impurities',[18] which, he notes, corresponds to A I.10. Based on these arguments, Lindtner himself has suggested that the precanonical conception of Nirvāṇa was as follows:

> The old conception (represented by *Dīgha Nikāya* I 223, *Udāna* 80 etc.) is one of a *place one can actually go to*. It is called *nirvāṇadhātu*, has no border-signs (*animitta*), is localized

> somewhere beyond the other six *dhātus* (beginning with earth and ending with *vijñāna*) but is closest to *ākāśa* and *vijñāna*. One cannot visualize it, it is *anidarśana*, but it provides one with firm ground under one's feet, it is *dhruva*; once there one will not slip back, it is *acyutapada*. As opposed to this world, it is a pleasant place to be in, it is *sukha*, things work well.[19]

Whether or not Lindtner realizes it, this description of Nirvāṇa corresponds exactly to the early Brahminic ideas that developed from the *Nāsadīyasūkta*, such as those found in Mbh XII.224.[20] But there is hardly any evidence for this sort of view in the Suttapiṭaka; only the passage from the *Udāna* to which Lindtner refers seems to state this:

> There is, O *bhikkhus*, a sphere (*āyatanaṃ*) where there is no earth, water, fire, wind; no sphere of the infinity of space, no sphere of the infinity of consciousness, no sphere of nothingness, no sphere of neither perception nor non-perception; no this world or the other world, no sun or moon. There, O *bhikkhus*, I say there is no coming, no going, no persisting, no falling away, no arising; it is unfounded (*appatiṭṭhaṃ*), uninvolved (*appavattaṃ*), without support. This is the end of suffering.[21]

This passage reflects the early Brahminic conceptualization of *brahman* very closely, as can be seen from the following Upaniṣadic verse:

> There the sun does not shine, nor do the moon or stars; lightning does not shine, let alone this fire here. . . .[22]

Lindtner also cites an untraced Sūtra fragment cited in Yaśomitra's *Sphuṭārthavyākhyā* on *Abhidharmakośabhāṣya* I.5:

> 'Earth is founded on what, O Gautama?'
> 'Earth is founded on the orb of water.'
> 'The orb of water is founded on what, O Gautama?'
> '[It is] founded on wind.'
> 'Wind is founded on what, O Gautama?'
> '[It is] founded on space.'
> 'Space is founded on what, O Gautama?'
> 'You go too far, great Brahmin, you go too far. Space, great Brahmin, is unfounded, it lacks a support.'
> Therefore according to the Vaibhāṣikas, space exists.[23]

Lindtner relates this to the passage on the genesis of the elements at TU II.1. Indeed some relationship between this ancient Sūtra fragment and

TU II.1 is undeniable. Thus the evidence presented by Lindtner, Schayer and Keith shows that diverse beliefs, which correspond to the views of the meditative mainstream, must have been current in early Buddhism. But I see no reason to think that these opinions characterize a 'precanonical Buddhism'. One of the problems with this theory is that the evidence for different beliefs is presented in the simplistic form of a dichotomy between 'precanonical Buddhism' vs. 'canonical Buddhism'. What does this dichotomy mean? The early Pāli scriptures were written down, and hence canonized, in Sri Lanka in the first century BC, during the reign of Vaṭṭagāmaṇī.[24] Lindtner obviously does not think that the lengthy period of almost four centuries before this is the period of 'precanonical Buddhism'. What he must mean is that his evidence pertains to a very early (or the earliest) phase of Buddhism, and that the vast amount of Suttapiṭaka material at odds with it comes from a later precanonical period than this. His theory, simply put, is that passages radically different from most of the early Buddhist literature must be very early, and in fact definitive of the early period.

But I fail to see how these conclusions follow from the textual evidence. It certainly shows that some of the early Buddhists were influenced by their Brahminic peers, but hardly any of it shows that the *nirvāṇadhātu* was thought to be 'a place one can actually go to'. The citation from the *Udāna* suggests such a view of Nirvana, but it shows only that some early Buddhists held Upaniṣadic beliefs; it does not mean that this view is that of the Buddha, or even that it existed in the earliest phase of Buddhism. On the contrary, if the theory about early Buddhism that I am proposing is correct, it means that these views cannot be traced back to the Buddha. I have tried to show that the Buddha rejected the early Brahminic teachings of Āḷāra Kālāma and Uddaka Rāmaputta, and that when he taught Brahminic renouncers his teaching appears to have been a radical departure from the old Brahminic beliefs. As I see it, substantialist beliefs that are typical of the early Upaniṣads, i.e. the theoretical counterparts to the early yogic practices, must have been rejected by the Buddha if he rejected the goals of the meditative mainstream by emphasizing mindfulness and liberating insight. The notion of liberation in life, and the refusal to consider the question of what happens after death, denies the Upaniṣadic ontology. This sort of teaching is perhaps what Lindtner would classify as characteristic of 'canonical Buddhism', but I have argued that it goes back to the Buddha himself. In short, Lindtner presents no criteria for ascribing his evidence to the earliest period of Buddhism.

How are we to explain the early Upaniṣadic beliefs in the Suttapiṭaka? I would address the problem as follows: if the Buddha taught an adapted version of early Brahminic *yoga* to Brahmins from Vedāntic milieux, some early Brahminic converts to Buddhism were bound to retain some of their old beliefs. If a new religion originates in close contact with the mainstream religion, and accepts converts from it, an ongoing influence from it is only to be expected. The passages cited by Lindtner *et al.* should therefore be seen as the literary product of some early Buddhists who were influenced by early Brahminism. The Buddhists who held these views were probably converts from early Brahminism who retained some of the old beliefs attached to their yogic practices. But these early Brahminic beliefs are incompatible with the original Buddhist meditation and its non-substantialist implications.

This evidence suggests that the Suttapiṭaka is not homogeneous, a fact I pointed out at the beginning of this book. That the early Buddhist literature on meditation is heterogeneous was suggested some time ago by Louis de La Vallée Poussin, in his famous article 'Musīla et Nārada'.[25] Although not all scholars accept the views of La Vallée Poussin,[26] the texts cited by Lindtner *et al.* seem to confirm La Vallée Poussin's opinion. I have argued that these texts can be made sense of by the theory of a Brahminic origin of Buddhist meditation. The same seems to be the case with some of the divergences noted by La Vallée Poussin. This material has baffled scholars of Buddhism, but I think it is now possible to see that at least some of it must be the product of early Buddhists who were influenced by the meditative mainstream of early Brahminism.

## An early Buddhist controversy: meditation or intellectualism?

La Vallée Poussin claimed that two different versions of the path are outlined in Indian Buddhist texts: one in which liberation was considered to be achieved by intellectual means, and the other in which liberation was achieved by concentration alone, the gradual suppression of all mental activity. Concerning the ancient material he makes this assertion on the basis of two texts. First, there is the *Mahā-Cunda Sutta* (A III.355–6 = *Chakka Nipāta* XLVI), in which we are told of *bhikkhus* 'devoted to the doctrine' (*dhammayogā bhikkhū*: 'intellectuals')[27] who disagree with 'meditating' *bhikkhus* (*jhāyī bhikkhū*). We find a brief statement of their views towards the end of the Sutta. The intellectuals, it is said, should praise the meditators because: 'Marvellous are those persons, venerable sirs, [and] hard to find in the world, those who touch the deathless realm with the body' (*amataṃ dhātuṃ kāyena phusitvā*).[28] Conversely, the meditators should praise those 'devoted to the doctrine' because: 'Marvellous are those venerable persons, [and] hard to find in the world, those who have vision by penetrating the profound words of the doctrine with understanding.'[29] This description of those 'devoted to the doctrine' implies that they valued an intellectual understanding of the *dhamma*; indeed, all the other references to the expression 'penetrating with understanding' (*paññāya ativijjha*) show that it denotes an intellectual understanding that excludes meditation.[30]

In a similar vein is the *Kosambi Sutta* (S II 115 = *Nidāna Saṃyutta* 68, *mahāvagga*), the Sutta that gave the name to Louis de La Vallée Poussin's article. It states that Musīla knows and sees (*etaṃ jānāmi etaṃ passāmi*) by himself (*paccattaṃ*) all the links in the chain of dependent origination in its reverse (*paṭiloma*) order, in both the origination (*samudaya*) and cessation (*nirodha*) modes.[31] This is an understanding apart from faith (*saddhā*), apart from one's intellectual inclination or belief (*ruciyā*) and apart from traditional teachings (*anussavā*). Musīla is asked by Saviṭṭha if he knows and sees that '*nibbāna* is the cessation of becoming (*bhavanirodho*)', to which he answers that he does know and see this. So when Saviṭṭha asks Musīla if he is an *arahant* with corruptions destroyed, he is silent, and the conclusion is that he is indeed an *arahant*.[32] However, Nārada claims to know and see exactly what Musīla does, but he denies that he is liberated.[33] He likens his condition to the state of a thirsty person who can see water in a well, but cannot touch it with his body (*na kāyena phusitvā vihareyya*). Nārada claims to have the correct intellectual understanding (he knows what *nibbāna* is or should be) but he does not consider this to be liberating. The simile of seeing water in a well but not touching it with the body might just indicate a state of having knowledge without being liberated. However, the expression 'he does not touch it with his body', coupled with its opposition to insight (*paññā*), likens Nārada's view to the view of the meditators in the *Mahā-Cunda Sutta*, where liberation is said to involve the 'touching' of the deathless realm with the body that is different from a mere intellectual understanding of the doctrine. For Nārada, it seems, liberation meant touching a deathless realm while in a meditative state (*amataṃ dhātuṃ kāyena phusitvā*), something different from having an idea about what it should be.

We have a serious problem here – two different and (according to the *Mahā-Cunda Sutta*) hostile versions of Buddhism. The most obscure line in these two texts is the expression describing how some meditative adepts 'touch' (*phusitvā*) a 'deathless realm' (*amatā dhātu*) with the body (*kāyena*). What does this mean? It surely refers to the attainment of liberation, and the other occurrences of the expression *amatā dhātu* in the Suttapiṭaka support this view.[34] But what type of meditation is a path to it? There are only two frequent contexts in which the expression *kāyena phusitvā* occurs, and in only one of these contexts are meditative states the subject of discourse.[35] These meditative states are the 'formless meditations' (*āruppā vimokkhā*) connected to Āḷāra Kālāma and Uddaka Rāmaputta, states that are said to be 'touched by the body' in a number of places in the Suttapiṭaka.[36] Does this mean that some early Buddhists used the practice of formless meditation as a way to attain the touching of the 'deathless realm' with the body? It seems natural to conclude this, although the formless meditations as listed in the Suttapiṭaka are never said to lead to the attainment of the 'deathless realm' (*amatā dhātu*). They are usually followed by the attainment of 'the cessation of perception and feeling' (*saññāvedayitanirodha*). But this merely begs the question: could the attainment of *saññāvedayitanirodha* be another way of describing how a *bhikkhu* touches the deathless realm with his body? Louis de La Vallée Poussin seems to have drawn this conclusion: he used the description of the *jhāyī bhikkhū* in the *Mahā-Cunda Sutta* to support his idea that the liberation according to the way of concentration (rather than the way of insight) is *saññāvedayitanirodha*.[37] And there is textual support for La Vallée Poussin's opinion. Verses occurring at two places in the *Itivuttaka* equate the attainment of cessation (*nirodha* = *saññāvedayitanirodha*) with the touching of the deathless realm by the body:

> Understanding the realm of form without, not abiding in the formless [realms], those people who are released in cessation (*nirodhe*) abandon death.
>
> Having touched the deathless element (*amataṃ dhātuṃ*) with the body, [that] which is without attachment (*nirūpadhiṃ*), realising the relinquishing of [all] attachment, being without defilements, the perfectly awakened one teaches the place which is without grief or defilement.[38]

The two items *nirodha* and *amatā dhātu* do not stand in apposition, but the implication is that they indicate the same thing. I think we can conclude that for some early Buddhists, the non-Buddhist yogic methods of the two teachers led to a sort of liberation referred to as 'touching the deathless realm with the body' or 'the cessation of perception and feeling'. As Louis de La Vallée Poussin has commented, 'this way has nothing specifically Buddhist about it':[39] the goal of meditation, formulated as 'the cessation of perception and feeling' or the 'deathless realm', does not seem to differ from the yogin's mystic union with *brahman*. Indeed, Schmithausen has noted that the notion of touching the deathless realm with the body is 'a temporary anticipation, still in this life, of the state of Nirvāṇa (which is attained definitively after death).'[40] This is exactly the conceptualization of liberation in the meditative mainstream of early Brahminism. Surely it was a Vedāntic belief, held by Buddhists who were influenced by the mainstream yogic ideas.

It is not surprising that some early Buddhists continued the pre-Buddhist yogic practices of Āḷāra Kālāma and Uddaka Rāmaputta, since the Buddha's dialogues with Upasīva and Posāla seem to have allowed this. What is harder to explain is the fact that some of these Buddhists thought of liberation in terms of the yogic ideology of the meditative mainstream. This seems to be completely at odds with the view of liberating insight described by the Buddha in the dialogues with Upasīva and Posāla. According to the theory formulated here, the Buddha cannot have been responsible for this development. He did not teach that liberation was attained in a deep meditative trance devoid of mental activity. If the approach to meditation and insight described in the dialogues with Upasīva and Posāla is definitive of the earliest form of Buddhism, then ideas such as 'touching the deathless realm with the body', 'the cessation of perception and feeling' (*saññāvedayitanirodha*) and the meditative scheme of 'gradual abidings' (*anupubbavihāra-s*: they impose the four formless spheres above the four *jhāna-s* and lead to *saññāvedayitanirodha*) must be indicative of a later period of thought.

## The intellectual tendency in early Buddhism

More difficult to understand is the view held by the opponents of the meditating *bhikkhus* in the *Mahā-Cunda Sutta*. If the expression 'penetrating with insight' (*paññā ativijjha*) refers to an understanding devoid of meditation,[41] it means that some early Buddhists thought liberating insight was an intellectual matter that did not require meditation. According to Gombrich, this tendency stems from the *Susīma Sutta*,[42] in which some *bhikkhus* claim to be liberated without attaining the formless spheres or supernatural powers that come after the four *jhāna-s*.[43] As the Pāli text reads, the statement by the group of *bhikkhus* that they have not attained the supernatural powers that come after the four *jhāna-s* – including the first two knowledges of three that effect liberation[44] – suggests that they have not attained the *jhāna-s*. Although there is no explicit statement that their liberation was achieved without meditation, this conclusion seems inevitable. This position is certainly at odds with what I have stated was the sort of meditation taught by the Buddha: although it is difficult to determine the nature of liberating insight in the dialogue with Posāla, it seems to depend upon meditation, and if we read it together with the teaching to Upasīva, we must understand that insight is a state beyond words (*vādapatha*).

The tendency towards intellectualism is evident throughout the Suttapiṭaka. The extreme view, of course, is that stated in the *Mahā-Cunda Sutta* and strongly suggested in the *Susīma Sutta*, i.e. that meditation is not necessary. But a less extreme view is stated at the conclusion of the *Anattalakkhaṇa Sutta*, in the account of the five *bhikkhus*' liberation: 'When this discourse was being spoken, the minds of the group of five *bhikkhus* were released from the corruptions without clinging.'[45] The point of this, it seems, is that pondering doctrinal teachings can result directly in liberation. This view does not take the extreme stance of making meditation unnecessary for liberation, for the composers of the passage would no doubt have assumed that the five *bhikkhus* were sufficiently adept in ascetic/meditative practices. But it implies that liberation is effected, in the end, not by an insight mediated through a transconceptual meditative attainment, but by a direct contemplation of Buddhist dogma that requires conceptual thought. Moreover, this account of the five *bhikkhus*' liberation is very different from the account in the *Ariyapariyesana Sutta*, where a period of time is envisaged during which the Buddha teaches them the *dhamma* so that they can practise it and finally attain their liberation, after a period of meditative development.[46] It seems that we have two alternative views of the same event. But which is the earliest?

For reasons given in Chapter 2, I think that the APS is likely to contain some of the oldest biographical material, and so it is likely that its account of the five *bhikkhus*' liberation is earlier than the account in the *Anattalakkhaṇa Sutta*. The latter must be indicative of a time when it was widely accepted that liberation could be attained by intellectual means. It is not entirely discordant with the view expressed in the dialogues with Upasīva and Posāla, where meditation is not an end in itself, and leads to insight. But the liberating insight taught to Posāla can hardly be described as intellectual, and according to the teaching given to Upasīva it leads to a non-intellectual state. At the least, the *Anattalakkhaṇa Sutta* and the dialogues with Upasīva and Posāla have a completely different feel to them. The Buddha tells Upasīva to live 'without talk' (Sn 1070: *virato kathāhi*) – it does not tell him to listen carefully while he speaks, in the hope that while he does so his mind will be released from the corruptions. Instantaneous liberation is not what the Buddha teaches to Upasīva, Udaya or Posāla. The *Anattalakkhaṇa Sutta*, the *Mahā-Cunda Sutta* and the *Susīma Sutta* show a trend towards intellectualism that cannot go back to the Buddha. And this trend towards intellectualism was not accepted by all the members of the early Buddhist *saṅgha*. I have pointed out elsewhere that the debate between intellectual and meditative theories of liberating insight is more widespread than La Vallée Poussin noted: it encompassed ideas such as liberating insight resulting from an understanding of the Four Noble Truths, and the different conceptions of the notion 'released on both sides' (*ubhatobhāgavimutti*).[47]

Whereas there is an easy explanation for the existence of meditative theories that exclude insight (the close contact with the meditative mainstream), there is no easy explanation for the origin of these intellectual theories of liberating insight. According to Gombrich, intellectualism might have been 'a kind of narrative accident due to Sangha apologetics';[48] Schmithausen has suggested that 'the Vedic belief in the extraordinary power of truth and knowledge may still have been influential among early Buddhists'.[49] Both these views explain the intellectual theories to some extent. Another explanation is that intellectualism was an unintended consequence of the Buddha's teachings on the necessity of liberating insight. I have argued that the Buddha taught a 'middle way' between pure meditation and cognitive practices. The states of absorption induced by meditation were considered useful and necessary, but in distinction from the meditative mainstream their ultimate aim was insight. For the Buddha it was vitally important that the meditative adept should apply his concentrative state to the practice of mindfulness (Sn 1070: *satimā*; Sn 1111: *ajjhattañ ca bahiddhā ca vedanaṃ nābhinandato*; Sn 1113: *ajjhattañ ca bahiddhā ca natthī ti passato*), and work towards the attainment of insight. According to this view meditation alone, the goal of the meditative mainstream would have been harshly criticized in the earliest Buddhism. The *Indriyabhāvana Sutta* illustrates this perfectly.[50] Here, the Buddha is told by the Brahmin Uttara that his master Pārāsariya teaches the 'cultivation of the senses' (*indriyabhāvana*) as follows:

> One does not see a form with the eye, or hear a sound with the ear.[51]

Pārāsariya's teaching accords well with the aims of the meditative mainstream. The name 'Pārāsariya' is not without interest. The Sanskrit equivalent 'Pārāśarya' appears a few times in the *Mokṣadharma*. In some cases it designates mythical sages,[52] but in one place the *bhikṣu* Pañcaśikha, teacher of King Janaka, is said to be from the same kin as Pārāśarya (*pārāśaryasagotra*).[53] It is possible that this tale has preserved some truth: even if the relationship between the early Brahminic teacher Pārāśarya and Pañcaśikha (himself a teacher of a sort of proto-Sāṃkhya at Mbh XII.211–12) is legendary, it is possible that the names have some significance and go back to historical figures. It may be the case, then, that the *Indriyabhāvana Sutta* has preserved the only historical information about Pārāsariya/Pārāśarya. If so, Pārāsariya was indeed a teacher in the early Brahminic-yogic tradition, but one whose teaching the Buddha ridiculed as follows:

> If it is so, Uttara, a blind man would have developed his senses, a deaf man would have developed his senses.[54]

The Sutta then goes on to teach that mindfulness with regard to one's sense impressions is the correct way to develop one's sense faculties. It is possible that this stress on the importance of mindfulness, i.e. the inculcation of a correct attitude with regard to one's cognitions, instead of the meditative goal of non-cognition, eventually led to intellectualism, especially given the harsh critique of meditation alone in the *Indriya-bhāvana Sutta*. If one must cognize something, rather than attain the yogic goal of 'not knowing', it is not surprising that the content of cognition began to be formulated in different ways, especially if Schmithausen is right in supposing that the 'Vedic belief in the extraordinary power of truth and knowledge' was influential among early Buddhists. Intellectualism was just waiting to happen, despite the fact that it was not what the Buddha taught.

## The four *jhāna-s* and their development

The 'middle way' between meditation and knowledge is expressed most succinctly in the scheme of four *jhāna-s*, although it seems to me that this scheme is poorly understood. Words expressing the inculcation of awareness, e.g. *sati*, *sampajāno*, *upekkhā*, etc., are mistranslated or understood as particular factors of the meditative states.[55] The translation of *sati* as 'mindfulness' and *upekkhā* as 'equanimity' do not do full justice to these terms. They give the misleading impression that the third and fourth *jhāna* are heightened states of meditative absorption characterized by some sort of indescribable inner calm. But these terms have quite distinct meanings in the early Buddhist texts: they refer to a particular way of perceiving of sense objects (which in the Buddhist analysis includes mental objects). Thus the expression *sato sampajāno* in the third *jhāna* must denote a state of awareness different from the meditative absorption of the second *jhāna* (*cetaso ekodibhāva*). It suggests that the subject is doing something different from remaining in a meditative state, i.e. that he has come out of his absorption and is now once again aware of objects. The same is true of the word *upek(k)hā*: it does not denote an abstract 'equanimity', for the root meaning of the verb *upa* + √*ikṣ* is 'to look at or on . . . to overlook, disregard, neglect, abandon'.[56] In other words, it means to be aware of something and indifferent to it. This much is clear in the numerous other occurrences in the Suttapiṭaka of the word *upekkhā*; I need only refer to the *Indriyabhāvana Sutta*.[57] The third and fourth *jhāna-s*, as it seems to me, describe the process of directing states of meditative absorption towards the mindful awareness of objects.[58] The culmination of this process is, of course, liberating insight.

The scheme of four *jhāna-s* appears to be in accordance with the teaching of the Buddha in the dialogues with Upasīva, Posāla, and especially Udaya. It seems to me that this scheme must go back in substance, and perhaps in word, to the Buddha. But even in this case it is likely that its transmission by later generations of Buddhists has not left it unchanged in its earliest form. One particular problem concerns the liberating insight that is the goal of the *jhāna-s*. In most places, most notably the accounts in the *Sīlakkhandhavagga* of the *Dīgha Nikāya*, liberation is effected by an insight into the Four Noble Truths and the corruptions (*āsava-s*). This seems to be an intellectual sort of insight; Schmithausen has argued that it is psychologically implausible[59] and 'cannot be accepted as representing the original account of Enlightenment [of the Buddha]'.[60]

It is easy to see why some early Buddhists conceived liberating insight to be a correct knowledge of the Four Noble Truths, for this list sums up Buddhism in a most coherent and simple way. Moreover, the content of the insight in the Buddha's teaching to Posāla consists of the understanding that delight (*nandī*) is the cause of the meditative experience of 'nothingness'. This insight approximates insight into the Second Noble Truth, i.e. the Truth that suffering is caused by thirst (*taṇhā*). Elsewhere, according to the *Mūlapariyāya Sutta* the content of a Tathāgata's liberating knowledge is the understanding 'Delight is the root of suffering' (*nandī dukkhassa mūlanti*).[61] It is easy to imagine that in the very beginning, liberating insight was imagined to be a non-conceptual, existential grasp of this fact. After this early period, there must have been a series of gradual shifts, which can be thought of as elaborations of the content of liberating insight, until eventually liberation was thought to be effected by an insight into the Four Noble Truths. Things did not stop there: ever more elaborate theories were formulated, such as the account of the Bodhisatta's awakening in the Vinaya,[62] and the notion of insight into the corruptions (*āsava-s*).

In fact, the notion of insight into the *āsava-s*, their origination, cessation and path leading to their cessation shows how complicated and incoherent the theoretical formulations became. As Schmithausen has pointed out, the notion of the origin of the *āsava-s* is absurd: 'According to two other passages,[63] it is Ignorance (*avidyā*); but Ignorance itself is, in our text as well as in the two other passages, enumerated as one of the Cankers!'[64] In other words, the list of *āsava-s* sum up the problem of the human condition. They characterize normal human experience and define what ought to be got rid of in order to experience liberation. But the attempt to work out their first cause makes no sense. The theory that a knowledge of their origin is part of the content of liberating insight is therefore implausible. Thus the scheme of *jhāna-s* became a support for different versions of intellectual insight; meditation became the means for an increasingly elaborate set of mental gymnastics.[65] And in the end some Buddhists dispensed with meditation altogether. This development was probably caused by a combination of factors, such as the polemic attitude to meditation alone, the belief in the efficacy of liberating insight, and the need for the early Buddhists to differentiate themselves and establish their own philosophical identity.

The processes involved in the doctrinal development of early Buddhist thought were no doubt complex. The above sketch is an approximation of what I think was probably the most likely course of events. Even if this sketch is incorrect, I think we are now in a better position to stratify the early literature and recover the historical development of the early doctrinal formulations. We can use the dialogues with Upasīva, Udaya and Posāla as the means to ascribe texts and certain teachings, such as the four *jhāna-s* to the Buddha. Thus I think we can discount the notion that the earliest conception of liberating insight was the insight into the Four Noble Truths. The content of liberating insight in the earliest teaching is unclear. Although I think it must have been something similar to that outlined in the Buddha's dialogue with Posāla, this teaching is obscure. The general principle that ought to be followed is that the simpler, non-intellectual versions of liberating insight are likely to be earliest. On this basis, a simple stratification of the early Buddhist literature is possible. The earliest period is described in the APS, where the Bodhisatta's meditative training under the two teachers and his rejection of their goals leads to the awakening and the teaching of the five disciples. The dialogues with Upasīva, Udaya and Posāla describe in more detail the meditative teachings of the Buddha, as does the scheme of four *jhāna-s*. Somehow, still in the early period before the first schism *c*.60 AB,[66] some Buddhists began to accept the ideology of early Brahminic meditation, probably because they had belonged to schools of Brahminic *yoga*, or been influenced by them beforehand. In the same period there is a tendency towards intellectualism and theories such as the one in which the Four Noble Truths are the content of liberating insight, partly as an extrapolation of the Buddhist critique of meditation alone, and partly in reaction to influence from the meditative mainstream. The content of liberating insight was further elaborated to include the teaching of dependent origination, and in the end some Buddhists dispensed with meditation altogether.

## The identification of authentic teachings of the Buddha

The evidence of Chapters 3 and 4 seems to show that formless meditation was borrowed from an early Brahminic source. But I have claimed more than this. I have claimed that this borrowing goes back to the Buddha himself, who was trained in the meditative practices of early Brahminism and then allowed these practices to be used by his followers. Moreover, I have claimed that this theory allows us to identify authentic teachings of the Buddha in the early literature. What are the criteria upon which this claim is made? The way in which I have attempted to establish authentic teachings of the Buddha is in principle quite simple. It depends in the first place on the deduction of historical facts from the early Buddhist literature. Facts, which I claim can be deduced from the *Ariyapariyesana Sutta*, suggest a particular intellectual background to the Buddha's early life. These facts allow us to form a theory about some aspects of the Buddha's teaching, a theory that can be put to the test by comparing it to some of the teachings contained in the early Buddhist literature. A text that seems to confirm this theory – the *Upasīvamāṇavapucchā* – is thus rooted in historical fact, and is most likely to be historically authentic.

One weakness in this method is that the source of historical facts deduced, the *Ariyapariyesana Sutta*, has nothing to say about what the Buddha taught. In other words, what I claim to be historical facts (in the APS) are not directly related to what I have identified as authentic teachings of the Buddha (in the *Upasīvamāṇavapucchā*). But it must be asked how else historical facts in the early literature could be used to deduce the teachings of the Buddha. The oral nature of early Buddhist literature means that doctrinal formulations, pericopes and even longer tracts (e.g. whole dialogues between the Buddha and a protagonist) could have been moved in and out of different texts at will.[67] This means that a direct relationship between the historical facts contained in a text and any doctrinal formulations adjacent to them cannot be assumed: the latter could easily have been added at a later time, and there is very little means of proving the opposite. Thus, an indirect relationship between historical facts deduced and the end to which they are applied is only to be expected. The important issue concerns how historical facts are used to prove that particular teachings of the Buddha are authentic.

I have attempted to answer this question by hypothesizing aspects of the Buddha's intellectual development from the historical facts deduced. If the Buddha really did have two teachers of meditation, as claimed in the texts, then we can build up a theory, as far as it is possible to do so, about the intellectual milieux of the teachers. In this way the facts deduced can be used to form some idea of the Buddha's intellectual history, which can in turn be used to hypothesize a few aspects of his teachings. Thus the knowledge that the Buddha was exposed to particular idea and responded to them in a certain way, presents us with some criteria that can be used to establish the authenticity of a teaching ascribed to him. Particular instances of the Buddha's teachings recorded in the early texts can be judged in the light of this hypothesis. What if, for example, we identify a dialogue in which the interlocutor of the Buddha professes ideas already shown to have been exactly those already rejected by the Buddha before his teaching career? And what if the Buddha's response to the interlocutor shows that he is well informed about the ideas in question, and in fact rejects them, as he is said to have done before? It would seem that the Buddha, of such a training and intellectual background as we have established him to be, responds exactly as expected to an adherent of his old beliefs. In such a case I would argue that this is no coincidence: provided the historical information on the personality of the Buddha is reliable, the correspondence most probably reveals an authentic teaching of the Buddha. This method of ascribing texts to the Buddha can be summed up as follows:

1. Historical facts about the Buddha's life, particularly those which pertain to his intellectual development, must first be established.
2. The intellectual content of these facts must be elaborated by whatsoever means of investigation are suggested by the facts themselves. This allows us a more detailed understanding of the Buddha's intellectual development.
3. Dialogues in the early literature must be identified in which the ideas discussed are those already shown to have been important in the Buddha's intellectual development. If the Buddha's teaching in the dialogue show that he fully understands these ideas, and responds to them in a way concordant with the theory of his intellectual development, the text is likely to be historically authentic.
4. The authenticity of the text(s) in question is further enhanced if the text contains its own evidence suggesting its antiquity and/or authenticity.

As can be seen, this hypothesis is based on a method of deduction: the deduction, in stage 1, of facts pertaining to the Buddha's life, and then the deduction, in stage 2, of the intellectual background suggested by these facts. On the basis of these deductions I have formed a theory about the intellectual history of the Buddha before his awakening (while he was still a Bodhisatta), i.e. I have supposed that the Buddha was knowledgeable about particular meditative practices and their philosophical background. I have then tried to show that the obscure dialogue between Upasīva and the Buddha portrays the latter in a manner that corresponds exactly to his intellectual background as hypothesized from the historical facts deduced. In other words, the above method has been used to establish some teachings of the Buddha as follows:

1 I have attempted to show that the Bodhisatta studied under Āḷāra Kālāma and Uddaka Rāmaputta, as claimed in the *Ariyapariyesana Sutta*.
2 I claim that the teachers of the Bodhisatta taught a sort of meditation similar to what is recorded in the early verse Upaniṣads and *Mokṣadharma*. This would mean that the Buddha emerged from an early Vedāntic milieu: his rejection of its soteriological goal allows us to form a hypothesis about the sort of ideas he rejected; the implicit non-rejection of its soteriological means – early Brahminic *yoga* – allows us to suppose that such methods were allowed in the Buddha's teachings. Most importantly, we can assume that the Buddha was well versed in the philosophical presuppositions of the early Brahminic thought.
3 The Buddha's answers to Upasīva show that he understands full well the Brahminical presuppositions of Upasīva's questions, i.e. that meditation is an inner concentration in which there should be no awareness of the world and that liberation is achieved at death. Moreover, the Buddha rejects these ideas, a fact that is concordant with his rejection of the goals of his two teachers. This suggests that he was indeed of such a training and intellectual background as suggested by the *Ariyapariyesana Sutta*.
4 The dialogue with Upasīva is of such a nature that it can hardly have been fabricated at a later date. It can be shown that the Buddha and Upasīva are for the most part speaking at cross-purposes, and that this is a demonstration of the Buddha's 'skill-in-means'. The interchange between the two men is so subtle that it is hardly likely to have been invented. Thus, it contains incidental evidence suggesting its historical authenticity, and this helps corroborate the theory elaborated in stages 1 and 2 of the argument.

In short, we can say that the Buddha's teachings to Upasīva are exactly what one would expect if the inferences drawn from the *Ariyapariyesana Sutta* are correct. In this way I have attempted to establish authentic teachings of the Buddha on the basis of historical facts deduced from the early literature. This approach to identifying the authentic teachings of the Buddha is in fact nothing new. The general method of deduction followed here has already been anticipated by T. W. Rhys Davids' argument for the authenticity of the long dialogues of the Buddha contained in the *Dīgha Nikāya*:

> On the hypothesis that [the Buddha] was an historical person, of that training and character he is represented in the Piṭakas to have had, the method is precisely that which it is most likely he would have actually followed.

Rhys Davids' argument, articulated in the abstract, is as follows: the Piṭakas suggest a person of a certain background and character; the background and character of the Buddha that emerge from the Piṭakas allow us to hypothesize the Buddha's manner of teaching; thus, particular instances of the Buddha's teaching that conform to what we have deduced to be his manner of teaching are likely to be historically authentic. This is a simpler formulation of the method followed here. I have attempted to establish the Buddha's 'training and character' by a more sophisticated identification of historical facts, but in substance the two methods differ little. Perhaps one could say that my method is a more rigorous elaboration of Rhys Davids' intuitions – this is, at least, what I am claiming.

# NOTES

## 1 INTRODUCTION

1 Discussions of some of the different doctrinal positions can be found in Bronkhorst (1985 and 1993), Gombrich (1996; in particular, Chapter 4: Retracing an Ancient Debate: How Insight Worsted Concentration in the Pali Canon), Schmithausen (1981) and Wynne (2002). An important study of some of the doctrinal differences concerning meditation is found in La Vallée Poussin (1937).

2 Lamotte (1988: 129–30).

3 This has been pointed out by Lambert Schmithausen (1990: 2): '[M]ethods of higher criticism will, at best, yield a relative sequence (or sequences) of textual layers and/or sequence (or sequences) of stages of doctrinal development. And it may not be easy to safely ascribe any such layer or stage (or layers/stages) to a definite date or even to the Buddha himself without additional criteria.'

4 De Jong (2000: 171).

5 De Jong (2000: 174–75).

6 Keith (1936: 2).

7 D II.137ff.

8 D II.156.1–2: *handa dāni bhikkhave, āmantayāmi vo: vayadhammā saṅkhārā, appamādena sampādethā ti.*

9 Gombrich (1990: 12).

10 This compound has been formed by haplology; its correct form is *viññāṇānañcāyatana*. See Geiger (1994: 57).

11 It seems methodologically preferable to maintain the possibility that some of the early Buddhist literature goes back to the Buddha, whatever one makes of its historicity. As pointed out by Bronkhorst (1993: vii): 'only those who seek may find'.

12 Schopen (1997: 23–24).

13 *Encyclopedia of Religion*, vol. II: 351.

14 Rhys Davids (1903: 174); Wynne (2005: 36).

15 I have recently attempted to substantiate Erich Frauwallner's hypothesis that the arrival of Buddhism in Sri Lanka was due to Buddhist missionaries connected to the court envoys of Aśoka c. 250 BC (Wynne 2005: 48–59; Frauwallner 1956: 1–24).

16 Norman (1978: 36).

17 Some of the most famous Buddhist stories are contained in the Theravādin commentaries, and so they must have reached Sri Lanka before Buddhaghosa. Norman (1997: 140) thinks that they were not inserted into the canon because 'at least the Vinaya- and Sutta-piṭaka had been closed at an earlier date'. Norman

(1997: 140) has also pointed out that certain Pāli works for which a North Indian origin is supposed, such as the *Milindapañha*, the *Peṭakopadesa* and the *Nettipakaraṇa*, contain 'a number of verses and other utterances ascribed to the Buddha and various eminent theras, which are not found in the canon . . . There was no attempt made to add such verses to the canon, even though it would have been a simple matter to insert them into the *Dhammapada* or the *Theragāthā*'. The point that the Pāli tradition received literature from other sects but excluded it from the canon had been made already by Oldenberg (1879: xlviii): 'These additions are by no means altogether unknown to the Singhalese church, but they have been there placed in the Aṭṭhakathās, so that the text of the Tipiṭaka, as preserved in Ceylon, has remained free from them.' See also Rhys Davids (1903: 175): 'It would seem, then, that any change that may have been made in these North Indian books after they had been brought to Ceylon must have been insignificant.'

18 This disproves the notion that correspondences between the Pāli canon and canonical texts of other texts, e.g. Buddhist texts in Sanskrit and Chinese, and the recently discovered Gandhāran manuscripts (see Salomon 1999 and 2003), were produced by a diffusion of texts in the sectarian period. In any case, the notion of a dissemination of texts in the sectarian period is unfeasible, for it would have required organization on a scale unknown in the ancient world.

19 Schopen (1997: 3).

20 Schopen (1997: 3).

21 King (1999: 148).

22 Thus Hallisey (1995: 36) has claimed that the textual construction of an idealized Buddhism by the Orientalists 'reinforced their impression that the Buddhism they saw around them was the result of a long process of decay'. See also Almond (1988: 37): 'And Buddhism, as it could be seen in the East, compared unfavourably with its ideal textual exemplifications contained in the libraries, universities, colonial offices, and missionary societies of the West. It was possible then, as a result of this, to combine a positive evaluation of a Buddhism textually located in the West with a negative evaluation of its Eastern instances.'

23 Said (1995: 11).

24 Reynolds (1976: 38): 'More recently, however, Buddhologists have come to recognize the inadequacy of both the purely mythic and the historical, essentially rationalistic, modes of interpretation, and have reached a rather widely shared consensus concerning a number of basic methodological issues.' He goes on to state that scholars are 'painfully aware that the available texts provide us with very little authentic information concerning the details of [the Buddha's] life' (1976: 39).

25 Tambiah (1992: 3). Tambiah has also disparaged what he calls 'the Pali Text Society mentality' (1984: 7).

26 The method of modern philologists follows that of the Orientalists closely and has been summed up by Tillemans (1995: 269) as follows: 'The important feature of most working philologists' approach is the conviction that by understanding in real depth the Buddhist languages, and the history, institutions, context and preoccupations of an author and his milieu, progress can be made towards understanding that author's thought and better grasping his world.' This approach has been called 'philological positivism' by Cabezón (1995: 245): 'In its philological variety, positivism sees a written text as complete and whole. It maintains that the purpose of scholarly textual investigation – and the use of science as a model for humanistic research here is always implied – is to reconstruct the original text (there is *only one* best reconstruction): to restore it and to contextualize it historically to the point where the author's original intention can be gleaned.' Cabezón contrasts this approach with what he calls 'interpretivism' (1995:

247–48): 'Interpretivists eschew the notion that there is a single achievable text that represents an author's original intention. Every move in the philological process represents an instance of personal choice, and these choices have their consequences.'

27 See p. 2 above.
28 Wynne 2004 (section 7).
29 Wynne 2004 (sections 5–6).
30 *Bhikkhupātimokkha, suddhāpācittiyā* 4 (Vin IV.14.20): *yo pana bhikkhu anusampannaṃ padaso dhammaṃ vāceyya pācittiyaṃ*. On this verse see Wynne (2004: 109).
31 See Wynne (2004: 108–12).
32 Collins (1987: 373).
33 The words 'enstasis' and 'stasis' were used by Mircea Eliade to translate the word *samādhi*, a term which for him indicated 'union, totality; absorption in, complete concentration of mind; conjunction' (1969: 77 n. 79). Although this use of the word 'enstasis' is based on the occurrence of the word *samādhi* in the *Yoga*-sūtras of Patañjali, Eliade generally applied it to meditative states that in the Indian sources are characterized by one-pointed concentration.
34 Although see pp. 27–28 below on Th 415.

## 2 ĀḶĀRA KĀLĀMA AND UDDAKA RĀMAPUTTA

1 This is called the *Pāsarāsi Sutta* in the VRI and Nālandā editions of the Burmese Chaṭṭhasaṅgāyana; the latter notes the name in the Sinhalese edition is the *Ariyapariyesana Sutta*. In the PTS edition of the *Majjhima Nikāya* commentary, the *Papañcasūdanī*, which is based on the Sinhalese, Burmese and Thai printed editions, the text is called the *Pāsarāsi Sutta* (Ps II.163), although its conclusion states that *Ariyapariyesana* is an alternative name (Ps II.193).
2 Bareau (1963: 14–16).
3 Mvu II.118.1ff.
4 SBhV I.97.4ff; Skilling points out that there is a Tibetan translation of this SBhV account, as well as a 'virtually identical' Mūlasarvāstivādin version, preserved in the Tibetan translation of the *Abhiniṣkramaṇa Sūtra* (Skilling 1981–82a: 101).
5 Vin I.7.14ff. According to Bareau (1963: 145–46), this episode also occurs in the Mahīśāsaka and *Dharmaguptaka Vinayas*, and in the Chinese Sarvāstivādin Sūtra that is parallel to the APS (where the same episode occurs at M I.169.33ff.). Elsewhere, the episode occurs in the SBhV at I.130.26ff., but it does not occur in the *Mahāvastu*.
6 La Vallée Poussin (1917: 163): 'Our texts clearly state that several of the Buddhist trances were practised by non-Buddhists, and scholars agree that the Buddhists did actually borrow from the common store of mystical devices.'
7 Zafiropulo (1993: 22–29); his arguments form a detailed argument against Bareau's attempt to show that the training under the two teachers was fabricated. As he comments (1993: 23): 'Ceci dit, nous affirmerons expressément n'avoir pu trouver aucune donnée de critique historique et textuelle nous permettent de traiter les peronnages *d'ĀRĀḌA KĀLĀMA* et *d'UDRAKA RĀMAPUTRA* d'une façon différente de celle qu'on applique généralement au cas des 'Six Maîtres Hérétiques' du *SĀMĀNAPHALA-S.* et autre sources. En effet et d'un commun accord, semble-t-il, l'historicité de tout les six paraît partout accepté.'
8 Vetter (1988: xxii): 'Furthermore, Bareau has shown that the well-known story in which the Buddha is said to have experienced the stages of formless meditation under the guidance of Ārāḍa Kālāma and Udraka Rāmaputra before becoming enlightened has no basis on historical fact.'

9 In spite of this sceptical assessment, all seem to accept La Vallée Poussin's opinion that the meditative states related to the teachers were originally non-Buddhist (see n. 6 of this chapter).
10 Bronkhorst (1993: 86).
11 Bronkhorst (1993: 86). Bareau's view is even more sceptical, for he seems to have thought that the two teachers probably never existed at all (1963: 20–1): 'Personnages absents, morts même avant que leurs noms ne soient cités, ils sont probablement fictifs. Plus tard, on s'interrogea sur ces deux mystérieux personnages et l'on en déduisit aisément qu'ils n'avaient pu être que les maîtres auprès desquels le jeune Bodhisattva avait étudié.'
12 The following comments are based upon Bareau's list of the *Mahīśāsaka Vinaya* contents (1963: 366).
13 Frauwallner (1956: 183).
14 See Bareau (1963: 365). This is noted by Zafiropulo (1993: 23–24).
15 See Zafiropulo (1993: 27) on SBhV I.130.19, I.131.4.
16 Ps II.171.3: *yena Āḷāro Kālāmo ti ettha Āḷāro ti tassa nāmaṃ, dīghapiṅgalo kira so. ten' assa Āḷāro ti nāmaṃ ahosi. Kālāmo ti gottaṃ.* In other words, he was called Āḷāra because he was long and tawny. The commentary on the *Mahāparinibbāna Sutta* repeats this; Sv II.569: *Āḷāro ti tassa nāmaṃ. dīghapiṅgalo kir' eso, ten' assa Āḷāro ti nāmaṃ ahosi.*
17 DPPN, s.v. *kālāma*.
18 A I.188ff. (= *Aṅguttara Nikāya, tikanipāta, mahāvagga* V). The town is called *Kesamutta* in the Burmese edition, which explains the Burmese title of the Sutta (*Kesamutti Sutta*).
19 Mp II.304.25: *Kālāmānaṃ nigamoti Kālāmā nāma khattiyā, tesaṃ nigamo.*
20 Sn 422: *ujuṃ janapado rāja himavantassa passato, dhanaviriyena sampanno Kosalesu niketino.*
21 M II.124.17: *bhagavā pi kosalako, aham pi kosalako.*
22 A I.276.26: *ekaṃ samayaṃ bhagavā Kosalesu cārikaṃ caramāno yena Kapilavatthu tad avasari.*
23 *Bharaṇḍu-Kālāma Sutta*, A I.276 (= *Tikanipāta, Kusināravagga* IV).
24 Mp II.375.3: *purāṇasabrahmacārī ti porāṇako sabrahmacārī. so kira āḷārakālāmakāle tasmiṃ yeva assame ahosi. taṃ sandhāy' evam āha.*
25 Conversely, the *Mahāvastu* claims that Ārāḍa Kālāma lived in Veśālī (Mvu II.118.1); Johnston (1935–36 Part II: 165) states that the *Lalitavistara* also places Arāḍa Kālāma in Vaiśālī. Another possibility is suggested by Aśvaghoṣa, who stated that Arāḍa Kālāma lived in the Vaiśvaṃtara hermitage (Bud XI.73), in the Vindhya mountains (Bud VII.54: *vindhyakoṣṭha*). The southern edge of the Ganges valley is bounded by the Vindhya range, although Gayā, the place of the awakening, seems to be far to the east of the Vindhyas. According to Rhys Davids (1870: 33), the hills surrounding Rājagṛha are 'the most northerly offshoot of the Vindhya mountains'. It may be that Aśvaghoṣa had in mind a location near to Rājagṛha. If so, Aśvaghoṣa's account is probably related to the tradition stated in the *Pabbajā Sutta* (Sn 405ff.), where the Bodhisatta is said to have travelled to Rājagaha and spoken to King Bimbisāra immediately after his renunciation. According to the sequence of events described in this tradition, the Buddha must have visited the two teachers after leaving Rājagṛha. But the historical value of this tradition is questionable, the talk with Bimbisāra being quite clearly legendary. I will argue on pp. 13–14 that there is a reliable tradition locating Uddaka Rāmaputta in Rājagṛha, but I find the incidental evidence of the *Bharaṇḍu-Kālāma Sutta* more convincing than the evidence of Aśvaghoṣa and the *Pabbajā Sutta*.
26 D II.130.1ff. According to Bareau (1970–71: 282), the story is found in all the other sectarian versions of the *Mahāparinibbāna Sutta*.

27 The story shows that Āḷāra Kālāma must have existed, but as Bronkhorst has shown (1993: x), it contradicts the teaching found in the *Indriyabhāvana Sutta*. On the *Indriyabhāvana Sutta*, see p. 122 below. Bareau (1970–71: 295), stating the obvious, suggested that the story is a Buddhist adaptation of a non-Buddhist story that eulogizes the concentrative power of heterodox ascetics.
28 Mp III.164.23: *samaṇe Rāmaputte ti Uddake Rāmaputte.*
29 D II.72.9ff. = A IV.17.11ff. (*Sattakanipāta, anusayavagga*, XX). He also appears in the *Gopaka-Mogallāna Sutta* (M III.7ff.), which is set in Rājagaha. At Vin I.228 (= D II.86.31ff., Ud 87), he and Sunīdha are in charge of the construction of Pāṭaligāma's defences.
30 There is also legendary material in Hiuen Tsang's *Si-Yu-Ki* that places 'Udra Rāmaputtra' in Rājagṛha (Beal 1981, Part II: 139ff.).
31 The following argument is based on points made by Thomas (1927: 63), Ñāṇamoli and Bodhi (1995: 258 n. 303) and Skilling (1981–82a).
32 M I.164.2: *so kho ahaṃ bhikkhave na cirass' eva khippam eva taṃ dhammaṃ pariyāpuṇiṃ. so kho ahaṃ bhikkhave tāvataken' eva oṭṭhapahatamattena lapitalāpanamattena ñāṇavādañ ca theravādañ ca.*
33 M I.164.6: *tassa mayhaṃ bhikkhave etad ahosi: na kho Āḷāro Kālāmo imaṃ dhammaṃ kevalaṃ saddhāmattakena sayaṃ abhiññā sacchikatvā upasampajja viharāmīti pavedeti; addhā Āḷāro Kālāmo imaṃ dhammaṃ jānaṃ passaṃ viharatī ti.*
34 M I.164.10: *atha khv āhaṃ bhikkhave yena Āḷāro Kālāmo ten' upasaṃkamiṃ, upasaṃkamitvā Āḷāraṃ Kālāmaṃ etad avocaṃ: kittāvatā no āvuso Kālāma imaṃ dhammaṃ sayaṃ abhiññā sacchikatvā upasampajja* [VRI: *viharāmīti*] *pavedesī ti? evaṃ vutte bhikkhave Āḷāro Kālāmo ākiñcaññāyatanaṃ pavedesi.*
35 M I.164.22: *yan nūnāhaṃ yaṃ dhammaṃ Āḷāro Kālāmo sayaṃ abhiññā sacchikatvā upasampajja viharāmī ti pavedeti, tassa dhammassa sacchikiriyāya padaheyyan ti? so kho ahaṃ bhikkhave nacirass' eva khippam eva taṃ dhammaṃ sayaṃ abhiññā sacchikatvā upasampajja vihāsiṃ.*
36 M I.165.27: *na kho Rāmo imaṃ dhammaṃ kevalaṃ saddhāmattakena sayaṃ abhiññā sacchikatvā upasampajja viharāmī ti pavedesi, addhā Rāmo imaṃ dhammaṃ jānaṃ passaṃ vihāsī ti.*
37 M I.165.32: *kittāvatā no āvuso Rāmo imaṃ dhammaṃ sayaṃ abhiññā sacchikatvā upasampajja* [VRI: *viharāmīti*] *pavedesī ti?*
38 M I.166.22: *iti yaṃ dhammaṃ Rāmo aññāsi, taṃ tvaṃ dhammaṃ jānāsi; yaṃ tvaṃ dhammaṃ jānāsi, taṃ dhammaṃ Rāmo aññāsi.* In this sentence, *dhammaṃ* indicates the meditative sphere attained by both Rāma and the Buddha. Earlier, the Buddha is said to have mastered the *dhamma* (165.24 = 164.4–5), a statement that seems to refer to an intellectual understanding. Thus the word *dhamma* seems to mean 'doctrine/teaching' as well as meditative object/goal.
39 M I.165.3: *iti yāhaṃ dhammaṃ jānāmi, taṃ tvaṃ dhammaṃ jānāsi; yaṃ tvaṃ dhammaṃ jānāsi, tam ahaṃ dhammaṃ jānāmi.*
40 M I.165.5: *iti yādiso ahaṃ tādiso tuvaṃ, yādiso tuvaṃ tādiso ahaṃ. ehi dāni āvuso ubho va santā imaṃ gaṇaṃ pariharāmā ti. iti kho bhikkhave Āḷāro Kālāmo ācariyo me samāno antevāsiṃ maṃ samānaṃ attano samasamaṃ ṭhapesi, uḷārāya ca maṃ pūjāya pūjesi.*
41 M I.166.24: *iti yādiso Rāmo ahosi tādiso tuvaṃ, yādiso tuvaṃ tādiso Rāmo ahosi. ehi dāni āvuso tvaṃ imaṃ gaṇaṃ pariharā ti. iti kho bhikkhave Uddako Rāmaputto sabrahmacārī me samāno ācariyaṭṭhāne ca maṃ ṭhapesi, uḷārāya ca maṃ pūjāya pūjesi.*
42 See Skilling (1981–82a: 100–02).
43 Skilling (1981–82a: 100).

44 Horner (1954: 209–10), as pointed out by Bodhi and Ñāṇamoli (1995: 1217 n. 303). Jones (1949–56 vol. 18: 117), translator of the *Mahāvastu*, preserves the distinction between Rāma and Rāmaputra, but fails to notice that in the *Mahāvastu* Rāmaputra does not establish the Bodhisattva as an equal to him – it says that he established the Bodhisattva as teacher (Mvu II.120.15: *ācāryasthāne sthāpaye*). Jones translates: 'Udraka Rāmaputra . . . would make me a teacher on an equal footing with himself' (1949–56 vol.18: 117).

45 Bareau (1963: 20): 'Mais le parallélisme avec l'épisode suivant, l'ordre trop logique et le choix trop rationnel des points de doctrine d'Ārāḍa Kālāma et d'Udraka Rāmaputra nous laissent un arrière-goût d'artifice qui nous rend ces récits suspects.'

46 Zafiropulo (1993: 25) does not point out the difference between Rāma and Rāmaputta, but on the stereotyped description of the training under the two teachers he comments: 'Justement cela nous semblerait plutôt un signe d'ancienneté, caractéristique de la transmission orale primitive par récitations psalmodiées.'

47 Zafiropulo (1993: 20): 'En ce cas, les seuls éléments dont on aurait gardé le souvenir seraient le nom du maître du Bodhisattva et la matière du Bodhisattva et la matière de son enseignement.'

48 Norman (1976: 22).

49 Oberlies (2001: 80).

50 Norman (1970: 135–36) notes a few cases where the Aśokan edicts have a hyper-form with -p- instead of -v-, which shows that some scribes knew that the dialect of the original edicts occasionally had intervocalic -v- instead of -p- (e.g. *apaladhiyenā* at Rūpnāth, Minor Rock Edict I, line 4 = Hultzsch p. 167). If this dialect change was current in the Buddha's time, it could mean that the form *hupeyya* was a hyper-translation of *huveyya* by early Buddhists who knew that the Magadhan Prakrit underlying some of the early Buddhist literature had voiced -v- < -p-. It seems unlikely, however, that the form *huveyya* would not have been recognized and changed to *bhaveyya*. On the other hand, Geiger (1994: 30, §39.6) has listed a number of cases in Pāli where the voiced consonants *b* and *v* are represented by unvoiced *p*, and he explains that these are due to dialectic variation. This would appear to explain the form *hupeyya*, and shows that in some Magadhan dialects in the Buddha's lifetime intervocalic -v- (and -b-) was sporadically unvoiced.

51 M I.165.5: *iti yādiso ahaṃ tādiso tuvaṃ, yādiso tuvaṃ tādiso ahaṃ*. M I.166.24: *iti yādiso Rāmo ahosi tādiso tuvaṃ, yādiso tuvaṃ tādiso Rāmo ahosi*. The same anomaly is repeated in the other biographical Suttas of the *Majjhima Nikāya* (the MSS *et al*: the *Mahā-Saccaka Sutta*, the *Bodhirājakumāra Sutta* and the *Saṅgārava Sutta*), which all include verbatim accounts of the training under the two teachers.

52 Norman (1970: 140): 'It may be deduced that UPkt [the original Prakrit of the Aśokan edicts] usually resolved consonant groups by the evolution of an epenthetic vowel.' This says nothing about the dialect in use in Magadha in the Buddha's time, although it is a reasonable assumption that *svarabhakti* was a common feature of Māgadhī even then.

53 A variant *tvaṃ* is recorded in Trenckner's critical notes. Trenckner's edition is based on only two MS, one Sinhalese and one Burmese. Although the manuscript (M I. 544.8) evidence is insufficient (see MI. 544.8), *tuvaṃ* seems preferable on the principle of *lectio potior difficilior*.

54 Taisho 26. Bareau (1963: 14–15), Chau (1991: 153ff.).

55 If the Sarvāstivādins of Kaśmīra/Gandhāra and the Theravādins of Laṅkā originated with the missions said to have taken place in Aśokan times, the

similarities between the APS and its Chinese Sarvāstivādin parallel must predate c. 250 BC. The theory of the Buddhist missions was formulated in some detail by Frauwallner (1956: 1–23). A more recent reconsideration and defence of this theory is found in Wynne 2005 (section 5). Similar accounts of the Buddha's austerities are found in the extant literature of the different Buddhist sects (see Dutoit: 1905). The essential points in this account must therefore be pre-sectarian, like the account of the visits to the two teachers in the APS.

56 M I.240.29. In the *Mahāvastu* and *Lalitavistara*, the similes occur to the Bodhisattva when he is on Mount Gayāśīrṣa, after which he travels to Uruvilvā to practise breathless meditation and emaciation (Skilling 1981–82b: 109).

57 Plus I believe that the internal evidence of the Pāli canon shows that attempts were made to ensure a more or less verbatim oral transmission of early Buddhist literature (Wynne: 2004). There is no evidence for a relatively free oral transmisison, which would have been necessary for the random omission of various textual strata.

58 M I.21.33ff., M I.117.6ff.

59 M I.167.3: *tassa mayhaṃ bhikkhave etad ahosi: ramaṇīyo vata bho bhūmibhāgo pāsādiko ca vanasaṇḍo, nadī ca sandati setakā sūpatitthā ramaṇīyā, samantā ca gocaragāmo, alaṃ vat' idaṃ kulaputtassa padhānatthikassa padhānāyā ti. so kho ahaṃ bhikkhave tatth' eva nisīdiṃ: alaṃ idaṃ padhānāyā ti. so kho ahaṃ bhikkhave attanā jātidhammo samāno jātidhamme ādīnavaṃ viditvā ajātaṃ anuttaraṃ yogakkhemaṃ nibbānaṃ pariyesamāno ajātaṃ anuttaraṃ yogakkhemaṃ nibbānaṃ ajjhagamaṃ*. This is also the language used to describe how the Buddha's first five disciples attained liberation in the APS (M I.173.7). This must mean that the authors of the APS considered the awakening of the five disciples to be identical to the Buddha's.

60 *ajaraṃ, abyādhiṃ, amataṃ, asokaṃ, asaṅkiliṭṭhaṃ*.

61 Chau (1991: 153) translates it as follows: 'I sought the diseaseless, the supreme peacefulness, Nirvāṇa . . . and I obtained the ageless, deathless, griefless, despairless, blemishless, the supreme peacefulness, Nirvāṇa.' Assuming Chau's translation is correct, most of the adjectives qualifying Nirvāṇa in this Chinese text correspond to the ones in the equivalent Pāli Sutta ('ageless' = *ajaraṃ*, 'deathless' = *amataṃ*, 'griefless' = *asokaṃ*, 'blemishless' = *asaṅkiliṭṭhaṃ*).

62 M I.163.18: *yan nūnāhaṃ attanā jātidhammo (jarādhammo . . . byādhidhammo . . . maraṇadhammo . . . sokadhammo . . . saṅkilesadhammo) samāno, jātidhamme (jarādhamme . . . byādhidhamme . . . maraṇadhamme . . . sokadhamme . . . saṅkilesadhamme) ādīnavaṃ viditvā ajātaṃ (ajaraṃ . . . abyādhiṃ . . . amataṃ . . . asokaṃ . . . asaṅkiliṭṭhaṃ) anuttaraṃ yogakkhemaṃ nibbānaṃ pariyeseyyaṃ?* Chau (1991: 153): 'I am liable to disease . . . old age, death, sorrow, grief, despair, blemishes, why should I foolishly seek what is liable to old-age. . . blemishes? What now if I seek the diseaseless . . . the ageless, deathless, griefless, despairless, blemishless, the Supreme peacefulness, Nirvāṇa.'

63 M I.249.4ff: *so evaṃ samāhite parisuddhe pariyodāte anaṅgaṇe vigatūpakkilese mudubhūte kammaniye ṭhite ānejjappatte āsavānaṃ khayañāṇāya cittaṃ abhininnāmesiṃ. so idaṃ dukkhan ti yathābhūtaṃ abbhaññāsiṃ ayaṃ dukkhasamudayo ti yathābhūtaṃ abbhaññāsiṃ ayaṃ dukkhanirodho ti yathābhūtaṃ abbhaññāsiṃ ayaṃ dukkhanirodhagāminī paṭipadā ti yathābhūtaṃ abbhaññāsiṃ. ime āsavā ti yathābhūtaṃ abbhaññāsiṃ ayaṃ āsavasamudayo ti yathābhūtaṃ abbhaññāsiṃ ayaṃ āsavanirodho ti yathābhūtaṃ abbhaññāsiṃ ayaṃ āsavanirodhagāminī paṭipadā ti yathābhūtaṃ abbhaññāsiṃ. tassa me evaṃ jānato evaṃ passato kāmāsavā pi cittaṃ vimuccittha bhavāsavā pi cittaṃ vimuccittha avijjāsavā pi cittaṃ vimuccittha. vimuttasmiṃ vimuttam iti ñāṇaṃ*

*ahosi: khīṇā jāti vusitaṃ brahmacariyaṃ kataṃ karaṇīyaṃ nāparaṃ itthattāyā ti abbhaññāsiṃ.*

64 M I.167.9ff: *so kho ahaṃ bhikkhave attanā jātidhammo samāno jātidhamme ādīnavaṃ viditvā ajātaṃ anuttaraṃ yogakkhemaṃ nibbānaṃ pariyesamāno ajātaṃ anuttaraṃ yogakkhemaṃ nibbānaṃ ajjhagamaṃ. . . ñāṇañ ca pana me dassanaṃ udapādi: akuppā me vimutti, ayam antimā jāti, natthi dāni punabbhavo ti.*

65 Mvu II.133.5–12.

66 It is found in a few more places in the Suttapiṭaka: S I.46.13, S II.278.19, A I.162.35 = A III.214.19, It 104.17, Sn 204, Th 1165, Thī 113.

67 The *Pariyesati Sutta* (AN, *catukka-nipāta* 252, *abhiññāvagga*; A II.247.17) is similar to the APS description, but it is not a description of the attainment of liberation. It seems to have been abstracted from the APS to form a text in its own right.

68 M I.167.27: *ñāṇañ ca pana me dassanaṃ udapādi: akuppā me vimutti, ayam antimā jāti, n'atthi dāni punabbhavo ti.* The pericope that occurs in the parallel Sarvāstivādin Sūtra, extant in Chinese, is translated by Bareau as follows: 'Fixées sont les choses (*dharma*) de la classe de la Voie (*mārga*), mes naissances sont épuisées, ma conduite pure (*brahmacarya*) est établie, ma tâche est accomplie, je ne recevrai plus d'autre existence' (Bareau 1963: 72). This seems to be an expanded version of the Pāli pericope.

69 Apart from its application to the description of the five disciples' liberation in the APS (M I. 173.18). The pericope is also found at M III.162.24; Be reads *cetovimutti* for *vimutti*. The pericope appears at the following places but with *cetovimutti* for *vimutti*: S II.171.1, S II.172.11, S III.28.31, S III.29.29, S IV.8.1, S IV.8.25, *S IV.9.30, S IV.10.21, S V.204.11, S V.206.6*, S V.423.10 (= Vin I.11.29); *A.I.259.11/31*, A.IV.56.16, A IV.305.4, A IV.448.18. For each reference (apart from those in italics) there are MS variants *vimutti* for *cetovimutti*. The failure to note this variant is probably due to errors made by the PTS editors. Be reads *vimutti* in all places except M III.162.24, A IV.305.4, A IV.448.18. As stated above, the only persons to whom the pericope is applied apart from the Bodhisatta are the five *bhikkhus* who are the first disciples of the Buddha in the APS. This indicates that this episode in the APS is probably as old as the episode describing the Buddha's liberation.

70 In all the references in the note above the pericope occurs in autobiographical Suttas. Each Sutta follows the same pattern, the only difference being the content of the Bodhisatta's liberating insight. All these references have no biographical importance; their uses of the simple liberation pericope are clearly secondary developments. The other most important occurrence of the pericope is in the *Dhammacakkappavattana Sutta* (S V.423.10 = Vin I.11.29). On the content of the Buddha's enlightenment in this Sutta, Schmithausen has commented: 'It is not likely that this rather sophisticated and schematic account of the Enlightenment of the Buddha is the original one.' (Schmithausen 1981: 203).

71 Thus the pericope is simply omitted at S II.173.18ff., S IV.12.1ff., S IV.13.7ff., A IV.260.14ff.

72 Although given the fact that this pericope is applied to the five disciples in the APS, at first the formula cannot have been thought to be special. That the pericope came to be viewed as a special formula to be applied to the Buddha alone is supported by the autobiographical accounts in the Theravādin Vinaya and the *Mahāvastu*. The former, in the account of the awakening at Vin I.11.29, uses the simple liberation pericope, but does not apply it to the liberation of the five

*bhikkhus*. The latter event is described at Vin I.14.34, where it is said that the disciples' minds were released from the corruptions as they listened to the discourse on not-self (*imasmiñ ca pana veyyākaraṇasmiṃ bhaññamāne pañcavaggiyānaṃ bhikkhūnaṃ anupādāya āsavehi cittāni vimucciṃsu*). Compared to description of the five *bhikkhus*' liberation in the APS, where the simple liberation pericope is applied to them (see p. 26 n. 69), the biography in the Vinaya appears to be the later account: there is every reason to differentiate the five disciples' liberation from the Buddha's (by making the former inferior in order to elevate the status of the Buddha), but little reason to change the fact that the two were originally described in different terms. In the *Mahāvastu*, the simple liberation pericope is slightly different: *jñānaṃ ca me udapādi akopyā ca me cetovimuktiḥ prajñāvimuktiḥ sākṣīkṛtā* (Mvu III.333.16). This is obviously a re-working of a pericope similar to the one found in the Suttapiṭaka. And it is different from the pericope applied to five *bhikṣu-s* at Mvu III.337.3, which mirrors the account of their liberation found in the Theravādin Vinaya: *imasmiṃ ca punar vyākaraṇe bhāṣyamāṇe āyuṣmata Ājñātakauṇḍinyasyānupādāyāśravebhyaś cittaṃ vimuktaṃ, caturṇāṃ ca bhikṣūṇāṃ virajaṃ vigatamalaṃ dharmeṣu dharmacakṣu viśuddhaṃ*. The *Mahāvastu* supports the idea that after the composition of the pre-sectarian version of the APS, the simple liberation pericope came to be applied to the Buddha alone. The SBhV does not have the simple liberation pericope at I.136.7, but there is little doubt that its account is later than the Pāli and Mahāsāṅghika accounts. The *Lalitavistara* has a version of the simple liberation pericope applied to the Buddha at I.418.16 (it is almost identical to the one in the *Mahāvastu*), but it does include any account of the liberation of the five *bhikṣus*.

73 This is the view of Bareau (1963: 72–74).

74 Bronkhorst (2000: 68) has stated that the description of the training under Āḷāra Kālāma and Uddaka Rāmaputta was merely anti-Jain propaganda: 'Wir haben gesehen, wie eine angeblich autobiographische Darstellung des Buddha benutzt wurde, um die Nutzlosigkeit der selbstquälerischen Pratiken der Jainas zu beweisen. Man darf also vermuten, daß auch die Beschreibungen der Schṃlerschaft bei *Ārāḍa Kālāma* und bei *Udraka*, dem Sohne des *Rāma*, propagandistische Elemente enthalten könnten. Dies ist tatsächlich der Fall.'

75 E.g. M I.165.10: *nāyaṃ dhammo nibbidāya na virāgāya na nirodhāya na upasamāya na abhiññāya na sambodhāya na nibbānāya saṃvattati, yāvad eva ākiñcaññāyatanūpapattiyā ti.*

76 M I.169.34: *ayaṃ kho Āḷāro Kālāmo paṇḍito viyatto medhāvī dīgharattaṃ apparajjhakajātiko, yan nūnāhaṃ Āḷārassa Kālāmassa paṭhamaṃ dhammaṃ deseyyaṃ? so imaṃ dhammaṃ khippam eva ājānissatī ti.*

77 M I.246.20: *ye kho keci atītam addhānaṃ samaṇā vā brāhmaṇā vā opakkamikā dukkhā tippā kaṭukā vedanā vedayiṃsu, etāvaparamaṃ na-y-ito bhiyyo. ye pi hi keci anāgatam addhānaṃ samaṇā vā brāhmaṇā vā opakkamikā dukkhā tippā kaṭukā vedanā vedayissanti, etāvaparamaṃ na-y-ito bhiyyo. ye pi hi keci etarahi samaṇā vā brāhmaṇā vā opakkamikā dukkhā tippā kaṭukā vedanā vediyanti, etāvaparamaṃ na-y-ito bhiyyo. na kho panāhaṃ imāya kaṭukāya dukkarakārikāya adhigacchāmi uttariṃ manussadhammā alamariyañāṇadassanavisesaṃ. siyā nu kho añño maggo bodhāyā ti*? Almost exactly the same passage occurs in the *Mahāvastu* (Mvu II.130.7–14).

78 E.g. M I.441.7ff., S IV.301.11ff., A III.15ff.

79 Hence, in the MSS *et al.*, immediately after contemplating that the ascetic practices got him nowhere, the Bodhisatta remembers attaining the first *jhāna* as a boy (M I.246.30), and wonders if this is the way to liberation (M I.246.35: *siyā nu kho eso maggo bodhāya*).

80 The concept of 'inclusivism' was originally formulated by Paul Hacker. On this concept, see Oberhammer (1983), Olivelle (1986) and Halbfass (1988: 403–18; 1995: 244–45).
81 M I.165.13/166.32: *so kho ahaṃ bhikkhave taṃ dhammaṃ analaṅkaritvā tasmā dhammā nibbijjāpakkamiṃ.*
82 Schmithausen (1981: 200).
83 Schmithausen (1981: 200).
84 See p. 14 n. 34.
85 Bareau (1963: 14–15, 24–25).
86 Bud XII.63–65.
87 K. R. Norman (1990: 26) has drawn the opposite conclusion: 'We may deduce from this that the concept of the attainment of *nibbāna* existed, even though the Buddha (while a Bodhisatta), and his teachers, were unable to achieve it.'
88 Bareau (1963: 24).
89 Bareau (1963: 25): 'le recueillement sans perception ni absence de perception.'
90 Bud XII.85: *saṃjñāsaṃjñitvayor doṣaṃ jñātvā hi munir Udrakaḥ, ākiṃcayāt paraṃ lebhe 'saṃjñāsaṃjñātmikāṃ gatim.*
91 Johnston (1935–36, Part II: xxxv).
92 See Chapter 5 on the *Upasīvamāṇavapucchā.*

## 3 FORMLESS MEDITATION AND EARLY BRAHMINISM

1 On this verse, see below p. 68.
2 See also: Mbh XII.232.13, Mbh XII.238.12, Mbh XII.304.11.
3 As pointed out by Hopkins (1901b: 35).
4 GDhp 275 (Brough 2001: 163): *yo du upadida kodhu radha bhada va dhara'i, tam aho saradi bromi rasviggaha idara jaṇa.*
5 See p. 5 n. 15.
6 Mbh III.202.20–21ab: *ṣaṇṇām ātmani yuktānām indriyāṇām pramāthinām, yo dhīro dhārayed raśmīn sa syāt paramasārathiḥ. indriyāṇāṃ prasṛṣṭānāṃ hayānām iva vartmasu . . .* I follow Hopkins (1901b: 35) in reading *yuktā-* instead of *nityā-* in *pāda* 20a. The image of the charioteer is used in a more complex form to illustrate the yogic teaching at KaU III.3–9. According to Hopkins (1901a: 354; see p. 38 n. 53), the image of the yoked chariot ready for battle was common in early yogic circles. For other chariot metaphors, see ŚU II.9 and Mbh XII.289.36.
7 See also Mbh XII.46.2ab: *caturthaṃ dhyānamārgaṃ tvam ālambya puruṣottama.*
8 Mbh XII.188.15: *vicāraś ca vitarkaś ca vivekaś copajāyate, muneḥ samādadhānasya prathamaṃ dhyānam āditaḥ.*
9 For the classical Suttapiṭaka description of the four *jhāna-s*, see D I.73.20.
10 A V.7.19 (*Dasakanipāta* VI, *ānisaṃsavagga*): *siyā Ānanda bhikkhuno tathārūpo samādhipaṭilābho yathā neva paṭhaviyaṃ paṭhavisaññī assa, na āpasmiṃ āposaññī assa, na tejasmiṃ tejosaññī assa, na vāyasmiṃ vāyosaññī assa, na ākāsānañcāyatane ākāsānañcāyatanasaññī assa, na viññāṇañcāyatane viññāṇañcāyatanasaññī assa, na ākiñcaññāyatane ākiñcaññāyatanasaññī assa, na nevasaññānāsaññāyatane nevasaññānāsaññāyatanasaññī assa, na idhaloke idhalokasaññī assa, na paraloke paralokasaññī assa, saññī ca pana assā ti.*
11 D I.55.15ff. (the view of Ajita Kesakambalī), III.264.12, III.287.12; M I.287.14, I.401.32, III.22.13, III.52.13, III.71.27; S III.206.29, IV.348.24, IV.351.16, IV.355.12; A I.269.1, IV.226.14, V.265.22, V.284.7.
12 A V.8.7: *idh' Ānanda bhikkhu evaṃsaññī hoti: etaṃ santaṃ etaṃ paṇītaṃ yadidaṃ sabbasaṅkhārasamatho sabbūpadhipaṭinissaggo taṅhakkhayo virāgo nirodho nibbānan ti.*

13 The pericope is the object of a *bhikkhu's* concentration at M I.436.34 (*Mahā-Māluṅkya Sutta* =A IV.423.21); A I.133.1, A V.110.23. At V.319.15, V.320.21, V.322.15, V.354.9, V.355.27, V.357.1, V.358.14 it is used in exactly the same context as it is in the *Samādhi Sutta* (A V.8.7), but in a list of eleven rather than ten objects beginning with the four elements and four formless spheres.
14 D II.36.8; M I.167.36 (=M II.93); S I.136.15, V.226.6; A II.118.7, III.164.2.
15 AN V, *Dasakanipāta* VII, *ānisaṃsavagga* (A V.8.23).
16 A V.9.24: *bhavanirodho nibbānaṃ bhavanirodho nibbānan ti.* In the *Kosambi Sutta* (S, *Nidāna Saṃyutta VII, mahāvagga*), at S II.117.14, *bhavanirodho nibbānan ti* defines the object of liberating insight for Musīla, but not for Nārada. On this Sutta see p. 118 n. 33.
17 From 'this is calm, this is supreme' to 'the cessation of becoming is *nibbāna*'.
18 D III.135.9; S III.203.12ff., III.213.30ff., III.214.20, III.216.20, IV.73.4; A II.23.30, II.25.21; Ud 8.6; It 121.17. The sequence *diññhaṃ . . . sutaṃ . . . mutaṃ . . . viññātaṃ* . . . also occurs at M I.3.15ff., but defines objects of awareness for the unlearned normal person (*assutavā puthujjano*): each item does not indicate an object of meditation. See also Sn 790, 793, 797, 798, 887, 901, 914, 1083.
19 Although the final pericope is always *etaṃ santaṃ . . .;* see the references to A V in n. 13.
20 A V.318.21: *yam p'idaṃ diṭṭhaṃ sutaṃ mutaṃ viññātaṃ pattaṃ pariyesitaṃ anuvicaritaṃ manasā.*
21 Bronkhorst (1993: 92) has a different opinion; he thinks that these items 'can, but should not be used as objects of meditation'. I cannot think of any reason why they 'should not be used as objects of meditation', when in other places most of them do appear as objects of meditation.
22 D III.268.20: *dasa kasiṇāyatanāni: pathavīkasiṇam eko sañjānāti, uddhaṃ adho tiriyaṃ advayaṃ appamāṇaṃ. āpokasiṇam eko sañjānāti . . .pe . . . tejokasiṇam eko sañjānāti . . . vāyokasiṇam eko sañjānāti . . . nīlakasiṇam eko sañjānāti . . . pītakasiṇam eko sañjānāti . . . lohitakasiṇam eko sañjānāti . . . odātakasiṇam eko sañjānāti . . . ākāsakasiṇam eko sañjānāti . . . viññāṇakasiṇam eko sañjānāti, uddhaṃ adho tiriyaṃ advayaṃ appamāṇaṃ.* Identical descriptions of the *kasiṇāyatana-s* are found at D III.290.16; M II.14.3; A I.41.14.
23 It also refers to Skt *kārtsna* and *kārtsnya* (s.v.).
24 DOP s.v. *kasiṇa.*
25 DOP s.v. *kasiṇāyatana.*
26 PED s.v. *kasiṇa*. PED also derives *kasiṇa* from Skt *kṛtsna*, and gives an adjectival meaning corresponding to DOP 1.
27 CPD s.v. *kasiṇa*. CPD also gives an adjectival meaning corresponding to DOP 1.
28 In MMW and BR, the abstract form *kārtsnya* is also given; this is the only abstract form of *kṛtsna* given in Apte (s.v.). We should probably derive *kasiṇa* from *kārtsna*, for the Middle Indian derivation of *kārtsnya* would probably have had the cerebralized conjunct *ññ*, i.e. giving something like *kasiñña*. Oberlies (2001: 105) and Geiger (1994: 50) both derive *kasiṇa* from *kṛtsna*, the former via **kaṣṇa*.
29 Apart from A I.41.14 where they are simply listed without any introduction, and the attainment is described as *pathavīkasiṇaṃ bhāveti* . . . etc.
30 Edited by T. W. Rhys Davids, London: PTS.
31 Eliade (1969: 194) refers to Woodward's translation *Manual of a Mystic* (p. 145ff.) on the assumption that it was composed during the sixteenth and seventeenth centuries. He also describes the various colours associated with meditation on each element (1969: 195–96).
32 Goudriaan (1978: 194–95); also see Eliade (1969: 130–31).

33 D II.110.5ff., D III.260.8ff., M II.14.1ff., A IV.305.1ff., A V.61.3ff.

34 BU IV.5.13: *sa yathā saindhavaghano 'nantaro 'bāhyaḥ kṛtsno rasaghana eva, evaṃ vā are 'yam ātmānantaro 'bāhyaḥ kṛtsnaḥ prajñānaghana eva.*

35 e.g. BU I.40: *kulaṃ kṛtsam*, the whole family; IV.18: *kṛtsnakarmakṛt*, the agent of every action; IX.8: *bhūtagrāmam imaṃ kṛtsnam*, this entire collection of beings.

36 BhG VII.6: *kṛtsnasya jagataḥ*; X.42: *idaṃ kṛtsnam*; XI.7, 13: *ekasthaṃ jagat kṛtsnaṃ*; XIII.33: *kṛtsnaṃ lokam imaṃ; . . . kṣetraṃ kṛtsnaṃ*. At BhG III.29cd, *kṛtsna* appears to mean something like 'perfect' (*tān akṛtsnavido mandān kṛtsnavin na vicālayet*).

37 BhG VII.29: *brahma . . . kṛtsnam.*

38 Mbh XII.305.21: *gacchet prāpyākṣayaṃ kṛtsnam ajanma śivam avyayam, śāśvataṃ sthānam acalam duṣprāpam akṛtātmabhiḥ*; 'He should go having attained the imperishable, whole, unborn, auspicious, intransient, perpetual place which is unmoving, hard to attain by normal people.'

39 Mbh XII.211.6, 299.4: *mahīṃ kṛtsnāṃ;* 289.20: *kṛtsnāṃ mahīm*; 289.21: *kṛtsnaṃ jagat*; 290.5: *kṛtsnān paiśācān viṣayāṃs*; 291.19: *kṛtsnaṃ trailokyam*; 302.1: *kṛtsnasya jagatas*; 328.52: *jagat kṛtsnaṃ;* 330.51: *kṛtsnā lokāḥ;* 335.66: *lokān kṛtsnān.*

40 Goudriaan (1978: 180) on Mbh III.148.10–39.

41 Goudriaan (1978: 182).

42 M I.185.12.

43 D III.247.19, M III.239.17, A I.176.1.

44 M III.62.21, S III.231.4, S III.234.12.

45 Five *dhātu-s* are mentioned at M I.421–23; six are listed at M III.31.15, M III.240.19ff., M III.260.19, S II.248.21, S II.251.17, S III.227.19.

46 M I.421.33: *yā c' eva kho pana ajjhattikā paṭhavīdhātu yā ca bāhirā paṭhavīdhātu, paṭhavīdhātur ev' esā. taṃ: n' etaṃ mama, n' eso 'ham asmi, na m' eso attā ti. evam etaṃ yathābhūtaṃ sammappaññāya daṭṭhabbaṃ. evam etaṃ yathābhūtaṃ sammappaññāya disvā paṭhavīdhātuyā nibbindati, paṭhavīdhātuyā cittaṃ virājeti.*

47 TU II.1: *tasmād vā etasmād ātmana ākāśaḥ saṃbhūtaḥ, ākāśād vāyuḥ, vāyor agniḥ, agner āpaḥ, adbhyaḥ pṛthivī.* On Mbh XII.195 and Mbh XII.224, see pp. 37–38 and p. 64–65.

48 See pp. 114–115: the only evidence is the non-existent *Ṣaḍdhātu Sūtra* and a Sūtra fragment inYaśomitra's *Sphuṭārthāvyākhyā* on *Abhidharmakośabhāṣya* I.5.

49 Mbh XII.247.13d: *bhūtaprabhāvād bhava śāntabuddhiḥ.*

50 Mbh XII.195.1: *akṣarāt khaṃ tato vāyur vāyor jyotis tato jalam, jalāt prasūtā jagatī jagatyāṃ jāyate jagat.*

51 Mbh XII.195.2–3: *ime śarīrair jalam eva gatvā jalāc ca tejaḥ pavano 'ntarikṣam, khād vai nivartanti na bhāvinas te ye bhāvinas te param āpnuvanti* (2). *noṣṇaṃ na śītaṃ mṛdu nāpi tīkṣṇaṃ nāmlaṃ kaṣāyaṃ madhuraṃ na tiktam, na śabdavan nāpi ca gandhavat tan na rūpavat paramasvabhāvam* (3).

52 Mbh XII.195.4–5: *sparśaṃ tanur veda rasaṃ tu jihvā ghrāṇaṃ ca gandhāñ śravaṇe ca śabdān, rūpāṇi cakṣur na ca tatparaṃ yad gṛhṇanty anadhyātmavido manuṣyāḥ* (4). *nivartayitvā rasanaṃ rasebhyo ghrāṇaṃ ca gandhāc chravaṇe ca śabdāt, sparśāt tanuṃ rūpaguṇāt tu cakṣus tataḥ paraṃ paśyati svaṃ svabhāvam* (5).

53 These words are explained by Hopkins (1901a: 354) as follows: 'we must remember the position of the chariot-guards, *pṛṣṭhagopas* and *pārśvagopas*, or as they are called in a similar description of another allegorical war-car, viii.34.45, *pṛṣṭharakṣas* and *paripārśvacaras*. For the van and rear and flank are technically known (adverbially) as *purataḥ*, *pṛṣthe*, and *pārśvayoḥ* . . . while *yoga*, in camp parlance, is hitching up or harnessing up.' See also v. 12 (n. 56), which relates the practice of *yoga* to the yoking of a chariot.

54 Mbh XII.228.13–15: *sapta yo dhāraṇāḥ kṛtsnā vāgyataḥ pratipadyate, pṛṣṭhataḥ pārśvataś cānyā yāvatyas tāḥ pradhāraṇāḥ* (13). *kramaśaḥ pārthivaṃ yac ca vāyavyaṃ khaṃ tathā payaḥ, jyotiṣo yat tad aiśvaryam ahaṃkārasya buddhitaḥ* (14). *avyaktasya tathaiśvaryaṃ kramaśaḥ pratipadyate, vikramāś cāpi yasyaite tathā yuṅkte sa yogataḥ* (15).

55 This seems to be the view of Barnes (1976: 67): 'Thus it would seem that an evolutionary doctrine of world-creation in which all is derived from the first principle and must return thither is linked with the practices of *Yoga* . . . The *Yoga*-practices are themselves arranged step-wise according to the spheres or entities in evolution, and the yogin himself goes through the series and enters into them at the different stages. He is thus able to recapitulate the creation process in the reverse order and so enter into Brahmā.'

56 Mbh XII.228.12: *atha saṃtvaramāṇasya ratham etaṃ yuyukṣataḥ, akṣaraṃ gantumanaso vidhiṃ vakṣyāmi śīghragam.*

57 Mbh XII.197.2–3, 8–12, 17–18: *yathāmbhasi prasanne tu rūpaṃ paśyati cakṣuṣā, tadvat prasannendriyavāñ jñeyaṃ jñānena paśyati* (2). *sa eva lulite tasmin yathā rūpaṃ na paśyati, tathendriyākulībhāve jñeyaṃ jñāne na paśyati* (3). *jñānam utpadyate puṃsāṃ kṣayāt pāpasya karmaṇaḥ, athādarśatalaprakhye paśyaty ātmānam ātmani* (8). *prasṛtair indriyair dukkhī tair eva niyataiḥ sukhī, tasmād indriyarūpebhyo yacched ātmānam ātmanā* (9). *indriyebhyo manaḥ pūrvaṃ buddhiḥ paratarā tataḥ, buddheḥ parataraṃ jñānaṃ jñānāt parataraṃ param* (10). *avyaktāt prasṛtaṃ jñānaṃ tato buddhis tato manaḥ, manaḥ śrotrādibhir yuktaṃ śabdādīn sādhu paśyati* (11). *yas tāṃs tyajati śabdādīn sarvāś ca vyaktayas tathā, vimuñcaty ākṛtigrāmāṃs tān muktvāmṛtam aśnute* (12). *buddhiḥ karmaguṇair hīnā yadā manasi vartate, tadā saṃpadyate brahma tatraiva pralayaṃ gatam* (17). *asparśanam aśṛṇvānam anāsvādam adarśanam, aghrāṇam avitarkaṃ ca sattvaṃ praviśate param* (18).

58 Mbh XII.199.25: *jñānena nirmalīkṛtya buddhiṃ buddhyā tathā manaḥ, manasā cendriyagrāmam anantaṃ pratipadyate.*

59 The feminine noun *prakṛti* is in the masculine locative case.

60 Mbh XII.304.11–16: *niśāyāḥ prathame yāme codanā dvādaśa smṛtāḥ, madhye suptvā pare yāme dvādaśaiva tu codanāḥ* (11). *tad evam upaśāntena dāntenaikāntaśīlinā, ātmārāmeṇa buddhena yoktavyo 'tmā na saṃśayaḥ* (12). *pañcānām indriyāṇāṃ tu doṣān ākṣipya pañcadhā, śabdaṃ sparśaṃ tathā rūpaṃ rasaṃ gandhaṃ tathaiva ca* (13). *pratibhām apavargaṃ ca pratisaṃhṛtya maithila, indriyagrāmam akhilam manasy abhiniveśya ha* (14). *manas tathaivāhaṃkāre pratiṣṭhāpya narādhipa, ahaṃkāraṃ tathā buddhau buddhiṃ ca prakṛtāv api* (15). *evaṃ hi parisaṃkhyāya tato dhyāyeta kevalam, virajaskam alaṃ nityam anantaṃ śuddham avraṇam* (16).

61 Brereton (1990: 121–22).

62 This is a reformulation of an argument made by Bronkhorst (1993: ix): 'An element that is (i) rejected at some places in the Buddhist texts, (ii) accepted at others, and (iii) known to fit at least some non-Buddhist religious movements of the time, such an element is very likely to be a non-authentic intrusion into the Buddhist texts.' Bronkhorst (1993: 92) has noted the similarity between the meditative objects at Mbh XII.228.113–115 and A V.324 and comments: 'It remains none the less possible that both these lists – the one from the Mahābhārata and the one from the *Aṅguttara Nikāya* – derive from a common ancestor.' I fully agree with this statement, but I hope the logic of my reasoning has led to the correct conclusion that the common ancestor originated in Brahminic circles. There is in fact no other likely source of the different meditation schemes.

63 MāU 7: *nāntaḥprajñaṃ na bahiḥprajñaṃ nobhayataḥprajñaṃ na prajñānaghanaṃ na prajñaṃ nāprajñam. adṛṣṭam avyavahāryam agrāhyam alakṣaṇam acintyam*

*avyapadeśyam ekātmapratyayasāraṃ prapañcopaśamaṃ śāntaṃ śivam advaitaṃ; caturthaṃ manyante. sa ātmā, sa vijñeyaḥ.*

64 Which is said to be 'a disease, a tumour, a barb' (M II.231.16: *saññā rogo saññā gaṇḍo saññā sallaṃ*).

65 M II.231.17.

66 Jayatilleke (1998: 41).

67 BU II.4.13/IV.5.14: 'I do not mean bewilderment' (*na vā are 'haṃ mohaṃ bravīmi*).

68 Yājñavalkya's own explanation of *na pretya saṃjñāstity* is: 'When there is some sort of duality . . . one can perceive the other' (BU II.4.14/IV.5.14: *yatra hi dvaitam iva bhavati . . . tad itara itaraṃ vijānāti*). This implies that Yājñavalkya denied only that the self was conscious of objects after death, not that it was completely unconscious.

69 E.g. D II.70.28ff.

70 E.g. M I. 159.10ff.

71 E.g. D II.71.12: *sabbaso ākiñcaññāyatanaṃ samatikamma nevasaññānāsaññāyatanaṃ upasampajja viharati.*

72 This fact is made clear in the *Mahāvedalla Sutta*, where its attainer is said to be like a corpse because his activities of body, speech and mind have stopped (M I.296.10ff.). Griffiths has termed the state a 'cataleptic trance' (1981: 608); La Vallée Poussin similarly described it as a 'crise cataleptique' (1937: 212). According to Bronkhorst, 'there are no ideations in this 'stage of Neither ideations nor Non-ideations'.' (1993: 81 n. 8). He draws this conclusion because he thinks that at D II.69 beings without ideations (*asaññasattā*) occupy the sphere of 'neither perception nor non-perception'. But this is wrong: at D II.69.21, 'the sphere of beings without perception' (*asaññasattāyatana*) and 'the sphere of neither perception nor non-perception' are two different spheres, as indicated by the introduction to the tract on *viññāṇaññhiti-s* and *āyatana-s* at D II.68.25 (*. . . dve ca āyatanāni*). This reference shows exactly the opposite of what Bronkhorst claims, i.e. that 'the sphere of neither perception nor non-perception' is not occupied by beings without consciousness (*asaññasattā*). The later differences of opinion among different Buddhist sects on this issue, as noted by Bronkhorst – some thinking that *nevasaññānāsaññāyatana* is with consciousness, some without – seem to be later scholastic attempts to deal with the non-Buddhist notion of consciousness without an object.

73 Bareau (1963: 16–17) has argued that the name 'Āḷāra Kālāma' is not Indo-European, suggesting that he belonged to a non-Brahminic milieu. Even if this is true, we have no idea if the early Brahminic yogins and philosophers excluded non-Brahmins or indigenous peoples from their ascetic groups. On this point, see Zafiropulo (1993: 25).

74 CU VI.12.1: *. . .kim atra paśyasīti? na kiṃcana bhagava iti.*

75 CU VI.12.3: *sa ya eṣo 'ṇimaitad ātymam idaṃ sarvaṃ. tat satyam. sa ātmā. tat tvam asi Śvetaketo iti.*

76 CU VI.2.1–3: *sad eva somyedam agra āsīd ekam evādvitīyam. tad dhaika āhur asad evedam agra āsīd ekam evādvitīyam. tasmād asataḥ saj jāyata.* (1). *kutas khalu somyaivaṃ syād iti hovāca? katham asataḥ saj jāyeteti? sat tv eva somyedam agra āsīd ekam evādvitīyam* (2).

77 TU II.7.1: *asad vā idam agra āsīt tato vā sad ajāyata.*

78 TU II.6.1: *asann eva sa bhavati asad brahmeti veda cet.*

79 CU III.19.1: *asad evedam agra āsīt. tat sad āsīd. tat samabhavat. tad aṇḍaṃ niravartata.*

80 D III.126.17: *Uddako sudaṃ Cunda Rāmaputto evaṃ vācaṃ bhāsati: 'passan na passatī ti'. kiñ ca passan na passatī ti? khurassa sādhunisitassa talam assa passati,*

*dhārañ ca kho tassa na passati. idaṃ vuccati Cunda 'passan na passatī ti'. taṃ kho pan' etaṃ Cunda Uddakena Rāmaputtena bhāsitaṃ hīnaṃ gammaṃ pothujjanikaṃ anariyaṃ anatthasaṃhitaṃ khuram eva sandhāya. yañ ca taṃ Cunda sammā vadamāno vadeyya: passan na passatī ti idam eva taṃ sammā vadamāno vadeyya: passaṃ na passatī ti. kiñ ca passaṃ na passatī ti? evaṃ sabbākārasampannaṃ sabbākāraparipūraṃ anūnaṃ anadhikaṃ svākkhātaṃ kevalaparipūraṃ brahmacariyaṃ suppakāsitan ti, iti h' etaṃ passati. idam ettha apakaḍḍheyya: evan taṃ parisuddhataraṃ assā ti, iti h' etaṃ na passati. idam ettha upakaḍḍheyya: evan taṃ paripūraṃ assā ti, iti h' etaṃ na passati. idaṃ vuccati: passan na passatī ti.*

81 Referring to this episode, Nakamura has commented (1979: 276): 'In this instance Uddaka's words and expressions were modified to suit Śākyamuni's thought. Since such an expression as 'seeing and seeing not' was extremely unique and does not appear in the general Buddhist canon; we can assume that Uddaka actually preached in such a manner.' Rhys Davids refers to the expression as a 'mystic utterance' of Uddaka Rāmaputta (1908: 34). The aphorism also brings to mind an early Upaniṣadic statement about *yoga* found at KaU III.14cd: *kṣurasya dhārā niśitā duratyayā durgaṃ pathas tat kavayo vadanti* ('The sharpened blade of a razor is hard to pass over – the poets say that is the difficulty of the path').

82 See Gombrich (1996: 17–21).

83 D III.94.24; see Gombrich (1992: 163).

84 If true, it would mean that the Buddha dismissed the idea of consciousness without an object.

85 Hume's translation (1931: 137).

86 Hume (1931: 137) – who follows the *Kāṇva* recension – notes that the *Mādhyandina* recension has *tad draṣṭavyaṃ na* for *tan na* found in the *Kāṇva* text.

87 BU IV.3.23: *yad vai tan na paśyati paśyan vai tan na paśyati. na hi draṣṭur 'dṛṣṭer viparilopo vidyate 'vināśitvāt. na tu tad dvitīyam asti tato 'nyad vibhaktaṃ yat paśyet.*

88 Olivelle (1998: 115).

89 The use of √*dṛś* to designate awareness in general in the early Upaniṣads has been pointed out by Jayatilleke (1998: 58): 'Where the verbal forms of √*dṛś*- are used without mention of the other forms of sensing or sensory perception, it seems to denote not just visual sensing or perception but perception in general.'

90 Mbh XII.180.16–17: *sarvaṃ paśyati yad dṛśyaṃ manoyuktena cakṣuṣā, manasi vyākule tad dhi paśyann api na paśyati* (16). *na paśyati na ca brūte na śṛṇoti na jighrati, na ca sparśarasau vetti nidrāvaśagataḥ punaḥ* (17).

91 E.g. Mbh XII.294.17ab: *na cābhimanyate kiṃcin na ca budhyati kāṣṭhavat.* 'He does not think and is not aware of anything, like a log of wood.' See also Mbh XII.294.14: *mano buddhyā sthiraṃ kṛtvā pāṣāṇa iva niścalaḥ, sthāṇuvac cāpy akampaḥ syād girivac cāpi niścalaḥ.* 'Making the mind firm by the *buddhi*, one is without movement like a stone. One should be like a tree stump, untrembling, without movement like a mountain.' Also Mbh XII.188.5: *kāṣṭhavan muniḥ.*

## 4 THE PHILOSOPHY OF EARLY BRAHMINIC *YOGA*

1 Meditation seems to be suggested at BU IV.4.23, although Bronkhorst (1993: 112) thinks that this passage is 'later than the beginnings of Buddhism'. In any case, it is not evidence for any sort of 'cosmological' meditation.

2 The reading *prāptir* in *pāda* d) is unclear. The verse describes how the formless absolute emits the first creation, but some of the adjectives in the nominative case have variants in the accusative (e.g. *śambhuṃ*, *svayambhuvaṃ*), and some

adjectives in the accusative case have variants in the nominative (e.g. *viśvaḥ*, *īśāno*, *avyayaḥ*). Moreover, the masculine accusative adjective *mahāntaṃ* agrees with *bhūtaṃ*, whose gender is usually neuter. The variants probably indicate that opinion on the status of the creator and the first creation differed. Other variants such as *aṇimāṃ*, *laghimāṃ* and *jyotim* show that the verse was simply misunderstood. At least the process of creation is clear enough, even if the theological issues are not.

3 Mbh XII.291.14–28: *yugaṃ dvādaśasāhasraṃ kalpaṃ viddhi caturguṇam, daśakalpaśatāvṛttaṃ tad ahar brāhmam ucyate, rātriś caitāvatī rājan yasyānte pratibudhyate* (14). *sṛjati anantakarmāṇaṃ mahāntaṃ bhūtam agrajam, mūrtimantam amūrtātmā viśvaṃ śambhuḥ svayaṃbhuvaḥ, aṇimā laghimā prāptir īśānaṃ jyotir avyayam* (15). *sarvataḥpāṇipādāntaṃ sarvatokṣiśiromukham, sarvataḥśrutimal loke sarvam āvṛtya tiṣṭhati* (16). *hiraṇyagarbho bhagavān eṣa buddhir iti smṛtaḥ, mahān iti ca yogeṣu viriñca iti cāpy uta* (17). *sāṃkhye ca paṭhyate śāstre nāmabhir bahudhātmakaḥ, vicitrarūpo viśvātmā ekākṣara iti smṛtaḥ* (18). *vṛtaṃ naikātmakaṃ yena kṛtsnaṃ trailokyam ātmanā, tathaiva bahurūpatvād viśvarūpa iti smṛtaḥ* (19). *eṣa vai vikriyāpannaḥ sṛjaty ātmānam ātmanā, ahaṃkāraṃ mahātejāḥ prajāpatim ahaṃkṛtam* (20). *avyaktād vyaktam utpannaṃ vidyāsargaṃ vadanti tam, mahāntaṃ cāpy ahaṃkāram avidyāsargam eva ca* (21). *avidhiś ca vidhiś caiva samutpannau tathaikataḥ, vidyāvidye 'ti vikhyāte śrutiśāstrārthacintakaiḥ* (22). *bhūtasargam ahaṃkārāt tṛtīyaṃ viddhi pārthiva, ahaṃkāreṣu bhūteṣu caturthaṃ viddhi vaikṛtam* (23). *vāyur jyotir athākāśam āpo 'tha pṛthivī tathā, śabdaḥ sparśaś ca rūpaṃ ca raso gandhas tathaiva ca* (24). *evaṃ yugapad utpannaṃ daśavargaṃ asaṃśayam, pañcamaṃ viddhi rājendra bhautikaṃ sargaṃ arthavat* (25). *śrotraṃ tvak cakṣuṣī jihvā ghrāṇam eva ca pañcamam, vāk ca hastau ca pādau ca pāyur meḍhraṃ tathaiva ca* (26). *buddhīndriyāṇi caitāni tathā karmendriyāṇi ca, saṃbhūtānīha yugapan manasā saha pārthiva* (27). *eṣā tattvacaturviṃśā sarvākṛtiṣu vartate, yāṃ jñātvā nābhisocanti brāhmaṇās tattvadarśinaḥ* (28).

4 Edgerton (1965: 302) does not seem to understand this verse. On the other hand, van Buitenen comments: 'it may be gathered that the *ahaṃkāra*-born *bhūtas* are the *mahābhūtas*' (1957a: 24).

5 I see no other option but to take *ahaṃkāreṣu* as an adjective qualifying *bhūteṣu*, although the variant attested in M5 has the same meaning (*ahaṃkārāc ca*). Edgerton (1965: 302) translates as follows: 'the modification of the already modified (evolvents of matter) in the existing beings which constitute the I-faculties (or, are derived from the I-faculty).' This makes no sense at all.

6 Edgerton takes it differently, translating v. 25ab as follows (1965: 302): 'Thus (as the fourth creation) a group of ten (just named) was created all at once.' He therefore thinks that *evaṃ* in v. 25ab points back to v. 24. This must be wrong: although it is not incorrect to suppose that the material elements are created simultaneously, the five material objects must be derived from them, rather than created at the same time.

7 According to MMW, *evam* in compounds with √*vac* and (*śru* 'refers to what precedes as well as to what follows' (MMW s.v.).

8 Edgerton usually omits verses of an *adhyāya* when their inclusion is unnecessary, or when they are garbled and hard to understand. It is unfortunate that he has not followed this principle in Mbh XII.291, for the verses before v. 21 are both intelligible and necessary, and their omission gives the impression that the cosmogonic tract is to be read together with v. 29ff., which, as I point out above, is a separate tract.

9 Mbh XII.291.29: *etad dehaṃ samākhyātaṃ trailokye sarvadehiṣu, veditavyaṃ naraśreṣṭha sadevanaradānave.*

10 The twenty-fifth is Viṣṇu, the opposite of the destructible (*kṣara*). He is not a *tattva* but a refuge for the *tattva-s* (*tattvasaṃśraya*; v. 37: *pañcaviṃśatimo viṣṇur nistattvas tattvasaṃjñakaḥ, tattvasaṃśrayaṇād etat tattvam āhur manīṣiṇaḥ*). If this part of the *adhyāya* (v. 37ff.) is also an interpolation, it was probably placed there by an editor attempting to bring the older view up to date. This stratum does not differ from the earlier cosmogonic tract in substance: both accept a cosmic agent as creator and soteriological goal.

11 This is not noticed by Sutton (2000: 400), who thinks that the twenty-four principles mentioned before v. 28 form the manifest: 'These twenty-four principles make up the different bodies of all living beings. These are what is known as the manifest and because they pass away day by day they are called the destructible.' But only twenty-four principles are mentioned in the tract before v. 28: the unmanifest named in v. 21 is identical with *śambhu*. Van Buitenen is certainly correct in thinking that the creation doctrine is '*brahman* → *mahān* → *ahaṃkāra*' (1957a: 24); there is no stratum called *prakṛti* or *avyakta*.

12 According to Hacker (1961: 83), however, differences between the *parasmaipada* and *ātmanepada* are significant in these early emanation tracts.

13 Tāṇḍya Mahābrāhmaṇa 20.14.2; Van Buitenen (1957a: 18).

14 Van Buitenen (1957a: 17–18): 'The speculations on creation-by-naming are already old in that period, and in a state of transition'.

15 Van Buitenen (1957a: 19).

16 Van Buitenen (1957a: 22).

17 According to Van Buitenen, the term *ahaṃkāra* is usually mentioned in a cosmogonic rather than psychological context in the *Mokṣadharma* (1957a: 17): 'in this random collection of texts from many different milieux and schools we find that attention is centered, not on the psychological function of *ahaṃkāra* in the individual spirit, but on its evolutionary function in the process of world creation.' This may overstate the matter somewhat: it seems to me that the term *ahaṃkāra* in the *Mokṣadharma* refers to a psychological item as many times as it refers to a cosmogonic item.

18 Van Buitenen (1957a: 17).

19 BU I.4.1: *ātmaivedam agra āsīt puruṣavidhaḥ. so 'nuvīkṣya nānyad ātmano 'paśyat. so 'ham asmīty agre vyāharat. tato 'haṃnāmābhavat.*

20 Brereton (1999).

21 ṚV X.129: *nā́sad āsīn nó sád āsīt tadā́nīṃ, nā́sīd rájo nó vyòmā paro yat. kím ā́varīvaḥ kúha kásya śármann, ámbhaḥ kím āsīd gáhanaṃ gabhīrám.* (1) *ná mṛtyúr āsīd amṛtam ná tárhi, ná rā́tryā áhna āsīt praketáḥ. ā́nīd avātáṃ svadháyā tád ékaṃ, tásmād dhānyán ná paráḥ kíṃ canā́sa.* (2) *táma āsīt támasā gūḷhám ágre, 'praketáṃ salilám sárvam ā idám. tuchyénābhv ápihitaṃ yád ā́sīt, tápasas tán mahinā́jāyataíkam.* (3) *kā́mas tád ágre sám avartatā́dhi, mánaso rétaḥ prathamáṃ yád ā́sīt. satḍ bándhum ásati nír avindan, hṛdí pratī́ṣyā kaváyo manīṣā́.* (4) *tiraścī́no vítato raśmír eṣāṃ, adháḥ svid āsī́d upári svid āsīt. retodhā́ āsan mahimā́na āsan, svadhā́ avástāt práyatiḥ parástāt.* (5) *kó addhā́ veda ká ihá prá vocat, kúta ā́jāta kúta iyáṃ vísṛṣṭiḥ. arvā́g devā́ asya visarjanenā́thā kḍ veda yáta ābabhū́va.* (6) *iyáṃ vísṛṣṭir yáta ābabhū́va, yádi vā dadhé yádi vā ná. yḍ asyā́dhyakṣaḥ paramé vyòman, sḍ aṅgá veda yádi vā ná véda.* (7)

22 As noted by Brereton (1999: 249), *pāda* (b) is short of two syllables.

23 Jurewicz (1995: 142).

24 Brereton (1999: 251).

25 Brereton (1999: 251).

26 Brereton (1999: 251) notices the correspondence between the verbs *ā́varīvaḥ* and *ā́nīd*.

27 Jurewicz (1995: 143).
28 Jurewicz (1995: 144).
29 Brereton (1999: 253).
30 Brereton (1999: 253).
31 Brereton (1999: 253).
32 Brereton (1999: 254).
33 Brereton (1999: 254).
34 Brereton (1999: 254).
35 Brereton's translation of *nèva hí sán máno nèvā́sat* (1999: 254).
36 Brereton (1999: 258).
37 Macdonell (1999: 209).
38 Macdonell (1999: 209).
39 Jurewicz (1995: 145): 'That One warms up in the self-cognitive act.'
40 Brereton (1999: 255).
41 Brereton (1999: 258).
42 Brereton (1999: 258).
43 Hacker (1961: 77).
44 Hacker (1961: 80).
45 Hacker (1961: 84). This tract corresponds to Manusmṛti I: v. 5, v. 74cd, v. 75–78.
46 I follow Hacker in reading *vyaktāvyaktātmakaṃ* in *pāda* (d) instead of *tasmād vyaktātmakaṃ manaḥ*.
47 Mbh XII.224: *anādyantam ajaṃ divyam ajaraṃ dhruvam avyayam, apratarkyam avijñeyaṃ brahmāgre samavartata (11). sṛjate ca mahad bhūtaṃ tasmād vyaktātmakaṃ manaḥ* (31cd). *manaḥ sṛṣṭiṃ vikurute codyamānaṃ sisṛkṣayā, ākāśaṃ jāyate tasmāt tasya śabdo guṇo mataḥ* (35). *ākāśāt tu vikurvāṇāt sarvagandhavahaḥ śuciḥ, balavāñ jāyate vāyus tasya sparśo guṇo mataḥ* (36). *vāyor api vikurvāṇāj jyotir bhūtaṃ tamonudam, rociṣṇu jāyate tatra tad rūpaguṇam ucyate* (37). *jyotiṣo 'pi vikurvāṇād bhavanty āpo rasātmikāḥ, adbhyo gandhaguṇā bhūmiḥ pūrvaiṣā sṛṣṭir ucyate* (38).
48 Hacker (1961: 85).
49 Mbh XII.224.33: *aharmukhe vibuddhaḥ san sṛjate vidyayā jagat, agra eva mahābhūtam āśu vyaktātmakaṃ manaḥ.*
50 See above, p. 36–37.
51 MuU III.1.3: *yadā paśyaḥ paśyate rukmavarṇaṃ kartāram īśaṃ puruṣaṃ brahmayoniṃ, tadā vidvān puṇyapāpe vidhūya nirañjanaḥ paramaṃ sāmyam upaiti.*
52 MuU III.1.5: *satyena labhyas tapasā hy eṣa ātmā samyagjñānena brahmacaryeṇa nityam, antaḥśarīre jyotirmayo hi śubhro yaṃ paśyanti yatayaḥ kṣīṇadoṣāḥ* (5).
53 MuU II.2.5–8: *yasmin dyauḥ pṛthivī cāntarikṣam otaṃ manaḥ saha prāṇaiś ca sarvaiḥ, tam evaikaṃ jānatha ātmānam anyā vāco vimuñcathāmṛtasyaiṣa setuḥ* (5). *arā iva rathanābhau saṃhatā yatra nāḍyaḥ sa eṣo 'ntaś carate bahudhā jāyamānaḥ, om ity evaṃ dhyāyatha ātmānaṃ svasti vaḥ pārāya tamasaḥ parastāt* (6). *manomayaḥ prāṇaśarīranetā pratiṣṭhito 'nne hṛdayaṃ saṃnidhāya, tadvijñānena paripaśyanti dhīrā ānandarūpam amṛtaṃ yad vibhāti* (8).
54 Mbh XII.180.28–29: *taṃ pūrvāpararātreṣu yuñjānaḥ satataṃ budhaḥ, laghvāhāro viśuddhātmā paśyaty ātmānam ātmani* (28). *cittasya hi prasādena hitvā karma śubhāśubham, prasannātmātmani sthitvā sukham akṣayam aśnute* (29).
55 Mbh XII.197. 8: *jñānam utpadyate puṃsāṃ kṣayāt pāpasya karmaṇaḥ, athādarśatalaprakhye paśyaty ātmānam ātmani.*
56 Mbh XII.238.10: *cittaprasādena yatir jahāti hi śubhāśubhaṃ prasannātmātmani sthitvā sukham ānantyam aśnute.*
57 KeU II.5: *iha ced avedīd atha satyam asti na ced ihāvedīn mahatī vinaṣṭiḥ, bhūteṣu bhūteṣu vicitya dhīrāḥ pretyāsmāl lokād amṛtā bhavanti.*

58 KeU I.5: *yad vācānabhyuditaṃ yena vāg abhyudyate, tad eva brahma tvaṃ viddhi nedaṃ yad idam upāsate* (5). 'What is not uttered by speech, by which speech is uttered, know that alone as *brahman*, and not what they venerate here.'

59 'It's envisioned by one who envisions it not; but one who envisions it knows it not. And those who perceive it perceive it not; but it's perceived by those who perceive [it] not.' Olivelle's translation of KeU II.3: *yasyāmataṃ tasya mataṃ mataṃ yasya na veda saḥ, avijñātaṃ vijānatāṃ vijñātam avijānatām*. I doubt that these paradoxes indicate an intellectual gnosis. The juxtaposition of positive and negative terms is reminiscent of the expression *passan na passati* (D III.126; see above pp. 46–49); both seem to indicate an attempt to describe an intangible and logically inexplicable state of consciousness, i.e. a nondual state of consciousness produced by one-pointed concentration.

60 MuU III.2.6, 8: *vedāntavijñānasuniścitārthāḥ saṃnyāsayogād yatayaḥ śuddhasattvāḥ, te brahmalokeṣu parāntakāle parāmṛtāḥ parimucyanti sarve.* (6) *yathā nadyaḥ syandamānāḥ samudre 'staṃ gacchanti nāmarūpe vihāya, tathā vidvān nāmarūpād vimuktaḥ parāt paraṃ puruṣam upaiti divyam.* (8)

61 Mbh XII.231.18: *avyaktaṃ vyaktadeheṣu martyeṣv amaram āśritam, yo 'nupaśyati sa pretya kalpate brahmabhūyase.*

62 Mbh XII.289.35, 41: *tadvad ātmasamādhānaṃ yuktvā yogena tattvavit, durgamaṃ sthānam āpnoti hitvā deham imaṃ nṛpa* (35). *sa śīghram amalaprajñaḥ karma dagdhvā śubhāśubham, uttamaṃ yogam āsthāya yadīcchati vimucyate* (41).

63 Van Buitenen (1957: 37).

## 5 MEDITATION IN THE *PĀRĀYANAVAGGA*

1 See p. 42 n. 62.

2 This is indicated when the Buddha tells the five disciples that his doctrine is to be practised just as he teaches it (M I.172.34: *ahaṃ dhammaṃ desemi, yathānusiṭṭhaṃ tathā paṭipajjamānā. . .*).

3 It belongs to the *Khuddaka Nikāya*. The introductory verses to the *Pārāyanavagga* (Sn 976–1031: *Vatthugāthā*) are not commented on in the *Niddesa*, and were probably not originally part of the text (see Norman's note, 2001: 395).

4 Norman (2001: xxxii).

5 Norman (2001: xxxvi).

6 Norman (2001: xxxviii-xxxix).

7 Norman (2001: xxix). De Jong (2000: 173): '[I]t would be hazardous to rely too much on metrical grounds for distinguishing older and newer verses.'

8 Norman (2001: xxxiii): 'Nevertheless, the fact that what we can, on other grounds, consider to be the original core of verses in the Aṭṭhaka-v, is in Triṣṭubh metre, which is generally a sign of an early composition in Pāli, supports the argument that the Aṭṭhaka-v is old.'

9 Norman (2001: xxxiii-iv). Schmithausen (1992: 113 n. 18) notes the differences of opinion on these identifications; see also Hultzsch (1991: 174 n. 1).

10 Norman (2001: xxii).

11 Following Gombrich (1992: 258); see also Gombrich (1988: 17) and Cousins (1991: 58–59).

12 The story of *bhikkhus* reciting the *Aṭṭhakavagga* to the Buddha is found in all extant Vinayas, and Frauwallner concludes: 'This piece of evidence means, that at the time of the composition of the *Skandhaka* the *Arthavargīyāṇi Sūtrāṇi* already existed and were a popular sacred text.' (1956: 149).

13 Vetter (1990: 42).

14 Vetter (1990: 38–39). The verses Vetter has in mind are: 1035–36, 1039, 1041, 1053–54, 1056, 1062, 1066–67, 1070, 1085, 1095, 1104, 1110–11, 1119.

15 These are the verses 1035–36 according to Vetter (1990: 40).
16 Vetter (1990: 39) on Sn 1119.
17 I reproduce the PTS edition of the *Upasīvamāṇavapucchā*, although I will suggest emendations for v.1071 and 1072.
18 Following Norman (2001: 136; see also pp. 412–13), who reads *cavetha* instead of *bhavetha*.
19 Norman (2001: 136–37).
20 On the word *ogha*, CPD comments 'the flood of *saṃsāra*'. According to PED (s.v.), the 'flood' is a metaphor for the 'ignorance and vain desires which sweep a man down'.
21 According to Nakamura (1979: 272), this dialogue states that 'in the primitive Buddhism non-Buddhist thought was adopted and the state of non-existence was a goal'. But the meditative state of nothingness is certainly not the goal in the dialogue with Posāla. Nakamura's view depends upon taking the compound *saññāvimokkhe* in v. 1071–72 as the goal identical to nothingness. In one place he translates this as 'emancipation by thought' (p. 272), but in another place (p. 273) he translates it as 'deliverance from thought', a translation that implies that the compound *saññāvimokkha-* refers to a state different from the meditative state of nothingness. It is hard to take Nakamura's argument seriously considering these conflicting translations of *saññāvimokkha-*. See p. 80 n. 34 on Nakamura's reading of the dialogue with Upasīva.
22 Norman does not indicate how he understands this enigmatic expression. His translation suggests that liberation is described in v. 1071–72 ('released in the highest release from perception'). If so, *sīti-siyā* for Norman must be what happens to somebody who has already been liberated for a number of years. It is possible that Norman understands the compound *sīti-siyā* in v. 1073–74 to refer to the death and final liberation (*parinibbāna*) of the liberated person.
23 Vetter (1990: 41).
24 Nidd II, PTS edition pp. 23–24.
25 The reading is *vimutto* in Nidd II's repetition of the *Pārāyanavagga* verses (VRI p. 10 = Be p. 12), but the *Niddesa* itself (i.e. the commentary on the verses) reads *'dhimutto* (VRI p. 94 = Be p. 105).
26 Ne KN I p. 430.5/9.
27 Ne KN IV.II p. 111.20.
28 As Norman notes (2001: xlii): 'Pj II presumes the existence of Nidd – its comments are frequently identical'.
29 Pj II 594.2ff., Ne KN IV.II p. 112.19ff.
30 Ne KN IV.II (Nidd II), p. 112.9ff: *saññāvimokkhe paramedhimutto ti. saññāvimokkhā vuccanti satta saññāsamāpattiyo. tāsaṃ saññāsamāpattīnaṃ ākiñcaññāyatanasamāpattivimokkho aggo ca seṭṭho ca viseṭṭho ca pāmokkho ca uttamo ca pavaro ca, parame agge seṭṭhe viseṭṭhe pāmokkhe uttame pavare adhimuttivimokkhena adhimutto tatrādhimutto tadadhimutto taccarito tabbahulo taggaruko tanninno tappoṇo tappabbhāro tadadhimutto tadadhipateyyo ti – saññāvimokkhe paramedhimutto*. This explanation is given for the expression in both the verses 1071–72.
31 Pj II 594.1: *saññāvimokkhe parame ti sattassu saññāvimokkhesu uttame ākiñcaññāyatane.*
32 E.g. the sequence *pakkhandati pasīdati santiṭṭhati adhimuccati/vimuccati* at M I. 186.4, M I. 435.16ff., M III. 104.21ff. The same sequence is found with only the reading *vimuccati* at D III.239.19ff. (= III.278); M III.112.3; A II. 166.2ff., A III.245.7ff., IV. 235.5, IV. 438.23ff. It is probable that the lack of the variant *adhimuccati* in these places is due to an editorial error, or else a lack of MS.

33 Norman's note on v. 1071–72 (2001: 412) refers to the *v/dh* alteration: he suggests that the variant *°dhimutto* reflects a dialect change *vi* → *dhi*, or a different system of orthography giving this change. Thus he implies that the correct reading should really be *vimutto*, and so he reads and translates. But this fails to take into account that derivations of *adhi* + √*muc* have a distinct meaning in Pāli: nominal forms mean 'conviction' or 'meditative concentration'. This use cannot be explained away as a dialectic or orthographic way of representing *vi* + √*muc*. The same derivations of *adhi* + √*muc* are not unusual in Buddhist Sanskrit texts (BHSD s.v.). It seems that *adhimutto* was a real word in ancient India, and different from *vimutto*; it was not a corruption of the latter. If so it is probable that the *v/dh* variation, i.e. *dh* appearing for *v* in Pāli texts, whether due to scribal practice or ancient dialectic variation, has blurred this fact.

34 Hajime Nakamura suggested that nothingness was the goal in v. 1070–71, but this view depends upon taking *vimutto* to mean 'liberated'. Reading *°dhimutto* and understanding only meditative concentration instead of liberation does not support a view that in earliest Buddhism 'the state of non-existence was a goal and for that purpose meditation was practiced' (1979: 273). Nakamura also suggested that Sn 874 shows that the state of *nevasaññānāsaññā* (which he translates as 'thoughtless thought') was a goal in early Buddhism. According to him, this represents a later stage of Buddhism in which the goal of *ākiñcañña* had been usurped (1979: 273). But Sn 874 ought to be read as part of the verses in the *Aṭṭhakavagga* for which a state without *saññā* is thought to be liberating. It follows that there is very little support for the following statement (1979: 273–74): 'When Buddhism underwent dramatic evolution (in the post-Aśokan period, or possibly after the reign of King Nanda), the concepts of the periods A [goal = *ākiñcañña*] and B [goal = *nevasaññānāsaññā*] were no longer acceptable to the contemporary people and new ideas became necessary. As a result, the concept of non-existence was attributed to Āḷāra Kālāma and the theory of thoughtless-thought attributed to Uddaka, son of Rāma, while Buddhism itself set forth new ideas.'

35 Norman (2001: 412).

36 Stede published the PTS edition of Nidd II in 1918, and on p. 23 he reads *°dhimutto* in v. 1071, recording *vimutto* as a variant. Given his preference for *°dhimutto*, it is difficult to explain his translation of *anuyāyin* in PED. Perhaps the PED translation of *anuyāyin* was the work of Rhys Davids.

37 CPD s.v. notes that *aviccamāno* is a variant, probably corrupt, for the reading *avedhamāno* in the PTS edition of Nidd II at 86.25. In Ne *avedhamāno* (from the Siamese edition of 1926) is cited as a variant for *aviccamāno*.

38 Ne KN IV.II (Nidd II), p. 112.16ff: *tiṭṭhe nu so tattha anānuyāyī ti. tiṭṭhe nu ti: saṃsayapucchā vimatipucchā dveḷhakapucchā anekaṃsapucchā. evaṃ nu kho, nanu kho, kiṃ nu kho, kathaṃ nu kho ti tiṭṭhe nu. tatthā ti: ākiñcaññāyatane. anānuyāyī ti: anānuyāyī aviccamāno avigacchamāno anantaradhāyamāno aparihāyamāno pe . . . athāvā arajjamāno adussamāno amuhyamāno akilissamāno ti.*

39 Ne KN IV.II (Nidd II), p. 113.26ff: *tiṭṭheyyā ti: tiṭṭheyya saṭṭhikappasahassāni.*

40 Ne KN IV.II (Nidd II), p. 114.11.

41 This view is based on the argument from silence, but not one in which the absence of terms in individual verses is thought to be significant. The absence of terms in a large collection of verses is surely significant.

42 Pj II 594.2ff: *tiṭṭhe nu so tattha anānuyāyī ti so puggalo tattha ākiñcaññāyatanbrahmaloke avigacchamāno tiṭṭhe nū ti pucchati. ath' assa bhagavā saṭṭhikappasahassamattaṃ yeva ṭhānaṃ anujānanto tatiyagātham āha.*

43 As far as I am aware, the idea is only made explicit in a couple of canonical texts. At A I.267.3 (*Tikanipāta* 114, *āpāyikavagga* 4), it is said that a disciple of the

Buddha who dies having attained either the 'sphere of the infinity of space', the 'sphere of the infinity of consciousness' or 'the sphere of nothingness' will exist as a *deva* in those spheres for 20,000 aeons, 40,000 aeons or 60,000 aeons respectively, before attaining *parinibbāna*. It seems that Nidd II and Pj II follow this canonical source in holding that the span of life in the sphere of nothingness is 60,000 aeons. At A II.160.3 (*Catukkanipāta* 172, *sañcetanikavagga* 2), the Buddha says that someone who attains *nevasaññānāsaññāyatana* in this life exists in that sphere as a deity after death; if he had abandoned the worldly fetters in life (*orambhāgiyāni saṃyojanāni pahīnāni*), then he will not come back to earth, i.e. he will attain liberation from that sphere.

44 See p. 123 n. 57 on the similar use of these words in *Indriyabhāvana Sutta*.

45 Barnes (1976: 184).

46 This interpretation of the word *satīmā* is supported by the teachings given by the Buddha to Udaya and Posāla (see p. 105).

47 The fact that *sītisiyā* is a verb in the optative mood whereas *vimutto* is a past passive participle does not matter: it is possible to take *vimutto* as logically rather than grammatically equivalent to *sītisiyā*, giving a translation such as 'and would become cool right there, i.e. released'.

48 At this point, Ne KN IV.II (Nidd II), p. 114.25 reads: *punabbhavapaṭisandhiviññāṇaṃ nibbatteyya kāmadhātuyā vā rūpadhātuyā vā arūpadhātuyā vāti*: 'would consciousness connecting to re-becoming be produced in the realm of sensual pleasures, the realm of form, or the realm without form?' This sentence is at odds with the previous one, where the word *cavetha* in the main text is interpreted as *caveyya, ucchijjeyya, nasseyya, vinasseyya, na bhaveyya*, and is clearly about the annihilation of the *viññāṇaṃ* and not its connection to re-becoming. In other words, the sentence does not connect with what precedes it (the annihilation of the *viññāṇa*) or the summary of the two views that follows (eternalism or nihilism). However, the second interpretation Nidd II offers of 1073c-d interprets *cavetha viññāṇaṃ* almost verbatim: *puna paṭisandhiviññāṇaṃ nibbatteyya kāmadhātuyā vā rūpadhātuyā vā arūpadhātuyā vāti*. It is likely that this phrase has migrated from this position into the first explanation above, probably as a scribal mistake. The passage makes no sense if it is read as it is. Having read Stede's notes (p. xii) about the state of the Singhalese MS upon which the PTS edition of Nidd II is based, it is not surprising to find some textual corruption in this passage.

49 Ne KN IV.II (Nidd II), p. 114.22ff: *tatth' eva so sītisiyā vimutto cavetha viññāṇaṃ tathāvidhassā ti.* 1) *tatth' eva so sītibhāvam anuppatto nicco dhuvo sassato avipariṇāmadhammo sassatisamaṃ tath' eva tiṭṭheyya?* 2) *athavā, tassa viññāṇaṃ caveyya ucchijjeyya nasseyya vinasseyya na bhaveyyā ti? [punabbhavapaṭisandhiviññāṇaṃ nibbatteyya kāmadhātuyā vā rūpadhātuyā vā arūpadhātuyā vā ti]* (– see the previous note on why this sentence should not be read in this position) *ākiñcaññāyatanaṃ samāpannassa sassataṃ ca ucchedaṃ ca pucchati. udāhu*: 1) *tatthe 'va anupādisesāya nibbānadhātuyā parinibbāyeyya?* 2) *athavā, tassa viññāṇaṃ caveyya punapaṭisandhiviññāṇaṃ nibbatteyya kāmadhātuyā vā rūpadhātuyā vā arūpadhātuyā vā ti? ākiñcaññāyatanaṃ upapannassa parinibbānaṃ ca paṭisandhiṃ ca pucchati.*

50 Pj II.594.20: *atha bhagavā ucchedasassataṃ anupagamma tattha uppannassa ariyasāvakassa anupādāya parinibbānaṃ dassento 'accī yathā ti' gāthām āha.*

51 Pj II.594.13: *tatth' eva so sītisiyā vimutto ti so puggalo tatth' evākiñcaññāyatane nānādukkhehi vimutto sītibhāvaṃ patto bhaveyya, nibbānappatto sassato hutvā tiṭṭheyyā ti adhippāyo.*

52 Pj II.594.16: *cavetha viññāṇaṃ tathāvidhassā ti udāhu tathāvidhassa viññāṇaṃ anupādāya parinibbāyeyyā ti ucchedaṃ pucchati. paṭisandhigahaṇatthaṃ vāpi vibhaveyyā* [= PTS, Be = *bhaveyya*] *ti paṭisandhim pi assa pucchati.*

53 Sn 1075: *atthaṅ gato so uda vā so natthi, udāhu ve sassatiyā arogo? tam me munī sādhu viyākarohi, tathā hi te vidito esa dhammo.*

54 D I.30.24ff.

55 Bedekar (1963) distinguishes the path of *japa* from that of *sāṃkhya* and *yoga*, but comments (1963: 65): 'A Jāpaka can, however, renounce the household and can even attain to the highest stage of self-realisation which the follower of the *Yoga* reaches.' The passage quoted above on the liberation of the *jāpaka* clearly follows standard yogic ideas about liberation.

56 The critical edition refers to the commentary of Vidyasāgara, in which this word is interpreted as *śarīrahīnaḥ*.

57 Reading: *amṛtaś* for *amṛtāc* in *amṛtāc cāmṛtaṃ prāptaḥ*.

58 Mbh XII.192.118–123: *prayāti saṃhitādhyāyī brahmāṇaṃ parameṣṭhinam, atha vāgniṃ samāyāti sūryam āviśate 'pi vā* (118). *sa taijasena bhāvena yadi tatrāśnute ratim, guṇāṃs teṣāṃ samādatte rāgeṇa pratimohitaḥ* (119). *evaṃ some tathā vāyau bhūmyākāśaśarīragaḥ, sarāgas tatra vasati guṇāṃs teṣāṃ samācaran* (120). *atha tatra virāgī sa paraṃ gacchaty asaṃśayaṃ, param avyayam icchan sa tam evāviśate punaḥ* (121). *amṛtaś cāmṛtaṃ prāptaḥ śītībhūto nirātmavān, brahmabhūtaḥ sa nirdvaṃdvaḥ sukhī śānto nirāmayaḥ* (122). *brahmasthānam anāvartam ekam akṣarasaṃjñakam, aduḥkham ajaram śāntaṃ sthānaṃ tat pratipadyate* (123).

59 Twelve MS read *śāntī/śānti-bhūto*.

60 See pp. 43–44.

61 M I.256.13: *idaṃ viññāṇaṃ sandhāvati saṃsarati anaññan ti.* Norman (1991: 4) relates this view of Sāti to the teachings of Yājñavalkya in the *Bṛhadāraṇyaka Upaniṣad.*

62 DOP, MMW, PED s.v.

63 E.g. *nāmarūpaṃ* (D II.32.17), *nāmarūpamhā* (D II.32.29), *nāmarūpasmiṃ* (Sn 756), *nāmarūpassa* (D II.62.32), *nāmarūpe* (D II.32.14).

64 E.g. D II.62.14: *yehi Ānanda ākārehi yehi liṅgehi yehi nimittehi yehi uddesehi nāmakāyassa paññatti hoti, tesu ākāresu tesu liṅgesu tesu nimittesu tesu uddesesu asati, api nu kho rūpakāye adhivacanasamphasso paññāyethā ti?*

65 Nett 27, 28, 41, 69, 77, 78; Paṭis I.183.

66 *Dutiyarāga Sutta*, It 57.18: *yassa rāgo ca doso ca avijjā ca virājitā so 'maṃ samuddaṃ sagahaṃ sarakkhasaṃ [sa]ūmibhayaṃ duttaram accatāri. saṅgātigo maccujaho nirūpadhi pahāsi dukkhaṃ apunabbhavāya. atthaṅgato so na pamāṇam eti amohayi maccurājan ti brūmī ti.* The same verse is found at S IV.158 where the context makes clear that it is a living and not a dead person who is said to be *atthaṅgato.*

67 M I.341.11: [*ekacco puggalo*] *diṭṭhe va dhamme nicchāto nibbuto sītibhūto sukhapaṭisaṃvedī brahmabhūtena attanā viharati.* Also at D III.233.1; M I.412.2, M II.159.14; A I.197.8, A II.206.3, A V.65.3.

68 M I.171.9 (= M II.93 = Vin I.8): *ahaṃ hi arahā loke ahaṃ satthā anuttaro, eko 'mhi sammāsambuddho sītibhūto 'smi nibbuto.*

69 Th 79, 298; the Thī version is *sītibhūt' amhi nibbuto*, which occurs at Thī 15, 16, 34, 66, 76, 101.

70 S I v.567, v.692; A I.138.4; Dhp 418 = Sn 642 =M II.96; Sn 542; Th 416, Thī 205, 360.

71 A II.198.30: *so kāyapariyantikaṃ vedanaṃ vediyamāno kāyapariyantikaṃ vedanaṃ vediyāmī ti pajānāti, jīvitapariyantikaṃ vedanaṃ vediyamāno jīvitapariyantikaṃ vedanaṃ vediyāmī ti pajānāti, kāyassa bhedā uddhaṃ jīvitapariyādānā idh' eva sabbavedayitāni anabhinanditāni sītī bhavissantī ti pajānāti.* Also S II.83.1, S III.126.14, IV.213.10, S IV.214.23, S V.319.25.

72 This distinction is applied to the terms *saupādisesā nibbāna* and *anupādisesā nibbāna* at It 38.4.
73 And almost identical to the *Itivuttaka* verse quoted above p. 91 n. 66 (*Dutiyarāga Sutta*, It 57.18: *atthaṅgato so na pamāṇam eti*).
74 Vetter's translation (1990: 41; 'When all things (*dhamma*) are abolished, then all ways of thinking, too, are abolished') is not quite correct: *vādapathā* does not mean 'ways of thinking'.
75 A recent study of *dhamma* in the *Nikāya-s* is found in Gethin (2004).
76 Sn 993, 1015, 1052–54, 1064, 1075, 1085, 1097, 1102, 1120, 1122.
77 Sn 982.
78 Sn 1002.
79 Sn 1053, 1066, 1087, 1095.
80 Sn 16.9, 141, 343, 140.14, 148.14.
81 The word *dhamma* seems to be used in the *Ariyapariyesana Sutta* in both senses, i.e. meditative object and teaching. See p. 15 n. 38.
82 See the previous note.
83 M I.487.24: *sace pana taṃ Vaccha evaṃ puccheyya: yo te ayaṃ purato aggi nibbuto, so aggi ito katamaṃ disaṃ gato, puratthimaṃ vā pacchimaṃ vā uttaraṃ vā dakkhiṇaṃ vā ti? evaṃ puṭṭho tvaṃ Vaccha kinti byākareyyāsī ti? na upeti bho Gotama, yaṃ hi so bho Gotama aggi tiṇakaṭṭhupādānaṃ paṭicca ajali, tassa ca pariyādānā aññassa ca anupahārā anāhāro nibbuto t' eva saṅkhaṃ gacchatī ti. evam eva kho Vaccha yena rūpena tathāgataṃ paññāpayamāno paññāpeyya taṃ rūpaṃ tathāgatassa pahīnaṃ ucchinnamūlaṃ tālāvatthukataṃ anabhāvakataṃ āyatiṃ anuppādadhammaṃ. rūpasaṅkhāvimutto kho Vaccha tathāgato gambhīro appameyyo duppariyogāho seyyathā pi mahāsamuddo. upapajjatī ti na upeti, na upapajjatī ti na upeti, upapajjatī ca na ca upapajjatī ti na upeti, neva upapajjati na na upapajjatī ti na upeti.*
84 I am indebted to Richard Gombrich for pointing this out (see Gombrich 1996: 67).
85 There is no evidence in the early Brahminic literature, as far as I am aware, of the metaphor of 'going out' referring to the liberation at death of the yogic adept. However, Collins has pointed out that the use of this metaphor by the Buddha at Sn 1074 plays on old Brahminic ideas: 'To be able to appreciate the full flavour of the phrase, one must bear in mind the fact that since Vedic times, the movement of the sun had been a major motif in representations of time and temporality.' (Collins 1982: 130).
86 Reading *hyasya* for *yasya*.
87 Mbh XII.180.2–6: *Bhṛgu uvāca: na śarīrāśrito jīvas tasmin naṣṭe praṇaśyati, yathā samitsu daghdāsu na praṇaśyati pāvakaḥ* (2). *Bharadvāja uvāca: agner yathā tathā tasya yadi nāśo na vidyate, indhanasyopayogānte sa cāgnir nopalabhyate* (3). *naśyatīty eva jānāmi śāntam agnim anindhanam, gatir hyasya pramāṇaṃ vā saṃsthānaṃ vā na dṛśyate* (4). *Bhṛgur uvāca: samidhām upayogānte sann evāgnir na dṛśyate, ākāśānugatatvād dhi durgrahaḥ sa nirāśrayaḥ* (5). *tathā śarīrasaṃtyāge jīvo hy ākāśavat sthitaḥ, na gṛhyate susūkṣmatvād yathā jyotir na saṃśayaḥ* (6).
88 The occurrence of the terms *śītībhūto* and *brahmabhūtaḥ* in the same *Mokṣadharma* verse (Mbh XII.192.122) suggests that the Pāli phrase *brahmabhūtena attanā* is similarly an adaptation of a Brahminic metaphor. The Buddhist *bhikkhu* becomes *brahman* in a metaphorical sense: unlike the Brahminic yogin, he is not absorbed into *brahman*. This is not what Pérez-Remón thinks. After the appearance of the pericope at M I.349 (in the *Kandaraka Sutta*), he comments (1980: 117): 'It would be a disappointing anticlimax to have to think at the conclusion of such brilliant

description that such a self is not a reality but a merely conventional name.' He also comments (1980: 118): 'It is evidence that all the passages, where *brahmabhūtena attanā viharati* is used, refer to a self that is free from all attachments and has attained to the quenching of *nibbāna*. Such a usage of *attā* gives the term a prominence that could not be expected from people utterly convinced that the basic teaching of early Buddhism was that of absolute *anattā*.' I do not accept this argument, which seems to be based on the notion that the early Buddhists were incapable of using metaphors. It is doubtful that the term *brahmabhūta* would have been used by someone who believed that the self does not exist, but this does not mean the opposite – that its use presupposes an *ātman* doctrine.

89 Rhys Davids (1899: 206–07), on the *Kassapasīhanāda Sutta*. Also quoted by Gombrich (1996: 17–18).

90 The verses Sn 1105–07 are quoted at A I.134.10–13.

91 Sn 1108–09 are repeated almost verbatim at S I.88 (v. 209–210). Norman translates *vicāraṇaṃ* in Sn 1108 as 'investigation' (2001: 141) whereas Bodhi translates it at S I.88 (v. 209) as 'means of travelling about' (2000: 131). I disagree with Norman, for by analogy with Sn 1108a the term must have a pejorative sense. Bodhi follows the commentary that glosses *vicāraṇa* as *pādāni*.

92 Sn 1105–11: *jhāyiṃ virajam āsīnaṃ (icc āyasmā Udayo) katakiccaṃ anāsavaṃ, pāraguṃ sabbadhammānaṃ atthi pañhena āgamaṃ: aññāvimokham pabrūhi avijjāya pabhedanaṃ* (1105). *pahānaṃ kāmacchandānaṃ (Udayā ti Bhagavā) domanassāna cūbhayaṃ, thīnassa ca panūdanaṃ kukkuccānaṃ nivāraṇaṃ*, (1106). *upekhāsatisaṃsuddhaṃ dhammatakkapurejavaṃ, aññāvimokhaṃ pabrūmi avijjāya pabhedanaṃ* (1107). *kiṃ su saṃyojano loko kiṃ su tassa vicāraṇaṃ, kiss' assa vippahānena nibbānaṃ iti vuccati* (1108). *nandīsaṃyojano loko vitakk' assa vicāraṇā, taṇhāya vippahānena nibbānaṃ iti vuccati* (1109). *kathaṃ satassa carato viññāṇaṃ uparujjhati, bhagavantaṃ puṭṭhuṃ āgamma taṃ suṇoma vaco tava* (1110). *ajjhattañ ca bahiddhā ca vedanaṃ nābhinandato, evaṃ satassa carato viññāṇaṃ uparujjhatī ti* (1111).

93 E.g. D I.71.21.

94 E.g. D I.75.30.

95 Brough (1962: 208).

96 According to Brough (1962: 208): 'The conclusion seems certain.'

97 D II.74.14–15: . . . *avitakkaṃ avicāraṃ samādhijaṃ pītisukhaṃ dutīyajjhānaṃ*.

98 The translation of v. 1112–13 is Norman's with a few changes.

99 *Vibhūtarūpasaññissa*. Vetter thinks that this 'reminds us of states without apperception which are in some passages of the Aṭṭhakavagga an aim in themselves' (1990: 40). But the compound only refers to a state without the apperception of form, not without all apperception. It is a description of a meditative state, not a description of a liberated state that is without *saññā*.

100 Vetter (1990: 40) thinks that this points towards going beyond a state without apperception, which might be the attainment of intellectual insight into the stations of consciousness (*viññāṇaṭṭhiti-s*, on which see v. 1114 and p. 104 n. 102). However, the question only concerns how a person may go beyond a meditative state without the apperception of forms, rather than going beyond a state completely without apperception.

101 Norman reads the words *tiṭṭhantam*, *vimuttaṃ* and *tappārāyanaṃ* as alternative conditions for the person whose condition the Buddha knows, so that he translates 'standing [in this world]', 'released' and 'destined for that [release]' respectively. But these adjectives must qualify the subject of the whole passage – the person who has attained the meditative state of nothingness (*ākiñcañña*). Thus *vimuttaṃ* probably refers to meditative release rather than liberation, just as *vi* + √*muc*

does in Sn 1071–72. Nidd II reads ˚*dhimuttaṃ*, and so the arguments put forward about the *Upasīvamāṇavapucchā* apply here; it is probably preferable to read ˚*dhimuttaṃ* rather than *vimuttaṃ*. If so, the three words must be synonymous and the word *pārāyana* probably refers not to the 'final aim' but the 'chief meditative object' of this person concentrated on *ākiñcañña* (PED s.v.).

102 Vetter thinks that this verse is a description of how one is to be 'led further': 'one has to know the *viññāṇaṭṭhitiyo* and the *viññāṇa*, and this knowledge might have consisted of the insight that *viññāṇa* and the four other constituents are nonpermanent, unsatisfactory and non-self' (1990: 40). However, the verse is not a prescription of how someone can attain liberating insight; it merely describes the Buddha's ability to know a person's meditative state.

103 Following Norman in reading Be *ākiñcañña-* instead of PTS *ākiñcaññā* in *pāda* (a), and Be *etaṃ* for the second *evaṃ* of Ee in *pāda* (c).

104 Sn 1112–15: *yo atītaṃ ādisati (icc āyasmā Posāla) anejo chinnasaṃsayo, pāraguṃ sabbadhammānaṃ atthi pañhena āgamaṃ* (1112). *vibhūtarūpasaññissa sabbakāyapahāyino, ajjhattañ ca bahiddhā ca natthi kiñcī ti passato, ñāṇaṃ Sakkānupucchāmi kathaṃ neyyo tathāvidho* (1113). *viññāṇaṭṭhitiyo sabbā (Posālā ti Bhagavā) abhijānaṃ tathāgato, tiṭṭhantam enaṃ jānāti vimuttaṃ tapparāyanaṃ* (1114). *ākiñcaññasambhavaṃ ñatvā nandīsaṃyojanaṃ iti, evam etaṃ abhiññāya tato tattha vipassati etaṃ ñāṇaṃ tathaṃ tassa brāhmanassa vusīmato ti* (1115).

105 Collins (1982: 215): 'the concept of stations of consciousness covers both meditative states and ethical attitudes of mind in the present life, and also destinies for it after death.'

106 Norman (2001: 141) does not read *nandīsaṃyojanaṃ* as a compound; he translates *nandī saṃyojanaṃ iti* as '[he thinks] "Enjoyment is a fetter"'. This does not alter the meaning much, although Norman's translation of *pāda-s* (a-b) gives the impression that the act of insight described by *ākiñciññasambhavaṃ ñatvā* is different from the thought content of *nandīsaṃyojanaṃ iti*, whereas it seems to me that the latter is the content of liberating insight indicated by the former. Reading a *karmadhāraya* compound *nandīsaṃyojanaṃ* is supported by Sn 1109.

107 Wynne (2004: 117).

## 6 CONCLUSION

1 See p. 49 n. 91.

2 Frauwallner (1953: 176): 'Und dass es sich um entlehnte ältere Vorstellungen handelt, ist auch daraus zu ersehen, dass die Sphäre jenseits von Bewusst und Unbewusst auch in Jinismus wiederkehrt.' Nakamura (1979: 272).

3 Bronkhorst (1993: 53).

4 Bronkhorst (1993: 45–53).

5 Bronkhorst (1993: 45).

6 Bronkhorst (1993: 53).

7 Bronkhorst (1993: 48 n. 11).

8 Bronkhorst (1993: 48).

9 Mbh XII.178.15–16, Mbh XII.294.8, Mbh XII.304.9. Breath restraint is also mentioned in the *Bhagavadgītā* at IV.29.

10 Bronkhorst (1993: 60), referring to Mbh XII.232.10–18.

11 The word 'not' inserted here is surely a mistake.

12 Lindtner (1997: 129).

13 Schayer (1935: 125, 131).

14 E.g. A I.10.5: *pabhassaram idaṃ bhikkhave cittaṃ tañ ca kho āgantukehi upakkilesehi upakkiliṭṭhan ti*; M I.329.30 (D I.223.12): *viññāṇaṃ anidassanaṃ anantaṃ sabhatopabhaṃ.*
15 Schayer (1935: 125).
16 Keith (1936: 6): 'But the six *dhātu* list suggests that we have a relic of a view which made consciousness the source whence the elements were derived, each less subtle than the preceding.'
17 Keith (1936: 6).
18 Keith (1936: 6).
19 Lindtner (1997: 116–17).
20 See p. 64ff.
21 *Udāna* 80.9 (Vagga VIII.1: *pāṭaligāmiyavaggo): atthi bhikkhave tad āyatanaṃ yattha n'eva paṭhavī na āpo na tejo na vāyo na ākāsānañcāyatanaṃ na viññāṇānañcāyatanaṃ na ākiñcaññayātanaṃ na nevasaññānāsaññāyatanaṃ nāyaṃ loko na paraloko no ubho candimāsuriyā tatra p' āhaṃ bhikkhave n' eva āgatiṃ vadāmi na gatiṃ na ṭhitiṃ na cutiṃ na upapattiṃ; appatiṭṭhaṃ appavattaṃ anārammaṇam eva taṃ. es' ev' anto dukkhassā ti.* Reading *no ubho candimāsuriyā tatra p'āhaṃ* for *ubho canimāsuriyā tad amhaṃ* (See Errata to the text). This seems to be the only place in the Suttapiṭaka where the form *viññāṇānañcāyatana* has not become *viññānañcāyatana* because of haplography, although Be reads the latter.
22 KaU V.15 (= ŚU VI.14, MuU II.2.11): *na tatra sūryo bhāti na candratārakaṃ nemā vidyuto bhānti kuto 'yam agniḥ.*
23 *Vyākhyā* on Akbh I.5 (Śastri, 1981:20): *pṛthivī bho gautama kutra pratiṣṭhitā? pṛthivī brāhmaṇa abmaṇḍale pratiṣṭhitā. abmaṇḍalaṃ bho gautama kutra pratiṣṭhitam? vāyau pratiṣṭhitam. vāyur bho gautama kutra pratiṣṭhitaḥ? ākāśe pratiṣṭhitaḥ. ākāśaṃ bho gautama kutra pratiṣṭhitam. atisarati mahābrāhmaṇa, atisarati mahābrāhmaṇa. ākāśaṃ brāhmaṇa apratiṣṭhitam anālambanam iti vistaraḥ. tasmād asty ākāśam iti vaibhāṣikāḥ.* See Qvarnström (1989: 120).
24 According to Collins (1990: 89) this was part of the strategy of legitimisation by the monks of the Mahāvihārin lineage in Ceylon in the early centuries of the first millennium AD.
25 La Vallée Poussin (1937).
26 E.g. Rupert Gethin (2001: xiii): 'While my study of the *bodhi-pakkhiyā dhammā* does not address directly all the specific points raised by those following in the footsteps of La Vallée Poussin and Frauwallner, it does at least, I think, place a question mark against some of the claims of "contradiction" and "inconsistency" in the way the texts (the Pali Nikāyas, the Abhidhamma, and the commentaries) present the theory of Buddhist meditation.' One can object that this is bound to be the conclusion if one studies a list made up of homogeneous items: Gethin's study shows that the separate items in the list of *bodhipakkhiyā dhammā* contain nothing of a heterogeneous nature. The fact is that this rather late list of thirty-seven *dhamma-s* does not have anything to do with the 'specific points raised by those following in the footsteps of La Vallée Poussin and Frauwallner'. It may systematize the meditative formulations of the Suttapiṭaka fairly well, but this is not surprising – it is not representative of the meditative formulations of the entire Suttapiṭaka. The one notable omission from this list and its extensions, as noted by Bronkhorst (1985: 306), is the list of four formless spheres. This led Bronkhorst to conclude that the formless meditations were not accepted in the earliest period of Buddhism (Bronkhorst 1993: xiii).
27 PED *yoga* s.v.: 'one who is devoted to the *dhamma*'.
28 A III.356.14: *acchariyā h' ete āvuso puggalā dullabhā lokasmiṃ, ye amataṃ dhātuṃ kāyena phusitvā viharanti.*

29 A III.356.20: *acchariyā h' ete āvuso puggalā dullabhā lokasmiṃ, ye gambhīraṃ atthapadaṃ paññāya ativijjha passantī ti.*

30 The phrase *paññāya ativijjha* usually occurs as half of a couplet, of which the other item is *kāyena phusitvā* or *kāyena paramaṃ saccaṃ sacchikaroti* (M I.480.10, II.173.24; S V.227.1, V.230.10; A II.115.12). In other words, according to the couplet, liberation must combine the different points of view of the *Mahā-Cunda Sutta*: *paññāya ativijjha* in the couplet refers to an intellectual insight different from meditation. Indeed, when it occurs alone, it refers to a sort of understanding: at M II.112.1 the expression *paññāya ativijjha* refers to the understanding of the Buddha; at A I.265.12 *paññāya ativijjha* refers to a non-liberated, intellectual understanding; at A IV.362.2 *gambhīraṃ atthapadaṃ paññāya ativijjha passati* refers to the understanding of a *dhamma*-preacher; and at A II.178.28 *paññāya cassa atthaṃ ativijjha passati* describes the disciple's (*sutavā*) understanding of the Four Noble Truths, the disciple being differentiated from the liberated person (*paṇḍito mahāpañño*). Moreover, the meaning of *atthapada* given in CPD is '1. a right or profitable word'; PED s.v. states: 'a profitable saying, a word of good sense, text, motto.' It must refer to doctrinal formulations in general.

31 Insight into the twelvefold chain of dependent origination, in its reverse (*paṭiloma*) order and its origintation (*samudaya*) and cessation (*nirodha*) modes, is said to be the original discovery of the Buddha and the six previous Buddhas at S II.5.7 (*Nidānavagga: Nidānasaṃyutta* IV-X). However, in the biographical account in the *Mahāvagga* (Vin I.ff.), insight into the twelve-fold dependent origination occurs after awakening; and does not constitute the content of the Bodhisatta's liberating insight. Therefore, we have two different theories of liberating insight: for Musīla at S II.115, the content of liberating insight is the twelve-fold list of dependent origination, a theory strongly suggested at S II.5.7ff. But for the authors of the biography in the *Mahāvagga*, the content of liberating insight is the Four Noble Truths (Vin I.11.1ff.), with insight into dependent origination being a later discovery of the Buddha. If insight into dependent origination was thought to be discovered by the Buddha after the awakening, as described in the Vinaya, it is easy to see how the idea arose that this must be what any *bhikkhu* must realize in order to attain liberation. If this is correct, it means that Musīla's theory of liberating insight was just that – a theory – and a theory preceded by the theory in the *Mahāvagga* that insight into the Four Noble Truths effected the Bodhisatta's liberation.

32 S II.117.15: *tenāyasmā Musīlo arahaṃ khīṇāsavo ti. evaṃ vutte āyasmā Musīlo tunhī ahosī ti.*

33 S II.118.1: *bhavanirodho nibbānan ti kho me āvuso yathābhūtaṃ sammapaññāya sudiṭṭhaṃ, na c' amhi arahaṃ khīṇāsavo.*

34 M I.435.36ff. (= A IV.423.2ff.), A I.282.17.

35 Its other occurrence is in the description of sense restraint that is usually a preliminary to the practice of *jhāna* e.g. D I.70.15: *kāyena phoṭṭhabbaṃ phusitvā phusitvā.*

36 M I.33.34, 477.26; S II.123.14, S II.127.18; A II.87.9, II 89.36ff., II 91.1, IV 316.2ff., V 11.23ff. At A IV.451.29ff., the expression *kāyena phusitvā* is applied not only to the formless meditations, but also to the four *jhāna-s*. It is likely that this singular occurrence represents a rather late development.

37 La Vallée Poussin (1937: 191): 'Cette voie aboutit, par une graduelle purification, par la graduelle suppression des idées *(saṃkalpa),* à un état d'inconscience – cessation de la pensée sous tous ses modes, *saṃjñāvedayitanirodha* ou simplement *nirodhasamāpatti* – qui met l'ascète en contact avec une réalité transcendante qui

est le *Nirvāṇa* (ancienne doctrine) ou qui est semblable au *Nirvāṇa* (scholastique Sarvāstivādin).' He then uses A III.355 as evidence to support this.

38 It 45.25ff. (= It 62.8): *rūpadhātupariññāya arūpesu asaṇṭhitā, nirodhe ye vimuccanti te janā maccuhāyino. kāyena amataṃ dhātuṃ phassayitvā nirūpadhiṃ, upadhippaṭinissaggaṃ sacchikatvā anāsavo, deseti sammāsambuddho asokaṃ virajaṃ padan ti.*

39 La Vallée Poussin (1937: 191): 'En principe, sinon en fait, ce chemin n'a rien qui soit spécifiquement bouddhique; la 'vue des vérités' n'y a pas de place; la connaissance spéculative (*prajñā*) n'y est pas mise en œuvre.'

40 Schmithausen (1981: 214).

41 See p. 117 n. 30: *paññāya ativijjha* in the couplet refers to an intellectual insight different from meditation.

42 S II.119.16 (*Nidānavagga: Nidāna Saṃyutta* 70 = *mahāvagga* IX).

43 Susīma's interview of these monks begins at S II.121.8. See Gombrich (1996: 96–134, especially 123–27).

44 I.e. the knowledge of past lives (*pubbenivāsānusatiñāṇa*), and the death and rebirth of other beings according to the law of *kamma* (*cūtūpapātañāṇa*).

45 S III.68.27 (= Vin I 14.34): *imasmiṃ ca pana veyyākaraṇasmiṃ bhaññamāne pañcavaggiyānam bhikkhūnam anupādāya āsavehi cittāni vimucciṃsū ti.* See p. 20 n. 72 on the equivalent episode in the Theravāda Vinaya and the Mahāsaṅghika *Mahāvastu*.

46 See p. 72 n. 2.

47 See Wynne 2002.

48 Gombrich (1996: 127). At the same time he notes: 'But I cannot exclude the possibility that the author of the Pali *Susīma Sutta* that has come down to us had views on the matter to put forward.'

49 Schmithausen (1981: 211).

50 This does not necessarily mean that the Sutta dates to the earliest period, although I think it probably does.

51 M III.298.13: *cakkhunā rūpaṃ na passati, sotena saddaṃ na suṇāti.*

52 At Mbh XII.314.23, 30 it refers to Vyāsa, and at Mbh XII.316.48 it refers to Śuka.

53 Mbh XII.308.24.

54 M III 298.16: *evaṃ sante kho, Uttara, andho bhāvitindriyo bhavissati, badhiro bhāvitindriyo bhavissati.*

55 E.g. bhikkhus Ñāṇamoli and Bodhi's translation of the description of the fourth *jhāna* (1995: 105): 'I entered upon and abided in the fourth *jhāna*, which has neither-pain-nor-pleasure and purity of mindfulness due to equanimity.' Translation of M I.22.7: *adukkkhaṃ asukhaṃ upekhāsatiparisuddhiṃ catutthaṃ jhānaṃ upasampajja vihāsiṃ.* The problem with this is that the translators seem to understand that simple adjectives such as *adukkhaṃ*, *asukhaṃ* and *upekhāsatiparisuddhiṃ* are 'factors' (*dhamma-s*?) of a meditative absorption. But this is misleading. The compounds *adukkhaṃ*, *asukhaṃ* and *upekhāsatiparisuddhiṃ* do not indicate 'factors' of/in the fourth *jhāna*, as if real 'things' contained in an objectively 'real' meditative state. The compounds are used to qualify a certain mental state that a practitioner of meditation can experience, one that can be *described* as an experience of the purification of mindfulness and indifference.

56 MMW s.v. *√upekṣ*.

57 See the meaning of *upekhā* at M III 299.15, 299.19, 299.24, 299.29 etc., where it denotes an indifference towards sense objects; and especially M III.301.17 where *upekhako* is combined with *sato sampajāno*.

58 This has been pointed out by Richard Gombrich. He writes (1997: 10): 'I know this is controversial, but it seems to me that the third and fourth jhānas are thus

quite unlike the second. I suppose that one can be "aware and cognisant" without being aware of anything in particular: the terms "aware and cognisant" could perhaps be described as a state of receptivity, of potential rather than actual thought. But I find this an unsatisfying argument. One has to ask whether a real meditator would or would not notice a flashing light or a loud noise in his vicinity. The natural explanation of the text, in my view, is that in the third and fourth jhāna he would, but in the second he would not. If that is correct, this description of the jhāna describes (and prescribes) two quite different cognitive states, and the later tradition has falsified the jhāna by classifying them as the quintessence of the concentrated, calming kind of meditation, ignoring the other – and indeed higher – element.'

59 Schmithausen (1981: 207–8).
60 Schmithausen (1981: 205).
61 M I.6.11.
62 Vin I.10ff. (= S V 422.3ff.); see Schmithausen (1981: 202).
63 M I.55.11 and A III.414.13.
64 Schmithausen (1981: 205).
65 As Griffiths puts it (1981: 616), the four *jhāna-s* are a sort of 'limbering up exercise for the mind, a way of making it supple and preparing it for the effort needed to gain insight into the real nature of the universe'.
66 See p. 120 n. 45 and p. 20 n. 72: the same intellectualist version of liberating insight is found in Theravādin and Mahāsaṅghika sources; the Sthaviras and Mahāsaṅghikas probably split some time after the second council 60 AB (Gombrich 1992: 258).
67 I have argued elsewhere that such a process was not ad hoc, but was a planned exercise carried out not by individual reciters but by redactional committees in the early Buddhist communities (Wynne 2004).

# BIBLIOGRAPHY

Almond, Philip C. (1988) *The British Discovery of Buddhism*, Cambridge: Cambridge University Press.

Apte, Vaman Shivaram (1998) *The Practical Sanskrit–English Dictionary* (revised and enlarged edition; first compact edition), Delhi: Motilal Banarsidass.

Bareau, André (1963) *Recherches sur la biographie du Buddha dans les Sutrapitaka et les Vinayapitaka anciens I: De la quête de l'éveil à la conversion de Sariputra et de Maudgalyayana*, Paris: École française d'Extrême-Orient.

—— (1970–71) *Recherches sur la biographie du Buddha dans les Sutrapitaka et les Vinayapitaka anciens II: Les derniers mois, le Parinirvana, et les funérailles*, Paris: École française d'Extrême-Orient.

Barnes, Michael Anthony (1976) *The Buddhist Way of Deliverance: A Comparison Between the Pali Canon and the Yoga-Praxis of the Great Epic*, Oxford: unpublished M.Litt. thesis.

Beal, Samuel (1906) *Si-Yu-Ki: Buddhist Records of The Western World*, London; reprinted Delhi: Motilal Banarsidass (1981).

Bedekar, V. M. (1963) 'The place of japa in the *Mokṣadharma* (Mbh 12 189–193) and the *Yoga* Sūtras: a comparative study', *Annals of the Bhandarkar Oriental Research Institute* 44, pp. 63–74.

Belvalkar, S. K. (1951–53) *Mahābhārata, Śāntiparvan: Mokṣadharma*; *fascicules 22–24 of the Critical Edition*, Poona: Bhandarkar Oriental Research Institute.

Bodhi, Bhikkhu (2000) *The Connected Discourses of the Buddha. A New Translation of the Saṃyutta Nikāya* (vol. I), Oxford: Pali Text Society.

Böhtlingk, Otto and Roth, Rudolph (1855–75) *Sanskrit-Wörterbuch herausgegeben von der Kaiserlichen Akademie der Wissenschaften*, St Petersburg: K. Akademie der Wissenschaften.

Brereton, Joel (1990) 'The Upanishads'. In *Approaches to the Asian Classics*, eds Wm Theodore de Barry and Irene Bloom, pp. 115–35, New York: Columbia University Press.

—— (1999) 'Edifying puzzlement*: Ṛgveda* 10.129 and the uses of enigma', *Journal of the American Oriental Society*, vol. 119, no. 2, 248–60.

Bronkhorst, Johannes (1985) 'Dhamma and Abhidhamma', *Bulletin of the School of Oriental and African Studies* 48, pp. 305–20.

—— (1986) *The Two Traditions of Meditation in Ancient India*, Stuttgart: Steiner Verlag; reprinted, New Delhi: Motilal Banarsidass (1993).

—— (2000) 'Die Buddhistische Lehre', *Der indische Buddhismus und seine Verzweigungen: Die Religionen der Menschheit*, Stuttgart: W. Kohlhammer, vol. 24, no. 1, pp. 23–213.

Brough, John (1962) *The Gāndhārī Dharmapada*, London: School of Oriental and African Studies; reprinted, Delhi: Motilal Banarsidass (2001).

Cabezón, José Ignacio (1995) 'Buddhist studies as a discipline and the role of theory', *Journal of the International Association of Buddhist Studies*, vol. 18, no. 2, pp. 231–68.

*Chaṭṭha Saṅgāyana*: CD-ROM version of the Burmese Tipiṭika, Rangoon 1954, Dhammagiri: Vipassana Research Institute, version 3.

Chau, Bhikkhu Thich Minh (1991) *The Chinese Madhyama Āgama and the Pāli Majjhima Nikāya: A Comparative Study*, Delhi: Motilal Banarsidass.

Collins, Steven (1982) *Selfless Persons; Imagery and Thought in Theravāda Buddhism*, Cambridge: Cambridge University Press.

—— (1987) 'Review of Bronkhorst 1993', *Journal of the Royal Asiatic Society* 1987, pp. 373–75.

—— (1990) 'On the very idea of the Pali Canon', *Journal of the Pali Text Society* XV, pp. 89–126.

Cone, Margaret (2001) *A Dictionary of Pali, Part I*, Oxford: Pali Text Society.

Cousins, L. S. (1991) 'The Five Points and the Origins of the Buddhist Schools'. In *The Buddhist Forum, vol. II*, ed. T. Skorupski, pp. 27–60, London: SOAS, University of London.

De Jong, J. W. (2000) 'The Buddha and His Teachings'. In *Wisdom, Compassion, and the Search for Understanding. The Buddhist Studies Legacy of Gadgin M. Nagao*, ed. Jonathan A. Silk, pp. 171–80, Honolulu: University of Hawaii Press.

Dutoit, Julius (1905) *Die Duṣkaracaryā des Bodhisattva in der buddhistischen Tradition*, Strasburg: Karl J. Trṃbner.

Edgerton, Franklin (1965) *The Beginnings of Indian Philosophy: Selections from the Rig Veda, Atharva Veda, Upaniṣads, and Mahābhārata, Translated from the Sanskrit with an Introduction, Notes and Glossarial Index*, London: George Allen & Unwin.

—— (1944) *The Bhagavad Gītā, translated and interpreted*, Cambridge: Harvard Oriental Series; reprinted, Delhi: Motilal Banarsidass (1994).

Eliade, Mircea (1954) *Le yoga. Immortalité et liberté*, Paris; trans. Willard R. Trask (1969) *Yoga, Immortality and Freedom*, London: Routlege & Kegan Paul.

—— (editor in chief) (1987) *The Encyclopedia of Religion*, New York, London: Macmillan.

Frauwallner, Erich (1953) *Geschichte der indischen Philosophie Band I: Die Philosophie des Veda und des Epos, der Buddha und der Jina, das Sāmkhya und das Klassische Yoga-system*, Salzburg: O. Müller: Instituto Italiano per il Medio ed Estreme Orientale.

—— (1956) *The Earliest Vinaya and the Beginnings of Buddhist Literature*, Rome: Instituto per il Medio ed Estremo Oriente.

Geiger, Wilhelm (1994) *A Pāli Grammar*, Oxford: Pali Text Society.

Gethin, R. M. L. (2004) 'He who sees *dhamma* sees *dhammas: dhamma* in early Buddhism', *Journal of Indian Philosophy*, vol. 32, pp. 513–24.

—— (1992) *The Buddhist Path to Awakening: A Study of the Bodhi-Pakkhiya Dhamma*, Leiden: Brill; reprinted, Oxford: Oneworld (2001).

Gnoli, Raniero (1978) *The Gilgit Manuscript of the Saṅghabhedavastu, Being the 17th and Last Section of the Vinaya of the Mūlasarvāstivādin, Part II*, Rome: Istituto Italiano per il Medio ed Estremo Oriente.

Gombrich, Richard F. (1988) 'The History of Early Buddhism: Major Advances since 1950'. In *Indological Studies and South Asian Bibliography – a Conference*, Calcutta: National Library Leeds: University of Leeds.

—— (1990) 'Recovering the Buddha's Message'. In *The Buddhist Forum: Seminar Papers 1987–1988*, ed. T. Skorupski, pp. 5–20, London: SOAS.

—— (1992) 'Dating the Historical Buddha: A Red Herring Revealed'. In *The Dating of the Historical Buddha, Part 2*, ed. Heinz Bechert, pp. 237–59, Göttingen: Vandenhoeck & Ruprecht.

—— (1996) *How Buddhism Began: The Conditioned Genesis of the Early Teachings*, London: Athlone Press.

—— (1997) 'Religious experience in early Buddhism?', *Eighth Annual British Association for the Study of Religion Lecture.*

Goudriaan, Teun (1978) *Māyā Divine and Human: A Study of Magic and its Religious Foundations in Sanskrit Texts, with Particular Attention to a Fragment on Viṣṇu's Māyā preserved in Bali*, Delhi: Motilal Banarsidass.

Griffiths, Paul (1981) 'Concentration or insight: the problematic of Theravāda Buddhist Meditation-theory', *The Journal of the American Academy of Religion*, vol. 49, no. 4, pp. 605–24.

Hacker, Paul (1961) 'The Sāṃkhyization of the Emanation Doctrine (shown in a critical analysis of texts)', *Wiener Zeitschrift fṃr die Kunde Sṃd- und Ostasiens und Archiv fṃr indische Philosophie* 5, pp. 75–112.

Halbfass, Wilhelm (1988) *India and Europe: An Essay in Understanding*, Albany NY: State University of New York Press.

—— (1995) *Philology and Confrontation: Paul Hacker on Traditional and Modern Vedanta*, Albany NY: State University of New York Press.

Hallisey, Charles (1995) 'Roads Taken and Not Taken in the Study of Theravāda Buddhism', in *Curators of the Buddha: The Study of Buddhism under Colonialism*, ed. D. Lopez, pp. 31–61 Chicago: University of Chicago Press.

Hopkins, E. W. (1901a) '*Yoga* technique in the Great Epic', *Journal of the American Oriental Society* 22, pp. 333–79.

—— (1901b) *The Great Epic of India*, New York, London.

Horner, I. B. (1954) *The Collection of Middle Length Sayings*, vol. I: *The First Fifty Discourses*, London: Luzac.

Hultzsch, E. (1925) *Corpus Inscriptionum Indicarum, Vol. I: Inscriptions of Aśoka*, Oxford: Clarendon Press for the Government of India; reprinted, New Delhi: The Director General Archaeological Survey of India (1991).

Hume, Robert Ernest (1931) *The Thirteen Principal Upanishads* (2nd revised edition), Oxford: Oxford University Press.

Jayatilleke, K. N. (1963) *Early Buddhist Theory of Knowledge*, London: George Allen & Unwin; reprinted, Delhi: Motilal Banarsidass (1998).

Johnston, E. H. (1935–36) *Aśvaghoṣa's Buddhacarita, or Acts of the Buddha. Complete Sanskrit Text with English Translation* (Parts I-III), Calcutta: Baptist Mission Press; reprinted, Delhi: Motilal Banarsidass (1984).

Jones, J. J. (1949–56) *The Mahāvastu: Translated from the Buddhist Sanskrit (Sacred Books of the Buddhists, volumes 16, 18, 19)*, London: Luzac.

Jurewicz, Joanna (1995) 'The Ṛgveda 10.129 – an attempt of interpretation', in *Cracow Indological Studies, volume I: International Conference on Sanskrit and Related Studies, September 23–26, 1992 (Proceedings)*, Cracow: The Enigma Press.

Kashyap, Bhikkhu J. (1959a) *Khuddaka Nikāya, vol I: Suttanipāta* (*Nālandā-Devanāgarī-Pāli-Series*), Bihar: Pāli Publication Board.

—— (1959b) *Khuddaka Nikāya, vol. IV, part II: The Cullaniddesa* (*Nālandā-Devanāgarī-Pāli-Series*), Bihar: Pāli Publication Board.

Keith, A. B. (1936) 'Pre-Canonical Buddhism', *Indian Historical Quarterly* XII, pp. 1–20.

King, Richard (1999) *Orientalism and Religion: Postcolonial Theory, India and 'The Mystic East'*, New Delhi: Oxford University Press.

Lamotte, Etienne (1958) *Histoire du Bouddhisme Indien, des origines a l'ère Śaka*, Louvaine: Bibliothèque du Muséon; trans. Sara Webb-Boin (1988) *History of Indian Buddhism, from the Origins to the Śaka Era*, Louvaine: Université Catholique de Louvain.

La Vallée Poussin, Louis de (1917) *The Way to Nirvāṇa: Six Lectures on Ancient Buddhism as a Discipline of Salvation*, Cambridge: The Hibbert Lectures, 1916.

—— (1937) 'Musīla et Nārada', *Mélanges chinois et boudhiques* 5, pp. 189–222.

Lefmann, S. (1902–08) *Lalitavistara: Leben und Lehre des Śākya-Buddha. Textausg., mit Varianten-, Metren-, und Wörterverzeichnis*, Halle, Halle: Buchhandlung des Waisenhauses.

Limaye, V. P. and Vadekar, R. D. (1958) *Eighteen Principal Upaniṣads*, Vol.1 (Gandhi Memorial Edition), Poona: Vaidika Saṃśodhana Maṇḍala.

Lindtner, Christian (1997) 'The problem of precanonical Buddhism', *Buddhist Studies Review*, vol. 14, no. 2, pp. 109–139.

Macdonell, A. A. (1917) *A Vedic Reader For Students*, Oxford: Oxford University Press; reprinted, Delhi: Motilal Banarsidass (1999).

Nakamura, Hajime (1979) 'A Process of the Origination of Buddhist Meditation in Connection with the Life of the Buddha'. In *Studies in Pali And Buddhism (A Homage Volume to the Memory of Bhikkhu Jagdish Kashyap)*, ed. Dr A. K. Narain, pp. 270–77, Delhi: B. R. Publishing Corp.

Ñāṇamoli, Bhikkhu and Bodhi, Bhikkhu (1995) *The Middle Length Discourses of the Buddha: A Translation of the Majjhima Nikāya*, Boston, MA: Wisdom Publications.

Norman, K. R. (1970) 'Some aspects of the phonology of the Prakrit underlying the Aśokan Inscriptions', *Bulletin of the School of Oriental and African Studies* XXXIII, pp. 132–43; reprinted in *Collected Papers*, vol. I, Oxford: Pāli Text Society, pp. 93–107.

—— (1978) 'The Role of Pāli in early Sinhalese Buddhism'. In *Buddhism in Ceylon and Studies on Religious Syncretism*, ed. Heinz Bechert, Göttingen: Vanderhock and Rupert pp. 28–47; reprinted in *Collected Papers*, vol. II, Oxford: Pāli Text Society, pp. 30–51.

—— (1990–2001) *Collected Papers*, vols I-VII, Oxford: Pāli Text Society.

—— (1990) 'Aspects of Early Buddhism'. In *Earliest Buddhism and Madhyamaka*, ed. David Seyfort Ruegg and Lambert Schmithausen, pp. 24–35; reprinted in *Collected Papers*, vol. IV, Oxford: Pāli Text Society, pp. 124–38 Leiden: Brill.

—— (1991) 'Death and the Tathāgata'. In *Studies in Buddhism and Culture (In Honour of Professor Dr. Egaku Mayeda)*, pp. 1–11, Tokyo; reprinted in *Collected Papers*, vol. IV, Oxford: Pāli Text Society, Sankibo Busshorin, pp. 251–63.

—— (1997) *A Philological Approach To Buddhism: The Bukkyo Dendo Kyokai Lectures 1994*, London: School of Oriental and African Studies.

—— (2001) *The Group of Discourses (Sutta-Nipāta)*, 2nd edition, Oxford: Pali Text Society.

Oberhammer, Gerhard (ed.) (1983) *Inklusivismus: Eine indische Denkform*, Vienna: Publications of the De Nobili Research Library.

Oberlies, Thomas (2001) *A Grammar of the Language of the Theravāda Tipiñaka*, Berlin, New York: Walter de Gruyter.

Oldenberg, Hermann (1879) *The Vinaya Piṭakaṃ: One of the Principal Buddhist Holy Scriptures in the Pāli Language, volume I, the Mahāvagga*, London: Williams and Norgate.

Olivelle, Patrick (1986) Review of Oberhammer 1983, *Journal of the American Oriental Society*, vol. 106, pp. 867–68.

—— (1998) *Early Upaniṣads*, Oxford: Oxford University Press.

Pérez-Remón, Joaquín (1980) *Self and Non-self in Early Buddhism*, The Hague: Mouton Publishers.

Qvarnstrom, O. (1989) *Hindu Philosophy in Buddhist Perspective: The Vedāntatat-tvaviniścaya Chapter of Bhavya's Madhyamakahṛdayakārikā*, Lund: Plus Ultra.

Reynolds, Frank E. (1976) 'The Many Lives of Buddha. A Study of Sacred Biography and Theravāda Tradition'. In *The Biographical Process. Studies in the History and Psychology of Religion*, eds Frank E. Reynolds and Donald Capps, The Hague, Paris: Mouton, pp. 37–61.

Rhys Davids, T. W. (1870) *Buddhism: Being a Sketch of the Life and Teachings of Gautama, the Buddha*, London: Society for Promoting Christian Knowledge; reprinted, New Delhi: Asian Educational Services (2000).

—— (1899) *Sacred Books of the Buddhists vol. II (Dialogues of the Buddha Part I)*, London; reprinted Oxford: Pali Text Society (1995).

—— (1903) *Buddhist India*, London T. Fisher Unwin; New York: G. P. Putnam's Sons.

—— (1908) *Early Buddhism*, London: Archibald Constable & Co.; reprinted New Delhi: Asian Educational Services (2002).

—— and Stede, William (1921–1925) *Pali-English Dictionary*, London: Pali Text Society.

Said, Edward W. (1978) *Orientalism*, London: Routledge & Kegan Paul; reprinted London: Penguin Books (1995).

Salomon, Richard (1999) *Ancient Buddhist Scrolls from Gandhara: The British Library Kharosthi Fragments*, London: British Library.

—— (2003) 'The senior manuscripts: another collection of Gandhāran Buddhist Scrolls', *Journal of the American Oriental Society*, vol. 123, no. 1, pp. 73–92.

Śastri, Swāmī Dwārikādās (1981) *Abhidharmakośa and Bhāṣya of Ācārya Vasubandhu with Sphuñārthā Commentary of Ācārya Yaśomitra, Part I (I to IV Kośasthāna)*, Varanasi: Bauddha Bharati.

Schayer, Stanislaw (1935) 'Precanonical Buddhism', *Archiv Orientální* VII, pp. 121–32.

Schmithausen, Lambert (1981) 'On Some Aspects of Descriptions or Theories of "Liberating Insight" and "Enlightenment" in Early Buddhism'. In *Studien Zum Jainism und Buddhism*, eds Klaus Bruhn and Albert Wezler, Wiesbanden: Franz Steiner, pp. 199–250.

—— (1990) Preface to *Earliest Buddhism and Madhyamaka: Panels of the VIIth World Sanskrit Conference*, eds Lambert Schmithausen and David Seyfort Ruegg, Leiden: Brill.

—— (1992) 'An Attempt to Estimate the Distance in Time between Aśoka and the Buddha in Terms of Doctrinal History'. In *The Dating of the Historical Buddha Part 2*, ed. Heinz Bechert, Göttingen: Vandenhoeck & Ruprecht, pp. 110–47.

Schopen, Gregory (1985) 'Two problems in the history of Indian Buddhism: the layman/monk distinction and the doctrines of the transference of merit', *Studien zur Indologie und Iranistik*, 10, pp. 9–47 (= Schopen (1997), pp. 23–55).

—— (1997) *Bones, Stones and Buddhist Monks. Collected Papers on the Archaeology, Epigraphy, and Texts of Monastic Buddhism in India*, Honolulu: University of Hawaii Press.

Senart, É. (1881–1897) *Le Mahāvastu, texte Sanscrit publié pour la première fois et accompagné d'introduction et d'un commentaire*, Paris: L'Imprimerie nationale.

Skilling, Peter (1981–82a) 'Uddaka Rāmaputta and Rāma', *Pāli Buddhist Review*, vol. 6, no. 2, pp. 99–105.

—— (1981–82b) 'The three similes', *Pāli Buddhist Review*, vol. 6, no. 2, pp. 105–13.

Sutton, Nicholas (2000) *The Religious Doctrines in the Mahābhārata*, Delhi: Motilal Banarsidass.

Tambiah, Stanley Jeyaraja (1984) *The Buddhist Saints of the Forest and the Cult of Amulets*, Cambridge: Cambridge University Press.

—— (1992) *Buddhism Betrayed. Religion, Politics and Violence in Sri Lanka*, Chicago, IL: The University of Chicago Press.

Thomas, E. J. (1927) *The Life of Buddha as Legend and History*, London: Kegan Paul.

Tillemans, Tom J. F. (1995) 'Remarks on philology', *Journal of the International Association of Buddhist Studies*, vol. 18, no. 2, pp. 269–77.

Trenckner, V. (1924) *A Critical Pali Dictionary,* continued and eds Dines Andersen, Helmer Smith and Hans Hendriksen, Copenhagen: Royal Danish Academy of Letters and Sciences.

Van Buitenen, J. A. B. (1957a) 'Dharma and Mokṣa', *Philosophy East and West* 7, pp. 33–40.

—— (1957b) 'Studies in Sāṃkhya II: Ahaṃkāra', *Journal of the American Oriental Society* 77, pp. 15–25.

Vetter, Tilmann (1988) *The Ideas and Meditative Practices of Early Buddhism*, Leiden: E. J. Brill.

—— (1990) 'Some Remarks on the Older Parts of the *Suttanipāta*', in *Earliest Buddhism and Madhyamake: Panels of the VIith World Sanskrit Conference*, Schmithausen, Lambert and Ruegg, 1990, Leiden: Brill, pp. 36–56.

Wynne, Alexander (2002) 'An interpretation of "released on both sides" (*ubhato-bhāga-vimutti*), and the ramifications for the study of early Buddhism', *Buddhist Studies Review*, vol. 19, no. 1, pp. 31–40.

—— (2004) 'The oral transmission of early Buddhist literature', *Journal of the International Association of Buddhist Studies*, vol. 27, no. 1, pp. 97–128.

—— (2005) 'The historical authenticity of early Buddhist literature: a critical evaluation', *Wiener Zeitschrift fṃr die Kunde Sṃdasiens* Band XLIX/2005, pp. 35–70.

Zafiropulo, G. (1993) *L'illumination du Buddha: de la quête à l'annonce de l'Éveil: essais de chronologie relative et de stratigraphie textuelle*, Innsbruck: Institut für Sprachwissenschaft der Universität Innsbruck.

# INDEX


*abhibhāyatana* 34
Abhidharmakośabhāṣya 115
*abhiṛñā* 105
*adhimutta* 78–9
*Aggañña Sutta* 47
*Aggi-Vacchagotta Sutta* 95–6
*agni* 96–7
*ahaṃkāra* 38, 41, 52–6
Ājīvikas 16
Āḷāra Kālāma: Buddhist appraisal of 22; Brahminic background of 44–5; Brahminic teaching of 108; meditative goal of *see* nothingness; name and location of 12–13; practices of *see* element meditation, formless meditation; spiritual attainment of 14–15; supposed Jaina background of 110
*Anattalakkhaṇa Sutta* 120–1
*anupubbavihāra-s* 44, 81, 120
Apadāna 73
Āpastamba Dharmasūtra 112
*Ariyapariyesana Sutta*: antiquity and historical authenticity of 16–17, 21, 23–4, 125–8; Chinese Sarvāstivādin parallel of 17, 19; circumstantial evidence of 107; peculiarities of 14–23, 110; simplicity of 24–5
argument from silence 10, 74, 149 n.41
Arthavargīya *see Aṭṭhavagga*
asceticism 112–13; *see also* breath restraint
Aśoka 5, 74
Aśvaghoṣa 25–6
*Aṭṭhavagga* 73–4, 78
*avyakta* 38–40, 52–4, 69

Bahuśrutikas 26
Bareau, A. 9–11
becoming cool metaphor 76–7, 84–5, 91–2, 97
*Bhagavadgītā* 34
Bharaṇḍu Kālāma 13
*Bharaṇḍu-kālāma Sutta* 12–13
*Bhayabherava Sutta* 18, 21
*Bhikkhu-pātimokkha* 7
*bodhi-pakkhiyā dhammā* 155 n.26
Bodhirājakumāra Sutta 9, 17; *see also* MSS *et al.*
Bodhisatta: asceticism and breathless meditation of 17–18, 23; critique of ascetic acts 22; early accounts of striving 9; rejection of the two teachers 23, 25, 108; renunciation 14–15; training under two teachers 14–15, 25, 110
Bodhisattva *see* Bodhisatta
*brahmabhūtaḥ* 89, 91
*Brahmajāla Sutta* 88
breathless meditation *see* Bodhisatta
breath restraint 112–13
Brereton, J. 42, 57–63
*Bṛhadāraṇyaka Upaniṣad* 43–5, 48–9, 55, 89, 111
Bronkhorst, J. 9–10, 21, 72, 111–13
Brough, J. 101
Buddha: account of own liberation 24; authentic teachings of 125–8; awakening 18–20; Brahminic

knowledge 106; death 2; decision to teach 9–12, 21–2; declaration of own liberation 16, 92; early biographies of 9; first teaching 72, 121; jokes 2; knowledge of own awakening 19–20; rejection of early Upaniṣads 116; skill in means 47, 73, 99, 103; *see also* Bodhisatta
*buddhi* 38–41, 52–4, 56
Buddhist missions 74, 129 n.15, 134 n.55

*Chāndogya Upaniṣad* 45, 111
chariot metaphor *see yoga*
consciousness: annihilation/rebirth of 76, 85–7; in early Brahminism 89–90; stations of 104; stopping of 102–3; as the ultimate reality 114; *see also buddhi, dhātu-s*, formless spheres, *kasiṇāyatana-s*
cosmogony *see* cosmology
cosmology: in early Buddhism 36–7; and meditation 39–42, 56, 65–6, 144 n.55; in the *Mokṣadharma* 36, 52–7, 64–5; in the *Nāsadīyasūkta* 57–64; in the Upaniṣads 36, 55
craving *see taṇhā*
*Cūḷaniddesa* 78

deathless realm 117–18
De Jong, J.W. 1
dependent origination 118
desire *see kāma*
*dhamma*: meditative object 14–15, 25; mental phenomena 77, 93–4, 100, 109; teaching 7, 117; teaching/mental phenomena 101
*Dhammacakkappavattana Sutta* 136 n.70
*Dhammacetiya Sutta* 12
*Dhammapada* 28, 105
*dhāraṇā* 38
*Dharmaguptaka Vinaya* 26
dhātu-s 35–7, 65–7; *see also* material elements, *Ṣaḍdhātu Sūtra*
*dhyāna* 29, 68, 75; *see also jhāna*
*Divyāvadāna* 73
*Dvedhāvitakka Sutta* 18, 21

early Buddhist literature: antiquity and historical authenticity of 1; heterogeneity of 1, 117; stratification of 1–2
Edgerton, F. 53–4
eight releases *see vimokkha-s*
element meditation: Brahminic source of 111; and colours 34–5; and formless meditation 29–31; in the *Mokṣadharma* 37–9; *see also kasiṇāyatana-s*, cosmology and meditation

first council 1
first schism 125
five aggregates 95–6
five *bhikkhu-s* 72, 120–1, 136 nn.69, 72
five hindrances 101
flame metaphor 76, 90–1, 95–8
flood metaphor *see ogha*
formless meditation *see* formless spheres
formless spheres 3, 115; Brahminic source of 42, 111; touched by the body 118; *see also anupubbavihāra-s, kasiṇāyatana-s, vimokkha-s*
Four Noble Truths 2, 102; *see* insight, three knowledges
Frauwallner, E. 11, 74, 110

Gāndhārī Dharmapada 28
Gethin, R. M. L. 155 n.26
going out metaphor 88
Gombrich, R. F. 2, 47, 120–1, 158 n.58
Goudriaan, T. 35
gradual abidings *see anupubbavihāra-s*

Hacker, P. 64–5
*hiraṇyagarbha* 53–4
Horner, I. B. 15
*hupeyya* 16–17

inclusivism 23
*Indriyabhāvana Sutta* 122–3, 133 n.27
insight 75, 117, 120; into the *āsavas* and Four Noble Truths 19–20, 121, 123–4; into dependent origination

118; instantaneous 120–1 n.72; *see also abhiññā*, intellectualism, three knowledges
intellectualism 75, 117–25
*Itivuttaka* 119

Jainism 110, 112–13
Jayatilleke, K. N. 43
*jhāna*: in accounts of the awakening 20–1, 24, 108; development of 122–5; early Brahminic borrowing of 29; first *jhāna* 22, 101–2; fourth *jhāna* 101; in the Pārāyanavagga 81, 101–2; second *jhāna* 102; supernatural powers of 120; as support for insight 123–4; *see also anupubbavihāra-s*, *dhyāna*
*jīva* 97
Johnston, E. H. 26
Jurewicz, J. 58–9

*kāma* 57, 60–2, 76, 100
*Kandaraka Sutta* 152 n.87
Kapilavatthu 12, 26
karma 40, 67–71, 113
*kasiṇāyatana-s* 31–5; *see also* cosmology and meditation
*Kassapasīhanāda Sutta* 99
*Kaṭha Upaniṣad* 8, 112
Keith, A. B. 2, 113–14, 116
*Kena Upaniṣad* 69
*Khaggavisāṇa Sutta* 73, 78
King, R. 6
Kosala 12–13, 26
*Kosambi Sutta* 118
*kṛtsna* 32–5
Kusinārā 2

*Lalitavistara* 15
Lamotte, E. 1
La Vallée Poussin, Louis de 9, 117–19
liberation at death 84, 88–90
Lindtner, C. 113–16

Macdonell, A. A. 61–2
Magadha 13, 26
Māgadhi 17
magical powers *see* Vedic recitation
*Mahā-Cunda Sutta* 117–18, 120
*Mahāparinibbāna Sutta* 2, 13–14
*Mahānidāna Sutta* 91
*Mahā-Rāhulovāda Sutta* 35
*Mahā-Saccaka Sutta* 9, 17, 18
*Mahā-Saccaka Sutta et al*; *see* MSS *et al.*
Mahāsāṅghikas 26, 114
*Mahātaṇhāsaṅkhaya Sutta* 89
*Mahā Upaniṣad* 112
*Mahāvastu* 9, 14, 20, 74
Mahīśasaka Vinaya 10–12
*Maitrāyaṇīya Upaniṣad* 112–13
Malalasekera, G.P. 12
*Māṇḍūkya Upaniṣad* 42, 111
Manusmṛti 64
material elements *see* cosmology, *dhātu-s*, element meditation
meditation 8; *see also* formless spheres, *jhāna*, *yoga*
mindfulness: as distinctly Buddhist 82, 122; and insight 75; and meditation 108, 121–2; in the *Posālamāṇavapucchā* 104–5; relationship with four *jhāna-s* 122–3; in the *Udayamāṇavapucchā* 101–2; in the *Upasīvamāṇavapucchā* 76, 82–4
*Moneyasutta* 74
MSS *et al.* 17–21, 24–5
*Muktikā Upaniṣad* 112
*Mūlapariyāya Sutta* 123
*Muṇḍaka Upaniṣad* 67–9
*Munigāthā* 74
*Munisutta* 74
Musīla 118

Nakamura, H. 110
*Nālaka Sutta* 74
*nāmarūpa* 55, 69, 91
*Nāsadīyasūkta* 43, 57–64, 67, 90, 111
Nārada 118
neither perception nor non-perception: Brahminic background to 43–4, 46–9; as a *dhamma* 15; in the *Dharmaguptaka Vinaya* 26; as an epithet of liberation 25–6; non-Buddhist origin of 12; supposed Jain origin of 110

*nibbāna see* Nirvana
Niddesa 73; *see Cūḷaniddesa*
Nirvana 19–20, 29–30, 101, 116, 118
Noble Eightfold Path 2
nondualism 108–9
Norman, K. R.: on *anānuyāyī* 80; on *dhamma* 93–4; on *hupeyya* 17; on *nāmakāyā* 90; on *saññāvimokkha* 79; on *satimā* 82; on *sīti-siyā* 84–6; on the *Suttanipāta* 73–4; translation of the *Upasīvamāṇavapucchā* 76; on *vimutto* 78
nothingness: non-Buddhist origin of 12; as a dhamma 15; as an epithet of liberation 25–6; Brahminic background to 44–5; as an eschatological destiny 81; in the *Posālamāṇavapucchā* 104–5; supposed Jain origin of 110; in the *Upasīvamāṇavapucchā* 76–87
not-self 75, 136 n.72, 138 n.87

Oberlies, T. 17
*ogha* 77
Olivelle, P. 48
orientalism 6–7

*Pabbajā Sutta* 132 n.25
Pāli canon: antiquity of 5; authenticity of 5–6; circumstantial evidence in 107; commentaries on 4–5; heterogeneity of 155 n.26; near synonyms in 85; oral repetition in 15–16; oral transmission of 5, 7, 135 n.57, 125; Upaniṣadic thought contained in 116–17; writing down of 116; *see also Ariyapariyesana Sutta*, early Buddhist literature
*paññā see* insight
Pañcaśikha 122
*Pañcattaya Sutta* 43–4
*Paramatthajotikā* 78
Pārāsariya/Pārāśarya 122
*parinibbāna* 84–7, 150 n.43
*Pāsādika Sutta* 14, 45–6
Pasenadi 12
*passan na passati* 46–9
Pérez-Remón, J. 152 n.87

Prajāpati 52, 54
*prāṇāyāma see* breath restraint
precanonical Buddhism 113–16
*pudgala* 114
Pukkusa Mallaputta 13

Rājagaha/Rājagṛha 1, 13–14
Rāhula 35
Rāma *see* Uddaka Rāmaputta
rebirth *see* consciousness
right view *see* this world and the other world
Rhy Davids, T. W. 5, 80, 99, 128

*Ṣaḍdhātu Sūtra* 114
Said, E. 6
*samādhi* 8, 30
*Samādhi Sutta* 29
Śambhu 52
Sāṃkhya 38, 52–3, 122
*saṃsāra* 76, 80
*Saṅgabhedavastu* 9, 11, 15
*Saṅgārava Sutta* 9, 17; *see also* MSS *et al.*
*saññā* 78–9, 148 n.21, 153 n.98
*saññāvedayitanirodha* 44, 81, 118–20
Ṣāriputta Sutta 30
Śaṭcaknirūpaṇa 32
*sati see* mindfulness
Sāti 90
*Sāriputtasutta* 74
Saviṭṭha 118
scepticism 4
Schayer, S. 113–14, 116
Schmithausen, L. 119, 121–2, 124
Schopen, G. 5
second council 74
sensual pleasure *see kāma*
simple liberation pericope 20
Skandhaka 74
skill in means *see* Buddha
soul *see jīva*
spheres of mastery *see abhibhāyatana-s*
Stede, W. 80
*Suttanipāta* 3
*Susīma Sutta* 120

supernatural power *see jhāna*
*svarabhakti* 17
*Śvetāśvatara Upaniṣad* 112–13

*Taittirīya Upaniṣad* 36–7, 45, 50, 111, 115
*taṇhā* 76, 101, 123
*Theragāthā* 27, 92
Theravāda Buddhism 114
Theravādin Vinaya 11
thirst *see taṇhā*
this world and the other world 30
three knowledges 20, 24
Trenckner, V. 16
*Triśikhabrāhmaṇa Upaniṣad* 112

*ubhatobhāgavimutti* 121
Udānā 114
Uddaka Rāmaputta: Brahminic background of 42–4, 46–9; Brahminic teaching of 108; Buddhist appraisal of 22; liberation of 13; supposed Jaina background of 110; meditative goal of *see* nothingness; name and location of 13–14; practices of *see* element meditation, formless meditation; relationship with Āḷāra Kālāma 25; relationship with Rāma 15–16; spiritual attainment of 14–15
Uddālaka Āruṇi 45
unmanifest *see avyakta*
*upādāna* 96
Upaka 16
*Upatisapasine* 74
Uruvilvā/Uruvelā 10–11, 17–18

Van Buitenen, J.A.B. 55, 70
Vassakāra 14
*Vassakāra Sutta* 13, 26
Vedānta 69
Vedic recitation 88–9
Vetter, T. 9, 74–5, 78–9
*vimokkha-s* 43
Viriñca 52, 54
Viṣṇu 35, 145 n.10
Viṣṇusmṛti 112

world ages 35, 52
wrong view *see* this world and the other world

Yājñavalkya 43–4, 89
Yājñavalkyasmṛti 112
*yoga* 8; Brahminic origin of 63–4, 143 n.1; chariot metaphor 28–9; difference from Buddhist meditation 82; followers of 38, 52–3; in the *Mokṣadharma* 37–8, 69–70; in the Pāli canon 27–8; as a pleasurable activity 112; *see also dhyāna*, element meditation, formless meditation, *kasiṇāyatana-s*, Vedic recitation
*Yogatattva Upaniṣad* 34
*yuga-s see* world ages

Zafiropulo, G. 9, 16

Lightning Source UK Ltd.
Milton Keynes UK

172142UK00003B/38/P

9 780415 544672